Damaged

Damaged

The Heartbreaking True Story of a Forgotten Child

Cathy Glass

W F HOWES LTD

This large print edition published in 2008 by
W F Howes Ltd
Unit 4, Rearsby Business Park, Gaddesby Lane,
Rearsby, Leicester LE7 4YH

1 3 5 7 9 10 8 6 4 2

First published in the United Kingdom in 2006
by HarperElement

A CIP catalogue record for this book is available
from the British Library

ISBN 978 1 40742 799 7

Typeset by Palimpsest Book Production Limited,
Grangemouth, Stirlingshire
Printed and bound in Great Britain
by MPG Books Ltd, Bodmin, Cornwall

FSC
Mixed Sources
Product group from well-managed
forests and other controlled sources
Cert no. SGS-COC-2953
www.fsc.org
© 1996 Forest Stewardship Council

In Britain today, there are over 75,000 children in the care of their local authority. These are the lucky ones. Concealed behind this figure are countless others; defiled, abused and undiscovered by Social Services, often until it's too late.

This book tells the true story of my relationship with one of these children, an eight-year-old girl called Jodie. I was her foster carer, and she was the most disturbed child I had ever looked after. I hope my story will provide an insight into the often hidden world of foster care and the Social Services.

Certain details, including names, places and dates, have been changed to protect the innocent.

To my family for your continuing love, patience and understanding.

ACKNOWLEDGEMENTS

My heartfelt thanks to David, Andrew Lownie, Kirsty Crawford, Carole Tonkinson and all the team at HarperCollins. Thank you all for making the book what it is.

CHAPTER 1

EMOTIONAL BLACKMAIL

The phone rang. It was Jill, my link worker from the fostering agency.

'Cathy, it's not two carers, but five,' she said. 'Five, since coming into care four months ago.'

'Good heavens.' I was astonished. 'And she's only eight? That must have taken some doing. What's she been up to?'

'I'm not sure yet. But Social Services want a pre-placement meeting, to be certain she doesn't have another move. Are you still interested?'

'I don't know enough not to be. When?'

'Tomorrow at ten.'

'All right, see you there. What's her name?'

'Jodie. Thanks, Cathy. If you can't do it, no one can.'

I warmed to the flattery; it was nice to be appreciated after all this time. Jill and I had been working together now for four years and had established a good relationship. As a link worker for Homefinders Fostering Agency, Jill was the bridge between the foster carers and social workers dealing with a particular case. She coordinated the needs of the

Social Services with the foster carers, and provided support and help as it was needed. An inexperienced foster carer often needed a lot of back-up and explanations of the system from their link worker. As Jill and I had been working together for some time, and I was an experienced foster carer, we were used to each other and got on well. If Jill thought I was up to the task, then I was sure she meant it.

But a pre-placement meeting? It had to be bad. Usually the children just arrived, with a brief introduction if they'd come from another carer, or with only the clothes they stood in if they'd come from home. I'd had plenty of experience of both, but none at all of a pre-placement meeting. Usually there was a meeting between everyone involved in the case as soon as the child had been placed in foster care, but I'd never been to one held beforehand.

It was my first inkling of how unusual this case was.

The following morning, we went about our normal, quiet routine of everyone getting up and dressed and having breakfast, and then the children made their way off to school. I had two children of my own, Adrian who was seventeen, and Paula, the youngest at thirteen. Lucy, who had joined the family as a foster placement two years ago, was fifteen and now a permanent member of our family, just like a daughter to me and a sister to Adrian and Paula. She was a success story: she had come to me hurt and angry and had, over time, learned to trust again, and eventually settled down to a normal existence where she had only the usual teenage angst to fret about, instead of the turmoil she had known as a child. I was proud of her, and she was testament to my belief that love, kindness, attention and firm boundaries are the basis of what any child needs to flourish.

As I saw the children off to school that morning, I felt a twinge of apprehension. The child I was going to learn about today would most certainly need all those things in abundance, and if I took her on I would have to be prepared to say goodbye to my relatively peaceful, steady routine for a while, until she learned to trust me and settled down, just as Lucy had. But that was the point of fostering – it wasn't easy by any means, but the rewards were so enormous. Besides, I had fostered almost continuously for over twenty years now and wasn't sure I could really remember what life before it had been like.

Once the children had left, I went upstairs and quickly changed from my joggers into a pair of smart navy trousers and a jumper, and headed for the Social Services offices. I'd been going there for years now, and the journey there was as familiar as the one to my own house. I also knew the drab grey décor, fluorescent lighting and air of busy activity and only-just-contained chaos very well indeed.

'Cathy, hello.'

As I entered the reception area, Jill came forward to meet me. She'd been waiting for my arrival, and walked up to me with a welcoming smile.

'Hi, Jill. How are you?'

'Oh, fine, thanks. You're looking well.'

'Yes – life is good at the moment. The children are doing well, completely wrapped up in their lives and in their schools. Time for another challenge, I suppose.' I smiled at her.

'We'd better get along to this meeting. I think they're ready for us.' Jill led me along the corridor to the meeting room. As we entered the room, it was obvious at once that this was a big case: there were already about a dozen people sitting round the enormous oblong mahogany table. What did it mean? From what Jill had told me, I could tell that this was not a run-of-the-mill fostering situation – not many children get through five carers in four months – but then, no child was ever run-of-the-mill. They were always unique and their troubles distinctly their own. Removing a child from its parents was never going to be a humdrum, everyday event; it was always traumatic, emotional and difficult.

Nevertheless, something told me that this was far more complex than anything I'd yet encountered. I felt another stab of apprehension, like I had when Jill first told me about the case the day before, but I was also interested. What could this child be like, to warrant so much involvement from so many people?

Jill and I took the two vacant chairs at the far end, and I felt every eye was on me, assessing my suitability.

The chairman was Dave Mumby, the Social Services team leader, and he began the round of introductions. On his left was Sally, the 'guardian ad litum': she was appointed by the courts to represent Jodie's interests. The lady next to her introduced herself as Nicola, Jodie's home tutor.

Home tutor? Why isn't the child in school? I wondered.

Next was Gary, Jodie's current social worker. He explained that he was about to leave the case, and hand Jodie over to Eileen, who was sitting next to him. I looked at Eileen carefully – if I was going to take Jodie, then Eileen and I would have to work closely together. At first glance she was nondescript: a woman in her forties with an unruffled and calm air about her. So far, so good.

I wasn't surprised that I was already witnessing a change of social worker. It happened all the time – it was the nature of the job that people had to move on – but it was unfortunate for the children and families involved, who were always having to learn new faces, build trust and forge fresh relationships with endless strangers. Although I knew it was something that couldn't be altered and was just part of the system, with all its flaws, nonetheless I felt for Jodie. Changing social worker would mean yet more disruption for her, and I wondered how many social workers she'd been through already.

Next, Deirdre introduced herself. She was the agency link worker for Jodie's current foster carers. Then it was my turn, and the eyes of everyone around the table turned to me.

I looked around the table, meeting the various gazes. 'I'm Cathy Glass,' I said, as clearly and confidently as I could. 'I'm a foster carer from Homefinders Fostering Agency.' There wasn't much more I could add at this stage, when I knew so little about what was going on, so I passed on to Jill.

After Jill came someone from the accounts department, followed by a member of the local authority's placement team. As they spoke, I looked over at Gary, Jodie's current social worker. He was young, and could only have been in his mid-twenties. How successful had he been at forging a relationship with Jodie? I wondered. Perhaps Eileen, as a woman, would fare better at empathizing with the little girl, so the change of social worker might be for the better in this case. I hoped so.

Once the introductions were complete, Dave thanked us for coming, and gave a brief outline of what had been happening, or to use the correct terminology: the case history to date. I warmed to Dave immediately. He was gently spoken but forthright, and looked directly at me as he spoke. I made a mental note of the salient points: Jodie had been on the 'at-risk' register since birth, which meant that Social Services had been monitoring the family for eight years. Although there had been suspicions of emotional and physical abuse by Jodie's parents, no steps had been taken to remove her or her younger brother Ben and sister Chelsea. Then, four months ago, Jodie had started a house fire by setting light to her pet dog – I shivered at this, struck by the peculiar cruelty of such an act – and that had been the catalyst for Social Services to take her and her siblings into care. Ben and Chelsea had both been placed with foster carers and were doing well. But Jodie exhibited 'very challenging behaviour'. I heard Dave deliver this euphemism and raised my eyebrows. All foster carers knew what that really stood for. It meant 'completely out of control'.

'I think it would be useful,' said Dave, looking at me, 'for you to hear from her social worker now. Gary's been on the case for two years. Feel free to ask any questions.'

Despite his youth, Gary was confident and methodical as he gave me an overview of Jodie and her family.

'I'm afraid that the general picture isn't good, as you'd expect. There's severe disruption inside the family. Jodie's mother is an intravenous drug user and her father is an alcoholic. In recent years, Jodie's suffered a number of injuries while at home, including burns, scalds, cuts, bruises and a broken finger. All of these were recorded at hospital, and although it was suspected that some of the injuries were non-accidental, it was impossible to prove that this was the case.'

Gary went on with his tale of neglect and misery while I concentrated on absorbing the facts. It was an appalling case history but I'd heard similar stories many times before. Nevertheless, it never ceased to amaze and horrify me that people could treat their children with such cruelty and indifference, and I was already feeling for this poor little girl. How could any child grow and be normal in such circumstances, and with such parents as her role models?

Gary continued, 'Jodie's no longer in school because of the recent moves, which is why she's been assigned a home tutor. She has learning difficulties and a statement of special needs.'

That was straightforward enough – I was used to looking after children with developmental delays and learning difficulties. I suspected that Gary was giving me the censored version of Jodie's case history. In all my years of fostering, I'd never heard of a child going through five carers in four months. When he paused and looked at me, I seized my opportunity.

'It would be helpful if you could tell me the make-up of the families of the previous carers,' I said, hoping to discover clues to explain why Jodie had gone through so many, so fast. 'How many children did they have, and were they older or younger? Had the carers had experience with this type of child before?'

Gary coughed and looked a little shifty. 'The previous placement breakdowns were purely circumstantial,' he said. 'One of the couples were first-time carers and Jodie should never have been placed with them – that was an error on our part and it's no surprise that it didn't work out.'

That was fair enough, but as he went through the other placements, he sounded unconvincing to my ears: the others had all been experienced professionals, and yet one couple had lasted only three days. Gary's explanation that circumstances were to blame was clearly a damage limitation exercise for Jodie's sake, so that I didn't get frightened off.

Deirdre, who was the link worker representing Jodie's present foster carers, felt obliged to speak up in their defence. After all, if Jodie was as harmless as Gary was making out, it didn't exactly reflect very well on their ability to cope.

'Jodie has delayed development,' she said. 'In most respects, she acts like a three- or four-year-old rather than an eight-year-old. She throws terrible tantrums and is consistently aggressive and uncooperative. Her behaviour is violent, abusive and destructive. Even though she's only been with Hilary and Dave a short time, she's already broken a number of objects, including a solid wooden door.'

I raised my eyebrows. Quite a feat for an eight-year-old.

But Deirdre wasn't finished yet, and she went on with her litany of Jodie's faults and shortcomings. Jodie's carers had described her as 'cold, calculating, manipulative, very rude and totally unlikeable'. Harsh words to pin on a little girl.

Surely, I thought, someone could say something nice about her, even if it was only that she liked her food. Children in care tend to eat ravenously, because in the past many of them haven't known when the next meal would arrive. But no, not so much as 'she does like her chocolate'. It appeared that Jodie did not have a single endearing feature. Instead, there was just a list of transgressions, with a footnote that her present carers had found her physically frightening: Jodie was a big girl, and she had threatened them.

I looked at Jill and we exchanged glances. Threatened them? I thought to myself. But she's only eight years old! How dangerous can she be? I began to feel as though I was on Jodie's side. What must it be like, having everyone dislike you so vehemently? No wonder she wasn't able to settle anywhere.

The next person to speak was Sally, the guardian ad litum, who briefly outlined the legal position: Jodie had been taken into the care of Social Services under what is known as an Interim Care Order; that meant she'd been removed from home against the parents' wishes and was now in the temporary care of the local authority. Proceedings to decide Jodie's future were now beginning; if the court judged that she was better off at home, and all the fears for her safety there were put to rest, then she would be returned to her parents' care. If not, and the court still considered that she would be in danger if returned home, her care order would become a Full Care Order, and Jodie would be permanently removed from her parents, to long-term fostering, adoption, or – the least likely option – some kind of residential care home. This whole process is lengthy and complicated, and while it is supposed to take as little time as possible, it usually takes at least a year, sometimes longer, before the court comes to a final decision.

When Sally had finished, she was followed by the home tutor, Nicola, who explained that she'd been teaching Jodie for a month, using material that was working towards Key Stage One, which is designed for pre-school children. This might sound shocking but, in my experience, it was not unusual. I had, in the past, cared for children who couldn't read or write long after their peers had mastered the three Rs. A difficult background and home life often seems to produce children who are unable to learn as quickly as those from a stable family.

Next, the finance representative confirmed that funding would be available to continue the tutoring until a school had been found. I glanced at the clock on the wall: nearly an hour had passed. Everyone had had their say, and Dave was looking hopefully at Jill.

11

'If Cathy doesn't take her,' he said, 'our only option will be a residential unit.'

This smacked of emotional blackmail, and Jill rose to my defence. 'We'll need to consider what's been said. I'll discuss it with Cathy and let you know tomorrow.'

'We need to know today,' said Deirdre bluntly. 'She has to be moved by midday tomorrow. They're adamant.'

There was silence around the table. We were all thinking the same thing: were these foster carers as unprofessional as they sounded? Or had Jodie somehow driven them to this level of desperation?

'Even so,' said Jill firmly, 'we'll need time to discuss it. While I haven't heard anything that would make me advise Cathy against it – she's very experienced – the decision must be hers.' She looked sideways at me.

I felt everyone's eyes on me, and a desperate desire to hear that I would be willing to take this little girl on. So far, I had heard from Gary that she was an innocent victim whose extraordinary record of getting through carers was nothing to do with her, and from Deirdre that she was a little devil incarnate, whose size, strength and sheer nastiness were completely out of proportion to her age. The truth, I felt, must lie somewhere in between. Even taking a balanced view, however, I could see that Jodie was a handful, to say the least.

I was unsure. Was I ready to take on a child with behavioural problems at this level? Could I – and more importantly, could my family – take on the kind of disruption it would surely involve? I couldn't help quailing a little at the thought of embracing the sort of challenge I was sure this child would pose. But on the other hand, my formula of love, kindness and attention mixed with firmness had not let me down yet, and when all was said and done, Jodie was only a child; a little girl who had been given a terrible start in life and who deserved the chance to begin again and have a little of the happiness every child needed. Could I really let her face the alternative? Now that I'd heard her story, could I really walk away?

I knew at that moment that I couldn't. I had to give her that chance. As soon as I'd walked into that room, I'd known in my heart that I would take Jodie. I wouldn't be able to turn my back on her.

'She's too young to go into a residential unit,' I said, meeting Dave's look. 'I'll take her and give it my best shot.'

'Are you sure?' asked Jill, concerned.

I nodded, and there was an audible sigh of relief, particularly from the accounts lady. It costs upwards of £3,000 a week to keep a child in a residential unit, so getting me to take her for £250 a week was a good piece of business.

'That's wonderful, Cathy,' said Dave, beaming. 'Thank you. We all think very highly of you, as you know, and we're delighted that you're willing to take this one on.'

There was a murmur of agreement and a general feeling of a burden being lifted. The meeting was over. For now, the problem of Jodie was solved. Everyone stood up, gathered their things and prepared to get back to work, move on to other cases and think about other situations.

But for me, a few words and a snap decision had changed my life. For me, the problem of Jodie was only just beginning.

CHAPTER 2

THE ROAD TO JODIE

I had started fostering twenty years before, before I had even had my own children. One day I was flicking through the paper when I saw one of those adverts – you might have seen them yourself. There was a black-and-white, fuzzy photograph of a child and a question along the lines of: Could you give little Bobby a home? For some reason it caught my eye, and once I'd seen it I couldn't stop thinking about it. I don't consider myself a sentimental person, but for some reason I couldn't get the picture out of my mind. I talked about it with my husband; we knew we wanted a family of our own at some point, and I was looking forward to that, but in the meantime I knew that I could give a good home to a child who needed it. I'd always felt a bond with children and had once had ambitions to teach.

'We've got the room,' I said, 'and I know I would love working with children. Why don't we at least find out a little bit more about it?'

So I picked up the phone, replied to the advertisement and before long we found ourselves on an induction course that introduced us to the world of foster care. Then, after we'd satisfied all the requirements and done the requisite training, we took in our first foster child, a troubled teenager in need of a stable home for a while. That was it. I was hooked.

Fostering, I discovered, is by no means easy. If a carer goes into it expecting to take in a little Orphan Annie, or an Anne of Green Gables, then he or she is in for a nasty shock. The sweet, mop-headed child who has had a little bad luck and only needs a bit of love and affection to thrive and blossom and spread happiness in the world doesn't exist. Foster children don't come into your home wide-eyed and smiling. They tend to be withdrawn because of what has happened to them and will often be distant, angry and hard to reach, which is hardly surprising. In worse cases, they can be verbally or even physically aggressive and violent. The only constant factor is that each one is different, and that they need attention and kindness to get through their unhappiness. It is never an easy ride.

The first year of fostering was by no means easy for me – and come to think of it, no year since has been what I would call 'easy' – but by the end of it I knew I wanted to continue. A foster carer will generally know almost at once if it is something they want to carry on doing or not, and certainly will by the end of that first year. I'd found something I had a talent for, and that was extremely rewarding and I wanted to carry on, even while I had my own children. I found that the difference I made to my foster children's lives, even if it was a small one, stayed with me. It was not that I was the most selfless being since Mother Teresa, or that I was particularly saintly – I believe that we do these things for our own ends, and mine was the satisfaction I got from the whole process of making things better for children who needed help.

While my children were small I fostered teenagers, as it's usually recommended that you take in children who are at a different stage to your own. As Adrian and Paula grew up, I began to take in younger ones, which meant that I never had to deal with the kind of serious drug problems that are endemic among a lot of teenagers these days – for which I am most grateful. My two grew up knowing nothing other than having foster children living with us, so it was something they accepted completely. Of course, when they were little, they were sometimes frustrated at having to share me with other children. Foster children, by definition, need a lot of time and attention and sometimes that felt never-ending to my two. After a day of pouring my energies into fostering, with its meetings and training, I would then have paperwork to see to, and that took its toll on the amount of time I had left over for my own family. But no matter how much they resented missing out on some of my time, they never took it out on the foster children who shared our home.

Somehow, they seemed to understand that these children had come from difficult backgrounds, and that they had had a rough start. In their own way, my children were sympathetic and did their best to make life a bit easier for whichever troubled child was living with us. It's something I've noticed in other children besides my own – there is often a lot more understanding and empathy there than we would expect.

Adrian and Paula have certainly had to put up with a lot over the years – particularly when my husband and I divorced – but they have never complained about all the troubled youngsters coming and going in their home. Over the years, we've experienced all types of children, most of whom have exhibited 'challenging behaviour'. The majority of children who come to me have suffered from neglect of one sort or another, and funnily enough that is something I find relatively easy to understand. When parents have addictions to drink or drugs, or suffer from mental problems, they are obviously in no fit state to care for their children properly and look after their needs in a way they might be able to if they could overcome their problems. This kind of parenting is not purposefully cruel in the way that actual physical and sexual abuse is cruel – it is a sad side-effect of a different problem. The ideal outcome is that a child will be returned to its parents once the factors that caused the neglect, such as addiction, have been remedied.

A child who has suffered from neglect will have had a miserable time and can arrive in my house in a very troubled state. They can be full of brashness and bravado, which is usually a disguise for a complete lack of self-esteem. They can often be out-and-out naughty, as a result of having no boundaries or parental guidance at home, and as a way of seeking attention. Their anger and resentment can stem from the unpredictable nature of life at home, where nothing was ever certain – would Mum be too drunk to function today? Would Dad be spaced out or violent? – and where the borders between who was the adult and who was the child, and who was caring for whom, were often blurred. They may try to destroy things, or steal, or be manipulative and self-seeking. And, to be honest, when you know what some of them have had to put up with in their short lives, who can blame them?

The way that I've found is usually best with children from this kind of background is fairly simple: I provide stability and a positive environment in which good behaviour is rewarded with praise. Most children desire approval and want to be liked, and most are able to unlearn negative behaviour patterns and accept different ones when they realize how much better and easier life is with the new order. For many of them, a regular routine provides a blessed relief to the chaos and unpredictability of life at home, and they soon respond to a calm, positive environment where they know certain things will happen at certain times. Something as simple as knowing for sure when and where the next meal is coming from can provide an anchor for troubled children who've only ever known uncertainty and disappointment. Routine is safe; it is possible to get things right inside a routine – and getting things right is lovely when it means being praised, approved of and rewarded.

Of course, simple as it may sound, it is never easy and straightforward. And sometimes children come to me who've suffered much more severe levels of abuse, and who need much more professional help to get through their experiences. Many have learning difficulties and special needs. Some are removed from home too late, when they're teenagers and have suffered so much that they are never able to get over what has happened; they're not able to respond to a positive environment in the way a younger child might, and their futures look a lot bleaker.

Nevertheless, almost all my fostering experiences have been good ones, and the child has left our home in a better place than when they arrived.

As I drove home from the meeting at Social Services that day having agreed to take on Jodie, I knew that this child might be more of a handful than most, and wondered how best to tell the children about our new addition. They wouldn't be best pleased. We'd had children before with 'challenging behaviour', so they knew what was in store. I thought of Lucy, who'd been with us for nearly two years, and was very well settled. I hoped Jodie's disturbed outbursts wouldn't set her back. Adrian, at seventeen, kept pretty much to himself, unless there was a crisis, or he couldn't find his shirt in the morning. It was Paula I was most worried about. She was a sensitive, nervous child, and even though Jodie was five years younger than her, there was a risk she could be intimidated. Emotionally damaged children can wreak havoc in a family, even a well-integrated one. My children had always reacted well to the other children who had joined our family, even though we'd had a few rocky times, and I had no reason to think that this time would be any different.

I suspected the children wouldn't be surprised by my news. It had been a few weeks since our last foster child had left, so it was time for a new challenge. I usually took a break of a couple of weeks between placements, to refresh myself mentally and physically, and give everyone time to regroup. I also needed to recover from the sadness of saying goodbye to someone I'd become close to; even when a child leaves on a high note, having made excellent progress and perhaps returning home to parents who are now able to provide a loving and caring environment, there is still a period when I mourn their going. It's a mini-bereavement and something I have never got used to even though, a week or two later, I'd be revved up and ready to go again.

I decided to raise the subject of Jodie over dinner, which was where most of our discussions took place. Although I consider myself liberal, I do insist that the family eat together in the evenings and at weekends, as it's the only part of the day when we're all together.

For dinner that night I served shepherd's pie, which was the children's favourite. As they tucked in, I adjusted my voice to a light and relaxed tone.

'You remember I mentioned I was going to a pre-placement meeting today?' I said, aware they probably wouldn't remember, because no one had been listening when I'd said it. 'They told me all about a little girl who needs a home. Well, I've agreed to take her. She's called Jodie and she's eight.'

I glanced round the table for a reaction, but there was barely a flicker. They were busy eating. Even so, I knew they were listening.

'I'm afraid she's had a rough start and a lot of moves, so she's very unsettled. She's had a terrible home life and she's already had some foster carers. Now they're thinking of sending her to a residential unit if they can't find someone to take her in, and you can imagine how horrible that would be for her. You know – a children's home,' I added, labouring the point.

Lucy and Paula looked up, and I smiled bravely.

'Like me,' said Lucy innocently. She had moved around a lot before she finally settled down with us, so she knew all about the disruption of moving.

'No. Your moves were because of your relatives not being able to look after you. It had nothing to do with your behaviour.' I paused, wondering if the discreet message had been picked up. It had.

'What's she done?' Adrian growled, in his newly developed masculine voice.

'Well, she has tantrums, and breaks things when she's upset. But she's still young, and I'm sure if we all pull together we'll be able to turn her around.'

'Is she seeing her mum?' asked Paula, her eyes wide, imagining what for her would be the worst-case scenario: a child not seeing her mother.

'Yes, and her dad. It will be supervised contact twice a week at the Social Services.'

'When is she coming?' asked Lucy.

'Tomorrow morning.'

They all glanced at me and then at each other. Tomorrow there would be a new member of the family and, from the sounds of it, not an easy one either. I knew it must be unsettling.

'Don't worry,' I reassured them. 'I'm sure she'll be fine.' I realized I'd better be quick, as once dinner was over they'd vanish to their rooms, so I cut straight to the chase and reminded them of the 'safer caring' rules that were always in place when a new foster child arrived. 'Now, remember, there are a lot of unknowns here, so you need to be careful for your own protection. If she wants you to play, it's down here, not upstairs, and Adrian, don't go into her room, even if she asks you to open a window. If there's anything like that, call me or one of the girls. And remember, no physical-contact games like piggy back until we know more. And, obviously, don't let her in your room, OK?'

'Yes, Mum,' he groaned, looking even more uncomfortably adolescent. He'd heard it all before, of course. There are standard codes of practice that apply in the homes of all foster carers, and my lot were well aware of how to behave. But Adrian could sometimes be too trusting for his own good.

'And obviously, all of you,' I said, addressing the three of them, 'let me know if she confides anything about her past that gives you cause for concern. She'll probably forge a relationship with you before she does with me.'

They all nodded. I decided that that was enough. They'd got the general picture, and they were pretty clued up. The children of foster carers tend to grow up quickly, as a result of the issues and challenges they're exposed to. But not as quickly as the fostered children themselves, whose childhoods have often been sacrificed on the pyre of daily survival.

After dinner, as expected, the children disappeared to their rooms and the peace of another quiet evening descended on the house. It had gone off as well as I could have expected and I felt pleased with their maturity and acceptance of the situation.

'So far so good,' I thought, as I loaded the dishwasher. Then I settled down myself to watch the television with no idea when I'd next have the opportunity.

CHAPTER 3

THE ARRIVAL

It was a wet and cold spring day in April. Rain hammered on the windows as I prepared for Jodie's arrival. She was due at midday, but I was sure she'd be early. I stood in what was to be her new bedroom, and tried to see it through the eyes of a child. Was it appealing and welcoming? I had pinned brightly coloured posters of animals to the walls, and bought a new duvet cover with a large print of a teddy bear on it. I'd also propped a few soft toys on the bed, although I was sure that Jodie, having been in care for a while, was likely to have already accumulated some possessions. The room looked bright and cheerful, the kind of place that an eight-year-old girl would like as her bedroom. All it needed now was its new resident.

I took a final look around, then came out and closed the door, satisfied I'd done my best. Continuing along the landing, I closed all the bedroom doors. When it came to showing her around, it would be important to make sure she understood privacy, and this would be easier if the ground rules had been established right from the start.

Downstairs, I filled the kettle and busied myself in the kitchen. It was going to be a hectic day, and even after all these years of fostering I was still nervous. The arrival of a new child is a big event for a foster family, perhaps as much as for the child herself. I hoped Jill would arrive early, so that the two of us could have a quiet chat and offer moral support before the big arrival.

Just before 11.30, the doorbell rang. I opened the door to find Gary, soaking wet from his walk from the station. I ushered him in, offered him a towel and coffee, and left him mopping his brow in the lounge while I returned to the kitchen. Before the kettle had a chance to boil, the bell rang again. I went to the door, hoping to see Jill on the doorstep. No such luck. It was the link worker from yesterday, Deirdre, along with another woman, who was smiling bravely.

'This is Ann, my colleague,' said Deirdre, dispensing with small talk. 'And this is Jodie.'

I looked down, but Jodie was hiding behind Ann, and all I could see was a pair of stout legs in bright red trousers.

'Hi, Jodie,' I said brightly. 'I'm Cathy. It's very nice to meet you. Come on in.'

She must have been clinging to Ann's coat, and decided she wasn't going anywhere, as Ann was suddenly pulled backwards, nearly losing her balance.

'Don't be silly,' snapped Deirdre, and made a grab behind her colleague. Jodie was quicker and,

I suspected, stronger, for Ann took another lurch, this time sideways. Thankfully, our old cat decided to put in a well-timed appearance, sauntering lazily down the hall. I took my cue.

'Look who's come to see you, Jodie!' I cried, the excitement in my voice out of all proportion to our fat and lethargic moggy. 'It's Toscha. She's come to say hello!'

It worked – she couldn't resist a peep. A pair of grey-blue eyes, set in a broad forehead, peered out from around Ann's waist. Jodie had straw-blonde hair, set in pigtails, and it was obvious from her outfit alone that her previous carers had lost control. Under her coat she was wearing a luminous green T-shirt, red dungarees and wellies. No sensible adult would have dressed her like this. Clearly, Jodie was used to having her own way.

With her interest piqued, she decided to take a closer look at the cat, and gave Ann another shove, sending them both stumbling over the doorstep and into the hall. Deirdre followed, and the cat sensibly nipped out. I quickly closed the door.

'It's gone!' Jodie yelled, her face pinched with anger.

'Don't worry, she'll be back soon. Let's get you out of your wet coat.' And before the loss of the cat could escalate into a scene, I undid her zip, and tried to divert her attention. 'Gary's in the lounge waiting for you.'

She stared at me for a moment, looking as though she'd really like to hit me, but the mention of Gary, a familiar name in an unfamiliar setting, drew her in. She wrenched her arms free of the coat, and stomped heavily down the hall before disappearing into the lounge. 'I want that cat,' she growled at Gary.

The two women exchanged a look which translated as, 'Heaven help this woman. How soon can we leave?'

I offered them coffee and showed them through to the lounge. Jodie had found the box of Lego and was now sitting cross-legged in the middle of the floor, making a clumsy effort to force two pieces together.

Returning to the kitchen, I took down four mugs, and started to spoon in some instant coffee. I heard heavy footsteps, then Jodie appeared in the doorway. She was an odd-looking child, not immediately endearing, but I thought this was largely because of the aggressive way she held her face and body, as though continually on guard.

'What's in 'ere?' she demanded, pulling open a kitchen drawer.

'Cutlery,' I said needlessly, as the resulting clatter had announced itself.

'What?' she demanded, glaring at me.

'Cutlery. You know: knives, forks and spoons. We'll eat with those later when we have dinner. You'll have to tell me what you like.'

Leaving that drawer, she moved on to the next, and the next, intent on opening them all. I let her look around. I wasn't concerned about her inquisitiveness, that was natural; what worried me more was the anger in all her movements. I'd never seen it so pronounced before.

With all the drawers opened, and the kettle boiled, I took out a plate and a packet of biscuits.

'I want one,' she demanded, lunging for the packet.

I gently stopped her. 'In a moment. First I'd like you to help me close these drawers, otherwise we'll bump into them, won't we?'

She looked at me with a challenging and defiant stare. Had no one ever stopped her from doing anything, or was she deliberately testing me? There was a few seconds' pause, a stand-off, while she considered my request. I noticed how overweight she was. It was clear she'd either been comfort eating, or had been given food to keep her quiet; probably both.

'Come on,' I said encouragingly, and started to close the drawers. She watched, then with both hands slammed the nearest drawer with all her strength.

'Gently, like this.' I demonstrated, but she didn't offer any more assistance, and I didn't force the issue. She'd only just arrived, and she had at least compromised by closing one.

'Now the biscuits,' I said, arranging them on the plate. 'I'd like your help. I'm sure you're good at helping, aren't you?'

Again she fixed me with her challenging, almost derisory stare, but there was a hint of intrigue, a spark of interest in the small responsibility I was about to bestow on her.

'Jodie, I'd like you to carry this into the lounge and offer everyone a biscuit, then take one for yourself, all right?'

I placed the plate squarely in her chubby, outstretched hands, and wondered what the chances were of it arriving intact. The digestives pitched to the left as she turned, and she transferred the plate to her left hand, clamping the right on top of the biscuits, which was at least safe, if not hygienic.

I followed with the tray of drinks, pleased that she'd done as I'd asked. I handed out the mugs of coffee as the doorbell rang, signalling our last arrival. Jodie jumped up and made a dash for the door. I quickly followed; it's not good practice for a child to be answering the door, even if guests are expected. I explained this to Jodie, then we opened it together.

Jill stood on the doorstep. She was smiling encouragingly, and looked down at the sullen-faced child staring defiantly up at her.

'Hi,' said Jill brightly. 'You must be Jodie.'

'I wanted to do it,' protested Jodie, before stomping back down the hall to rejoin the others.

'Is everything all right?' Jill asked as she came in.

'OK so far. No major disasters yet, anyway.' I took Jill's coat, and she went through to the lounge. I fetched another coffee, and the paperwork began. There's a lot of form filling when a child is placed with new carers, and a lot of coffee. Gary was writing furiously.

'I've only just completed the last move,' he said cheerfully. 'Not to mention the three-day one before that. Is it Cathy with a C?'

I confirmed that it was, then gave him my post-code and my doctor's name and address. Jodie, who'd been reasonably content watching him, and had obviously been party to the process many times before, decided it was time to explore again. She hauled herself up, and disappeared into the kitchen. I couldn't allow her to be in there alone; quite apart from the risk of her raiding the cupboards, there were any number of implements which could have been harmful in the wrong hands. I called her, but she didn't respond. I walked in and found her trying to yank open the cupboard under the sink, which was protected by a child lock, as it contained the various cleaning products.

'Come on, Jodie, leave that for now. Let's go into the lounge,' I said. 'I'll show you around later. We'll have plenty of time once they've gone.'

'I want a drink,' she demanded, pulling harder on the cupboard door.

'OK, but it's not in there.'

I opened the correct cupboard, where I kept a range of squashes. She peered in at the row of brightly coloured bottles.

'Orange, lemon, blackcurrant or apple?' I offered.

'Coke,' she demanded.

'I'm sorry, we don't have Coke. It's very bad for your teeth.' Not to mention hyperactivity, I thought to myself. 'How about apple? Paula, my youngest daughter, likes apple. You'll meet her later.'

'That one.' She tried to clamber on to the work surface to retrieve the bottle.

I took down the bottle of blackcurrant and poured the drink, then carried it through and placed it on the coffee table. I drew up the child-sized wicker chair, which is usually a favourite.

'This is just the right size for you,' I said. 'Your very own seat.'

Jodie ignored me, grabbed her glass, and plonked herself in the place I had vacated on the sofa next to Jill. I sat next to Gary, while Jill pacified Jodie with a game on her mobile phone. I watched her for a few moments. So this was the child who was going to be living with us. It was hard to make much of her so early on; most children displayed difficult behaviour in their first few days in a new home. Nevertheless, there was an unusual air about her that I couldn't quite understand: it was anger, of course, and stubbornness, mixed with something else that I wasn't sure I had seen before. Only time would tell, I thought. I observed Jodie's uncoordinated movements and the way her tongue lolled over her bottom lip. I noted almost guiltily how it gave her a dull, vacant air, and reminded myself that she was classified as having only 'mild' learning difficulties, rather than 'severe'.

A quarter of an hour later, all the placement forms had been completed. I signed them and Gary gave me my copies. Deirdre and Ann immediately stood to leave.

'We'll unpack the car,' said Ann. 'There's rather a lot.'

Leaving Jodie with Gary and Jill, I quickly put on my shoes and coat, and we got gradually drenched as we went back and forth to the car. 'Rather a lot' turned out to be an understatement. I'd never seen so many bags and holdalls for a child in care. We stacked them the length of the hall, then the two women said a quick goodbye to Jodie. She ignored them, obviously feeling the rejection. Gary stayed for another ten minutes, chatting with Jodie about me and my home, then he too made a move to leave.

'I want to come,' she grinned, sidling up to him. 'Take me with you. I want to go in your car.'

'I don't have a car,' said Gary gently. 'And you're staying with Cathy. Remember we talked about it? This is your lovely new home now.' He picked up his briefcase and got halfway to the door, then Jodie opened her mouth wide and screamed. It was truly ear piercing. I rushed over and put my arms around her, and nodded to Gary to go. He slipped out, and I held her until the noise subsided. There were no tears, but her previously pale cheeks were now flushed bright red.

The last person left was Jill. She came out into the hall and got her coat.

'Will you be all right, Cathy?' she asked, as she prepared to venture out into the rain. 'I'll phone about five.' She knew that the sooner Jodie and I were left alone, the sooner she'd settle.

'We'll be fine, won't we, Jodie?' I said. 'I'll show you around and then we'll unpack.'

I was half expecting another scream, but she just stared at me, blank and uncomprehending. My heart went out to her; she must have felt so lost in what was her sixth home in four months. I held her hand as we saw Jill out.

Now it was just the two of us. I'd been in this situation many times before, welcoming a confused and hurt little person into my home, waiting patiently as they acclimatized to a new and strange environment, but this felt different somehow. There was something in the blankness in Jodie's eyes that was chilling. I hadn't seen it before, in a child or an adult. I shook myself mentally. Come on, I cajoled. She's a little girl and you've got twenty years' experience of looking after children. How hard can it be?

I led her back into the living room and, right on cue, Toscha reappeared. I showed Jodie the correct way to stroke her, but she lost interest as soon as I'd begun.

'I'm hungry. I want a biscuit.' She made a dash for the kitchen.

I followed and was about to explain that too many biscuits aren't good, when I noticed a pungent smell. 'Jodie, do you want the toilet?' I asked casually.

She shook her head.

'Do you want to do a poo?'

'No!' She grinned, and before I realized what she was doing, her hand was in her pants, and she smeared faeces across her face.

'Jodie!' I grabbed her wrist, horrified.

She cowered instantly, protecting her face. 'You going to hit me?'

'No, Jodie. Of course not. I'd never do that. You're going to have a bath, and next time tell me when you want the toilet. You're a big girl now.'

Slowly, I led my new charge up the stairs and she followed, clumsy, lumbering and her face smeared with excrement.

What had I let myself in for?

CHAPTER 4

A NEW LITTLE SISTER

Foster carers aren't saints. We're just ordinary parents with space in our homes and hearts for one more. But as I turned on the shower, and helped Jodie out of her clothes and her soiled underwear, I wondered if my heart was truly big enough. I put her under the shower of hot water and began to sponge her down. My stomach lurched as the heat intensified the smell, and I closed my mouth and tried to breathe through my nose. I cleaned her face and hands, then between the folds of pale skin around her middle. Jodie was pear-shaped, which is unusual for a child, and she had hips like a middle-aged woman. She was docile, though, lifting her arms in the air and making no effort to help. She seemed to enjoy being treated like a baby. I consoled myself that at least the rest of the family weren't home to witness the new arrival's house-warming trick.

I couldn't help feeling puzzled by it – she hadn't been distressed by her accident at all, and it was unlikely that someone of her age had no bowel control and wasn't aware of when they were about to do a poo. So had it been deliberate? Surely not. It was probably anxiety.

I helped her out of the bath and wrapped a towel round her. 'Dry yourself, Jodie, while I put these in the wash.' I scooped up the soiled clothes and carried them downstairs to the washing machine. I added a few drops of disinfectant to the soap, and turned the dial to 80 degrees. The sound of Jodie talking to herself floated down from the bathroom and I could hear her muttering isolated words and phrases which didn't string together, and didn't make any sense.

Returning down the hall, I took the largest suitcase and heaved it upstairs. 'You OK, Jodie?' I called, as I crossed the landing.

Silence, then, 'Yeah,' before she lapsed into gobbledegook once again.

In her bedroom, I unzipped the case, and picked out joggers, a jumper and underwear, and carried them through to the bathroom. She was standing as I'd left her, wrapped in the towel but still dripping wet.

'Come on,' I encouraged, 'dry yourself. You're a big girl now.'

She shook her head sulkily, and I started patting her dry. She was like a seven-stone infant, and very cumbersome, and I was sure some of this was due to the rolls of fat.

'Don't want those,' she said, spying the clothes I'd brought in.

'OK, when you're dry we'll find some others.

You've got lots to choose from. Now come on before you get cold.'

She pulled out of the towel and darted naked along the landing to her room, where she began rummaging through the clothes. She held up a pair of pink shorts and a T-shirt. I tried to explain that they weren't suitable for the chilly weather, but I might as well have been talking Russian for all the response I got.

'How about these jeans?' I said, holding them up. 'And this blue top is nice and warm. Now find yourself some underwear and get dressed, come on, quickly.'

She held up a pair of knickers and struggled into them, then continued picking over the clothes. She was chattering continuously, but when I tried to join in the conversation she would stare at me blankly, before continuing with her search, and the next unintelligible monologue. Finally, she settled on a pair of black trousers and a grey jumper, and stood waiting for me to dress her. Just to hurry things along, I gave in to this demand, then began clearing up the heaps of discarded clothes, folding and hanging them in the drawers and wardrobe. Jodie had said nothing about her bedroom, and when I asked if she liked it, she responded with a blank, dismissive stare. She picked up a soft toy, and hurled it at the door. 'Not mine! Don't want it!' Her face screwed up in anger.

'OK, but don't throw it. I'm sure you've got lots

of your own. I'll put these away and find some of yours. You'd prefer that, wouldn't you?' I gathered up the other toys and moved towards the door.

'Where you going?' she demanded, her scowl intensifying.

'To put these away and bring up some of your own toys.' I smiled and left, aware another scene had been narrowly averted.

I dropped the unwanted toys on to my bed, then went downstairs and opened some of the holdalls. They were filled with clothes, a ridiculous amount; she couldn't possibly have worn them all if she'd changed three times a day for a fortnight. The next bag I opened was crammed full of small plastic toys: dolls, animals and gifts from McDonald's. It was like a school fête tombola. I lugged the bag upstairs.

'Have a look at these,' I said brightly, 'while I sort out the rest of your clothes. There's a toy box under the bed, you can put them in there.'

Her face softened, and we worked side by side for a few minutes, although I sensed the peace was tenuous. I wasn't wrong. Five minutes later she threw a plastic crocodile into the box, then ran out of the room, and into Adrian's bedroom next door.

I followed. 'Jodie, would you like to look around now? We can unpack later.' She was pressing the buttons on Adrian's mobile, which he'd left recharging by his bed.

I went over and gently took it from her. 'We won't

touch that, it's not ours. This is Adrian's room.'
She looked at me doubtfully. 'He's my son. He's
at school. You'll meet him later.'

She dropped the phone on the floor, then took
a flying leap on to the bed, where she started
clumsily bouncing up and down. I reached for her
hand. 'Come on, I'll show you the other rooms,
then fix you some lunch.'

The mention of lunch sealed it, and with another
leap she was beside me, floorboards juddering,
and then she dashed out, along the landing and
into the next bedroom.

'This is Lucy's room,' I said, catching up. 'She's
fifteen. She's been with us for two years and you'll
meet her later too.'

She rushed out of Lucy's room and round to
Paula's, where she spotted Paula's rag-doll pyjama
case propped on the bed.

'Mine. Mine!' she cried, snatching it to her chest.
'I want it.'

'It's Paula's,' I said gently. 'It's special, she got
it for her birthday.'

'Mine,' she growled. 'I want it. Get me one or
I'll kick you.'

I frowned and gently prised it from her arms.
Was that how she'd accumulated all those toys:
buy it or I'll kick you? I repositioned the doll
on the pillow, then took her hand and led her
out. I opened the door to my room just enough
for her to see in. 'This is where I sleep, but of
course it's private. All our bedrooms are private,

and we don't go into each other's unless we're asked.'

She grinned, with a strange grimace that gave her an unpleasant, malevolent air. She stared at the double bed. 'Have you got a man?'

I shook my head. 'No, I'm divorced. I have a big bed all to myself.'

She threw me a pitying look, and I decided she'd seen enough of my bedroom, and closed the door. On the landing I took the opportunity to re-inforce our privacy rule. 'Jodie, we all have our own bedrooms and they have our special things in them. No one will come into yours, and you mustn't go into anyone else's without being asked. Do you understand?'

She nodded vigorously, but I suspected her acquiescence was more to speed lunch along rather than a genuine commitment. 'I'm hungry! I want crisps and chocolate.' She lumbered down the stairs, bumping into the banister. I caught up with her in the kitchen, as she flung open the drawers and cupboards.

'OK, wait a minute, I'll find you something.' I took down a multipack of variety crisps and let her choose one. She wrenched open the packet of smoky bacon, and started cramming fistfuls into her mouth. 'What would you like in your sandwich? Ham? Cheese? Peanut butter? Or Marmite?'

'Marmite and chocolate spread.'

I laughed. 'Not in the same sandwich, surely?'

But she just stared at me, uncomprehendingly. 'I want a drink.'

'Can I have a drink, please?' I corrected, deciding it wouldn't do any harm to introduce some manners. I made one Marmite sandwich and one chocolate spread, then took down a glass and added some orange squash.

'Me do it,' she said, grabbing the glass from my hand.

'All right, but gently. Don't grab, it's not polite.' I showed her how to turn on the tap, then waited while she filled the glass. 'Do you like to help, Jodie? Did you used to help at home? At your other carers'?'

She plonked the glass down on the work surface, then adopted the pose of an overburdened house-wife, with her hands on her hips, her chin jutting out, and an expression of resolute grumpiness. 'Cooking! Cleaning! And you bleeding kids at me feet all day. Don't know why I 'ad you. You're a pain in the arse!'

I could see she was role-playing, probably repeating what she'd heard her mother say, but I suspected there was also some truth behind it. As the eldest of three, she was likely to have had some part in bringing up her brother and sister while her parents were too drunk or drugged to care. It reminded me why we were going through this experience, and the flash of insight Jodie had given me into her past helped me to gather my energy and face the volatile moods and constant demands that I knew were coming.

The afternoon passed, I'm not certain how. We didn't unpack, as all my time was taken up with trying to keep Jodie's attention for longer than two minutes. I showed her cupboards full of games, which we explored a number of times, trying to find something that would engage her. She liked jigsaws, but the only ones she had any hope of completing consisted of a handful of pieces, and were designed for two-year-olds. I had seen developmental delays before in children I'd fostered, and was used to dealing with learning difficulties. Nevertheless, I was beginning to suspect that Jodie was closer to the 'moderate' spectrum than the 'mild' that Gary had described.

We sat together on the carpet, but she hardly seemed to be aware of my presence. Instead, she muttered meaningless asides to people called Paul, Mike and Sean: 'See this bit. In there. It's a horse. I told you! I know. Where?'

They weren't the names of anyone in the immediate family that I knew of, so I assumed Jodie was playing with her imaginary friends. This kind of behaviour isn't unusual in children, even in eight-year-olds, but I'd never seen a child distracted to quite this extent.

'Who are these people?' I asked eventually.

She looked at me blankly.

44

'Paul, Mike and Sean? Are they your imaginary friends? Pretend ones, that only you can see?'

I was met with another uncomprehending gaze, then she looked menacingly over my left shoulder. 'Mike, if you don't watch what you're doing I'll kick you to death.'

When Paula and Lucy arrived home at 3.30, I was trying to manoeuvre Barbie into her sports car beside Ken. I heard the door close, followed by Lucy's reaction as she saw the bags I hadn't had time to move. 'Christ. How many have we got staying?'

'Only one,' I answered.

To prove it, Jodie jumped up and dashed down the hall. 'Who are you?' she demanded, hands on hips, assuming the grumpy housewife pose again.

The girls said nothing, but I knew what they were thinking. With her odd features and aggressive posture, she wasn't exactly the little foster sister they'd been hoping for.

'This is Jodie,' I said positively. 'She arrived at lunchtime. Jodie, this is Lucy and Paula.'

She stuck out her chin, in a take-me-on-if-you-dare attitude.

'Hello,' said Lucy, with effort.

'Hi,' Paula added weakly.

Jodie was blocking their path, so I gently placed a hand on her shoulder to ease her out of the way. She pulled against me. 'Get out!' she suddenly exploded at the girls. 'This is my home. You go!'

I was shocked. How could she believe this when I'd told her about the girls and shown her their rooms? They laughed, which was understandable, but not advisable. Before I could stop her, Jodie rushed at Paula, kicking her hard on the shin. She jumped back and yelped.

'Jodie! Whatever are you doing?' I shouted, as I turned her round to face me. 'That's naughty. You mustn't kick. This is their home as much as it is yours. We all live together. Do you understand?'

She grinned.

'Are you OK?' I asked Paula. She'd experienced aggression from foster siblings before – we all had – but never so immediate and pronounced.

She nodded, and I eased Jodie back as the girls went up the stairs. They always spent time unwinding in their rooms when they got home from school, while I prepared dinner. I took Jodie through to the kitchen, and reinforced again how we all lived as one family. I asked her if she'd like to help, but she folded her arms and leant against the worktop, muttering comments, most of which were impossible to follow. 'They're not mine,' she grumbled.

'The potatoes?' I responded. 'No, I'm peeling them for dinner for us all.'

'Who?'

'Who are these for? For all of us.'

'In the car?'

'No. You came here in the car. We're in the kitchen now.'

'Where?' she asked, lifting the lid on the pan I'd just set to boil.

'Be careful, Jodie,' I said. 'That's very hot.'

'I was walking,' she said, and so it went on, with Jodie mumbling disjointed phrases, as though she had a basket of words and pulled them out at random.

She helped lay the table, and I showed her which would be her place. We always sat in the same places, as the children preferred it, and it made life easier.

'Paula! Lucy! Dinner,' I called. Adrian was playing rugby that evening, so his dinner was waiting for him in the oven. The girls came down and we all took our places. Once she was seated Jodie suddenly became angry that she couldn't sit in Lucy's place.

'Lucy always sits there, Jodie,' I explained. 'It's her place. And that's your place.'

She glared at Lucy, then viciously elbowed her in the ribs.

'Jodie, no! That hurts. Don't do it. Good girl.' I knew I should ask her to apologize, but it was our first meal together so I let it slide. She was still staring at Lucy, who shifted uncomfortably away. 'Come on, Jodie, eat your meal,' I encouraged. 'You told me you like roast chicken.'

The front door opened and Adrian came in, still muddy from playing rugby. He was over six feet tall, and stooped as he entered the kitchen. I hoped Jodie wouldn't find him intimidating, but reassured myself that he had a gentle manner, and children usually warmed to him.

'Adrian, this is Jodie,' I said.

'Hi Jodie,' he smiled, taking his plate from the oven and sitting opposite her. She transferred her glare from Lucy to him, and then wriggled down in her chair, and started kicking him under the table.

'Jodie. Stop that,' I said firmly. 'No kicking or elbowing. It's not nice.'

She scowled at me, then finally picked up her knife and fork and started eating. I watched her out of the corner of my eye. She could barely grip the knife and fork, and her movements were so uncoordinated that her mouth had to be inches from the plate to have any chance of getting the food in.

'Would you like a spoon?' I asked after a while. 'If I cut it up first, it might be easier.'

'My gloves,' she said. 'It's hot.' Then, for no apparent reason, she jumped up, ran round the table three times, then plonked herself down, and started eating with her fingers. I motioned to the rest of the family to say nothing, and the meal passed in an unnatural, tense silence.

I was relieved when dinner was over, and I suggested to Jodie that she might like to help me load the dishwasher. As she came into the kitchen, she spotted Toscha sitting contentedly by the boiler.

'Why's it looking at me?' she demanded, as though the cat had some malicious intent.

'She's not looking at you, sweet. Cats often sit and stare into space. She's found the warmest spot.'

Jodie lurched towards the cat with large, aggressive strides, and I sensed another kick was about to be delivered. I quickly intercepted her. 'Come on, Toscha's old, we'll leave her there to sleep.'

I decided the dishwasher could wait until Jodie was in bed, and took her into the lounge. I tried to amuse her with more games and puzzles, while Adrian, Lucy and Paula did their homework upstairs. By seven, I was exhausted. She needed one-to-one attention to keep her involved in anything, and the meaningless chatter that never stopped was starting to get on my nerves.

'Let's go up and finish your unpacking before bedtime,' I suggested.

She stood up. 'I want the park.'

'Not today, it's too late. But we'll go tomorrow if it's nice.'

She turned her back and started talking to David, another imaginary friend. I caught the odd words – 'you see . . . in there! . . .' – but nothing that related to the park or the games we'd played, and I consoled myself that her imaginary world would fade in time as she started to feel safe with us. It took a mixture of coercion and repetition to persuade her upstairs, where we unpacked another bag, then changed and washed her ready for a story at eight. She found a book she'd brought with her: *The Three Little Pigs*. I read it to her twice, then coaxed her into bed and said goodnight. As I left, I went to turn off the light.

'No!' she screamed in panic. 'Not dark. I'm scared of the dark. You stop it!'

'All right, sweet. Don't worry.' I turned it on again, then dimmed it to low, but she still wasn't happy. She would only stay in bed if it was left on full.

'Would you like your door open or closed?' I asked, as I ask all the children on their first night. How they sleep is very important in helping them to feel secure and settled.

'Closed,' she said. 'Shut tight.'

I said goodnight again, blew her a kiss, then closed the door and came out. I paused on the landing and listened. The floorboards creaked as she got out of bed, and checked the door was firmly secured, before returning to bed.

At nine Adrian, Paula and Lucy came down to make a snack, and we sat together in the lounge. I had the television on, but I wasn't watching it. I was mulling over the day's events.

'Well, what do you think?' I asked, smiling at Lucy as she handed me a cup of tea.

'She's weird,' said Lucy, sitting down next to me.

'I don't like her,' said Paula, then looked at me sheepishly, expecting to be told off.

'And what about you, Adrian? What's your first impression?'

'She reminds me of that doll Chucky in the

horror film. You know, the one that's possessed by the devil.'

'Adrian!' I admonished, but I felt a cold shudder of recognition. With her broad forehead, staring blue-grey eyes, lack of empathy, and her detachment from the real world, she could easily have been possessed. I caught myself; whatever was I thinking? She was just a child who had been through some miserable times and needed our help – there was nothing more sinister to it than that. I had taken this challenge on and now I owed it to Jodie to see it through for as long as she needed me. Part of her problems no doubt stemmed from people falling at the first hurdle when it came to dealing with her, and passing her on for someone else to deal with. I couldn't do that to her again.

I tried to look relaxed. 'I'm sure she'll improve with time.'

CHAPTER 5

SELF-HARM

Perhaps I was haunted by the lingering image of the possessed doll, for suddenly I was awake, with my eyes open and my senses alert. I turned and looked at the alarm clock: it was nearly 2.15 a.m. I listened. The house was silent. Yet something told me all was not well; a sixth sense from years of looking after children.

I eased my feet from the duvet and felt for my slippers. The house was cold, as the central heating had switched off for the night. I fumbled to get my arms into my dressing gown, tied it loosely, and opened the bedroom door. Suddenly, I gasped in shock. Jodie was standing outside the door, her face covered in blood.

'What is it? What have you done?' I frantically searched her face and neck for the source of the blood. 'Where are you hurt? Tell me! Come on, quickly!' I couldn't find anything, but the blood was fresh.

In a trance-like state, she slowly raised her hands and showed me her palms. They were smeared with blood. but I still couldn't find any sign of a cut. I pulled up her pyjama sleeves, and then

I saw it. She had a cut on her left forearm, about an inch long, which was lightly seeping blood. I steered her into the bathroom, and took her to the sink. I turned on the tap and ran the cut under cold water. She didn't even flinch and I wondered if she might be sleepwalking.

'Jodie?' I said loudly. 'Jodie! Can you hear me?'

She grinned at her reflection in the mirror, and I knew that she was awake.

'What happened? How did you do this?'

She met my gaze in the mirror, but said nothing.

I washed the wound thoroughly and examined it. It wasn't deep, and wouldn't need stitches, so there shouldn't have been nearly this much blood. It seemed that she had smeared the blood deliberately, for maximum effect. But how? And why? No one had mentioned anything about Jodie self-harming, but I doubted this was the first time she'd done it. I looked closer, and saw there were other fine, pink scar lines running up both arms. How recent they were was difficult to tell.

'Stay here, Jodie,' I said. 'I'm going downstairs to fetch a bandage.'

She grinned again. That strange, mirthless smile seemed to hold meanings I couldn't fathom, and it gave me the shivers. I covered her arm with a clean towel, then went down into the kitchen, where I opened the first-aid box and took out a large plaster. My mind was reeling. She wasn't even distressed, which made it all the more worrying. Just as before, with her soiling herself, there was that cool calmness and detachment that was so strange in such a young child. It was as though she didn't feel the pain, or perhaps wasn't even aware of what she'd done. She couldn't have cried out when she'd cut herself, as I would have heard her – years of fostering had made me a light sleeper. I suddenly had an awful image of Jodie sitting silently in her room, squeezing the cut, then wiping the blood on her face.

Upstairs again, I found her looking in the mirror, grimacing, but not from pain. She appeared to be trying to make herself as ugly as possible, screwing up her face, and baring her teeth in a lopsided grin. I peeled the backing from the plaster, sealed the cut, then wet the flannel and wiped her face and neck clean. I washed my hands in hot soapy water, remembering too late that I was supposed to wear gloves when dealing with wounds, to prevent cross-infection. In the panic of the emergency, I'd forgotten.

When she was clean and dry again, I felt a sense of normality returning. 'All right, Jodie,' I said encouragingly. 'Let's get you back into bed.' She still didn't speak.

I led her round the landing as Lucy appeared at her door. 'You OK, Cathy?' she asked, her eyes only half-open.

'Yes, don't worry. I'll explain tomorrow.'

She nodded and shuffled back to bed.

In Jodie's room I found her duvet in a heap on the floor. There was no blood on it, but on top was a small fruit knife I'd never seen before. I picked it up. 'Where did you get this?' I tried to keep the accusation out of my voice.

She finally spoke. 'Hilary and Dave's.' Her previous carers.

'Do they know you've taken it?'

She shook her head mischievously, as though being caught out in a game. I could hardly tell her off. I was more annoyed with the carers for giving her access to it, but I did understand. I had learned only from experience that leaving a child for fifteen seconds in the vicinity of the kitchen could produce untold dangers. I'd once fostered a teenager who had self-harmed, but I'd never known a child of Jodie's age doing it. If a child has been physically abused at home, they can have very little respect for their bodies and are often careless about hurting themselves. Deliberate self-harm is relatively rare and is usually the preserve of teenagers. I'd never heard of an eight-year-old purposefully slashing herself with a knife. It was very worrying.

'Have you taken anything else?' I asked gently.

She shook her head, but I checked the room anyway, then remade the bed.

'Come on, in you get. We'll talk about this in the morning.'

She shook her head angrily. 'Park,' she demanded. 'I want to go to the park. You said.'

'It's the middle of the night, Jodie. We'll go tomorrow. No one goes to the park when it's dark. All the gates are locked.'

'Open them!'

'I can't. I haven't got the keys.' I realized the absurdity of this conversation. 'Jodie, get into bed and go to sleep before you wake the whole house.'

'No. Don't want to.' She made towards the door.

I caught her lightly round the waist and gently drew her to me. 'Come on, good girl, into bed and I'll tell you a story. We'll go to the park in the morning. When it's light.'

She struggled for a moment, then flopped against me. I eased her into bed, and drew the duvet up to her chin. I looked at her little head on the pillow, blonde hair falling over her face. I perched on the bed and stroked her forehead until her features relaxed. 'Jodie, you must be hurting very badly inside to cut yourself. Is there anything you want to tell me?'

But her eyes were already heavy with sleep. 'Story,' she mumbled. 'Free 'ickle pigs.'

'All right.' I continued to stroke her forehead, and began the story which I knew by heart. Her eyes closed and her breathing deepened. I kissed her cheek, then quietly came out and closed the door.

At five o'clock I was woken by a loud crash. I threw on my slippers and dressing gown, and staggered to her door, disoriented from lack of sleep. I gave a quick knock and entered. 'Jodie! Whatever are you doing?'

She was up and dressed, with a football in her

hand, and the contents of the shelves strewn across the floor.

'Put that away,' I said crossly. 'You don't play ball in here.'

'I do.' She clutched it protectively to her chest.

I went to take the ball from her, but she gripped it tighter. I was annoyed with myself, as I should have known it would only make her more defensive. I changed tack. 'OK, Jodie. You put it down and get back into bed. If you can't go to sleep, sit quietly and look at a book. I'll tell you when it's time to get up.'

I didn't wait for a reply, but came out and closed the door. Without a full-scale confrontation, I hoped she might do as I'd asked. I waited and listened. The room fell silent, so I returned to bed, and propped myself on the pillows. Five minutes passed, then I heard her door open, and then another. I ran along the landing in my nightdress and saw Adrian's door open. I rushed in and found her trying to climb into bed with him.

'Jodie! Come away,' I cried. 'Not in there.'

I eased her off. She was a big girl, and a dead weight without cooperation. Adrian groaned and turned over. I put my hands under her arms, and manhandled her out on to the landing. She plonked herself down on the floor, folded her arms, and set her face into a scowl. I took a deep breath, and knelt down beside her.

'Jodie, you can't stay here, pet. Come into your

bedroom and we'll put the television on. Everyone else is asleep.'

She thought about this for a moment, then threw herself on to all fours and started crawling towards her room, her hands and feet thumping on the floorboards. I followed her in, relieved that I'd had even this much cooperation. She sat on her bedroom floor, cross-legged, staring expectantly at the blank screen. I switched the TV on, and flicked through the channels. It was too early even for children's programmes, but the football seemed to capture her interest.

'Keep the volume down,' I whispered, 'then you won't wake the others.'

I wrapped the duvet around her shoulders, then returned to my room for my dressing gown and slippers. I went downstairs and turned the central heating on. It wasn't worth going back to bed. I wouldn't be able to sleep now – my thoughts were going nineteen to the dozen and my head was buzzing with everything that had happened.

I made a cup of coffee, and took it into the lounge. Jodie's room was directly above, and all was quiet. I sat on the sofa, resting my head back, and took a sip. Suddenly, the calm was shattered by a man's voice, booming loud with distortion. I gasped – the racket was bound to wake the whole house. I rushed upstairs to her room, and instinctively turned off the TV.

'It's mine,' she shrieked, and lunged at me with

her hands raised into claws. 'I want it. Get out! Get out of my fucking bedroom!'

I took her by the shoulders, and held her at arm's length. 'Jodie, calm down and listen to me. I told you to keep the volume low. Everyone is asleep and you'll wake them up with this noise. When you're calmer, we'll put it on again. Do you understand?'

She made eye contact. 'I want the TV.'

'I know, but shouting and swearing won't get it.'

I was too tired to give her a lengthy lecture. 'Now sit down and I'll switch it on, but keep the volume low.'

She resumed her cross-legged position on the floor, and I turned the TV on. I tucked the remote into my pocket, and returned to the lounge. I sat and yawned, as the sun rose on a crisp spring morning. Our first night together was over.

CHAPTER 6

A VERY TROUBLED CHILD

'You mustn't thump, kick, bite or push,' I said, for the third time that morning. 'Not Lucy, Paula, me or anyone. It hurts. It's bad. Do you understand?'

She said nothing. It was nearly 11.30 on Saturday, the day after Jodie had arrived, and the girls had come downstairs after their weekend lie-in. Lucy was greeted with a kick from Jodie.

'I don't want to have to tell you again, Jodie. Do I make myself clear?'

She pulled a face and stomped off down the hall.

'Sorry, Lucy,' I said. Lucy shrugged. We all knew there was not much to be done about Jodie's vicious behaviour except to keep reinforcing that it was bad and that she mustn't do it.

A moment later Jodie reappeared, her fists clenched and flaying the air. 'It's them! I'll kick you to death! Get out! I hate you all!'

Her eyes blazed as she tried to kick Paula this time, who deftly stepped out of the way. I went towards her, and avoided the kick aimed at me. 'Jodie,' I said evenly, 'Jodie. Calm down and come here.'

She screamed, then dropped to her knees and started thumping her face and head viciously. She badly wanted to hurt herself. As Jodie pounded her head with her fists, I knelt down behind her and took hold of her arms, crossing them in front of her body. She was still screaming, and her legs were thrashing, but with her arms enfolded she couldn't harm herself or me. I held her close, so that her back was resting against my chest. The screaming and thrashing reached a peak, and then eventually subsided. I waited patiently until she was calm, then slowly relaxed my hold.

'OK?' I asked gently, before I finally let go.

She nodded, and I turned her round to face me. We were both still on the floor. Her cheeks were red and blotchy, and she looked surprised, probably because I'd managed her anger, rather than fleeing for safety into another room. A moment later I helped her up, then took her into the kitchen, where I sponged her face and gave her a drink. She was calm now, calmer than I'd seen her since she first arrived. I hoped she'd got something out of her system.

Paula reappeared in the kitchen. 'Jodie, would you like to do a jigsaw puzzle with me?' she asked casually.

'That's a lovely idea,' I said, amazed at Paula's resilience and generosity. She understood that Jodie's violent behaviour wasn't directed at her personally; Jodie wanted to strike out at the whole world because she was hurting so much, and whoever was standing in her way would bear the brunt of her pain. Paula could sense this, and was prepared to forget and offer friendship and time. I was very proud of her.

'Shall we go to the cupboard and choose one?' Paula asked.

We found a jigsaw and went through to the lounge, where Paula and Jodie settled down to assemble the puzzle. I left them to it and returned to the kitchen to prepare lunch. I could hear Paula suggesting where the pieces should go, and Jodie replying, 'That's it, my girl. You can do it.' She was like a little old woman, but at least she was relating to Paula in a positive way.

With her short attention span, it didn't take long for Jodie to become bored, so Paula laid out some paper on the kitchen table, and tried to help her paint, while I made a cup of tea. Jodie could barely grip the paintbrush, and couldn't grasp the concept of painting a picture 'of' something.

'What's that you're painting, Jodie?' Paula asked.

'Dark.'

'Is it a sheep, or a horse? That looks a bit like a big horse.'

Jodie didn't respond, intent on her clumsy project.

'Maybe you could paint the sky with this nice blue?'

'No. Black,' Jodie said.

Despite Paula's encouragement, Jodie continued to paint nothing but large, dark splodges, with no interest in the other colours, and no apparent desire for the paintings to represent anything. I'd seen this before; children who have been abused and are hurting sometimes only use very dark colours. It's as if their senses have shut down and they don't notice anything about the world around them, so they don't see colours and shapes in the same way normal children do.

We ate lunch in relative calm, although it felt more like dinner to me, having been up for so long. The peace lasted into the afternoon, and I thought now would be a good time to take the photograph of Jodie that was required for the Social Services' records. I fetched my camera, and explained to Jodie why I was taking it.

'Is it all right to take your picture, sweet?' I asked. It was important to give Jodie as much control as possible, to increase her feeling of stability and security.

She shrugged, which I decided to take as consent. Paula moved to one side, so I had just Jodie in the picture. I looked through the lens, and framed her head and shoulders against the wall, centring her in the viewfinder.

'You can smile, Jodie,' I said. She was looking very stern.

I saw her mouth pucker to a sheepish grin, then an arm came up, and she disappeared from view. 'Very funny, Jodie. Come on, stand still.' I was still looking through the lens. Then her other arm came up, and with it her jumper.

I lowered the camera. 'Jodie, what are you doing?'

'Taking off my clothes.'

'Why?' asked Paula, and quickly pulled Jodie's top back into place.

She didn't answer. She was staring at me, but not scowling, so I quickly took the photograph and closed the camera. 'Jodie, we don't normally take our clothes off for a photograph,' I said. 'Why did you do that?'

She took a piece of the jigsaw and tried to place it. 'Want to,' she said, lowering her voice. 'Want to. My clothes.'

'I know, sweet, but why take them off for a photograph? I didn't ask you to.'

She turned to Paula. 'You helping, girl, or not?'

I smiled at Paula, and nodded for her to continue. I went over to my filing cabinet under the stairs and unlocked it. I wasn't going to jump to conclusions about Jodie's behaviour, but I had to make a note of it in the log. I took out the desk diary that the fostering agency had supplied and settled down to write everything that had happened so far. The 'log' is a daily record of a child's progress, and is something that all foster carers keep. It is used to update the social workers and to monitor the child's progress, and it's sometimes used as evidence during care proceedings in court. I was assiduous about keeping it up to date because I knew only too well how one incident could blend into another and how disturbed nights could all seem the same after a while. Detail was important: only with careful notes could a pattern of behaviour start to emerge. I made a note of exactly what had happened: the self-harming in the night and the strange detachment; the lashing out at other people and violent tantrums marked by Jodie's desire to hurt herself; and this strange and unsettling response to having her photograph taken. Why had she started to take her clothes off?

I was resolute that I would not rush into any hasty judgements. I needed to accept Jodie exactly as she was for the time being and then see what came from the pattern of her behaviour. I was uneasy, though, and also found it cathartic to be able to put it down on paper.

With the other two out for the day, Paula and I took it in turns to entertain Jodie throughout the afternoon, but despite this, and for no apparent reason, she threw another full-scale tantrum. I allowed her to continue for a few minutes, hoping it would run its course. When it didn't, and the high-pitched screaming became intolerable, I enfolded her in my arms as I had before, until she had calmed down. Later, I made another note of Jodie's erratic behaviour in the log. I was doing a lot of writing.

Our first weekend with Jodie was an exhausting and disturbing experience. Although none of us said anything, it was obvious that we were all thinking the same thing. But it was early days and we all knew from experience that children can settle down after an initial bout of odd behaviour.

'She's a very troubled child,' I said to Jill when she phoned the following Monday to see how things were going. I told her about the self-harming and the violent and aggressive tantrums.

'Yes, that is bad,' said Jill. 'It's very disturbed behaviour, particularly in such a young child. Do you think you can cope with her?'

'I'm determined to try,' I said. 'She's hardly been here five minutes. I want to give her as much of a chance as possible. Besides, we knew she was not going to be easy from the start so we can't be surprised if she's a handful at first. I'm keeping detailed notes of everything that happens, though.'

'Good. We'll just have to monitor it and see how it goes. You're definitely the best person she could possibly be with, so as long as you're happy, I know she's in safe hands.'

I listened out for Jodie – she was occupied watching a Tiny Tots video – and then went through my log for Jill, trying to think of something positive to say. 'She eats well. Actually, she gorges. I'm having to limit her intake. She nearly made herself sick yesterday. Apart from a healthy appetite, she doesn't have much else going for her at present, I'm afraid.'

'Do you think she can be contained within a family, Cathy? If she can't, the borough will have to start looking for a therapeutic unit, and they're few and far between. I have every faith in your judgement.'

I appreciated the compliment, but it was small comfort. I was already exhausted. I was worried about whether or not I'd be able to see this through and the prospect of failing before I'd even begun did nothing for my stamina. 'She's got contact with her parents tomorrow and her tutor's coming for a couple of hours next week. Perhaps a familiar face might help settle her. She's been seeing her tutor since September.'

'OK, Cathy, we'll see how it goes. I'll update Eileen. What are you going to do with her today?'

'Retail therapy. Courtesy of Tesco's.'

Jill laughed. 'I'll give it a wide berth.'

Jodie apparently loved food shopping, unlike the rest of my family who could think of nothing worse than a trip to the supermarket. She was in her element, pushing the trolley up and down, telling me what we should or shouldn't buy. In fact, she was so enthusiastic I had to limit her exuberance, and return some items to the shelves.

This wasn't unusual; children in care often seem to feel that all their problems can be solved by a bottomless purse. Children I'd looked after often had a desperate need for material goods. In the homes they had come from money was often short, and when there was any it was frequently spent on drink, drugs or cigarettes. When I started buying my foster children little treats, they would often find it very exciting and pleasurable: treats were something they had very little experience of. But I always had to be careful about managing their expectations, as they could very quickly become demanding and assume they'd be given anything they wanted. Jodie was a different case, though; from the looks of her luggage and her weight, treats had never been in short supply – which meant that she was used to getting anything she fancied. I hoped it wasn't going to be too much of a struggle restricting her to a sensible limit, but experience was already teaching me to expect a battle.

'Three packets of cereal is plenty,' I said. 'Choose one you'd like and we'll put the others back.'

She wanted them all, of course, and every packet of biscuits, and every dessert in the freezer cabinet, so I was spending as much time taking things out of the trolley as I was putting them in, but at least she was occupied and content.

It took nearly two hours to complete the weekly shop, and as we finally reached the check-out Jodie spotted the display of sweets, tantalizingly placed at the side of the aisle. I started unloading the trolley on to the belt, and told her to choose a bar of chocolate as a treat, because she'd been such a good girl and helped.

'One,' I repeated, as the bags of sweets started raining into the trolley. But I could see her previous cooperation was waning fast. 'Take the chocolate bonbons, you like those.'

'Want them all!' she shouted, and then sat on the floor defiantly.

The woman queuing behind us was clearly unimpressed by my parenting skills, and shot me one of those looks. I unloaded the last of the shopping, including the bonbons, onto the conveyor, and put the other sweets back on the rack. I watched Jodie out of the corner of my eye. Her anger was mounting, as she crossed her legs, folded her arms and set her face in a sneer. She kicked the trolley so that it jarred against my side. I clenched my teeth, pretending that it hadn't hurt. I pulled the trolley through the aisle and positioned it at the end, ready to receive the bags of shopping.

'Are you going to help me pack?' I said, trying to distract her. 'You were a big help earlier and I could do with your help now.'

She refused to make eye contact, and I began to wonder how I was going to remove her from the aisle, but I was determined that she wouldn't get what she wanted by making a scene in public.

'Don't want those sweets,' she suddenly yelled. 'Don't like them.'

I looked at her. 'Don't shout, please. I've said you can choose one, but hurry up. We've nearly finished.'

People were now openly staring. Petulantly, Jodie hauled herself to her feet, picked up a family-sized bag of boiled sweets and threw them at the cashier.

'Jodie!' I turned to the cashier, who was busy exchanging meaningful glances with the woman

69

behind us. 'I'm so sorry.' I paid, apologized again, and we left.

Outside, I ignored Jodie's screams for the sweets and pushed the trolley fast towards the car. I unlocked the doors and strapped her under her belt. 'Stay there while I load the bags into the boot. I'm cross, Jodie. That was very naughty.'

I watched her through the rear window. Her jaw was clenched as she muttered to herself and thumped the seat beside her. I knew how she felt; I was in the mood for thumping the seat myself. It had been a draining experience already and all I could do was prepare myself for more hurricanes and hysteria. Giving in to tantrums wouldn't help her or me in the long term.

I took the trolley back, then got into the front seat.

'Give me the sweets,' she growled. 'Want them now.'

'When you've calmed down and apologized, Jodie. I'm not having that behaviour in public.'

'Give me them, or I'll poo on your back seat,' she threatened.

'I beg your pardon? You most certainly will not!' So, I thought, she was prepared to soil herself if I didn't give her exactly what she wanted. Is that what had happened on the first day? Was this her trying to exert her will, rather than anxiety or poor bowel control? And much as I didn't want her to make a mess on the back seat, I wasn't prepared to give in to this kind of blackmail.

'Jodie, if you mess on the back seat deliberately you won't get any sweets all day. You can't just make a fuss and get everything you want. I'm sure you didn't at your previous carers.'

'Did. Everything. I made them.'

I started the car and pulled towards the exit. I didn't doubt that what she was saying was true. Given Jodie's appalling behaviour, it was no wonder her previous carers had given in to her demands, just to keep her quiet. Presumably, this was how she'd acquired the piles of clothes and toys that she'd arrived with. I glanced in the rear-view mirror. She stuck out her tongue, then started kicking the back of my seat.

'Jodie, I know it's a hard lesson, pet, but being naughty won't get you what you want. Just the opposite, in fact.'

'I had everything I wanted at home,' she said, suddenly more coherent.

'Really,' I replied, unimpressed.

'I made them, or I'd tell.'

I hesitated. 'Tell what, Jodie?'

There was a long silence. 'Nothing. Can I have my sweets now, Cathy? I'm sorry. I won't do it again.'

'OK, just as soon as we get home.'

As we pulled into the driveway, the sour smell coming from the back seat made me realize that she had made good on her threat. It would be another unwelcome date with the shower for us as soon as we got through the front door.

71

CHAPTER 7

CONTACT

'Did the previous carers say anything about defecation as a means of control?' I asked Eileen, Jodie's social worker, when she phoned the next day. It was the first time we had spoken since I'd met her at the pre-placement meeting, and I was glad to hear from her. A good social worker can make all the difference on the case, and I was hoping that Eileen and I would have a supportive working relationship. 'She threatens to make a mess if she doesn't get what she wants, and she's done it twice. The first time I put it down to anxiety but the last time was in the car when I wouldn't buy her all the sweets she wanted. She threatened to soil all over the back seat and then she did it.'

Eileen paused and I was sure that the answer would be yes, although it would probably be qualified. Jodie's modus operandi was too polished to have started when she came to me; she'd clearly been using defecation as a form of blackmail for a little while.

'There might be something in the file. Why? Is it going to be a problem?'

The idea that a child threatening to poo herself when she didn't get her own way and then carrying out her threat *not* being a problem almost made me want to laugh. I could hear in Eileen's voice the worry that I might be about to hand Jodie back, and the implication that, if so, I was over-reacting a bit. Constant soiling might not seem like a big issue to her, but then she wasn't the one who had to clean it up.

'If I'm going to be able to meet this child's needs,' I replied, 'it's important that I'm given all the relevant information. Could you check and get back to me, please?'

'I'll have a look in the file,' she said, but I doubted she would. If she hadn't familiarized herself with the case already, there was little compunction to do so now Jodie had been placed with me. I knew from long experience how these things worked.

Eileen changed the subject. 'Contact has been confirmed for tomorrow,' she said, using the social-work term meaning a meeting between a child and its natural parents. 'The escort will collect her at six, if that's OK.'

'That's fine. But why is it so late?'

'Jodie's father can't make it from work any earlier and he's most insistent on seeing her. He hasn't missed one yet.'

I heard Eileen's inference. Clearly she felt that this showed a commitment on his part, which suggested a strong attachment between father and daughter. If all went well over the next few months, and Jodie's parents could get their lives in order, there was a good chance Jodie would go back to them. Generally, the Social Services try to rehabilitate families wherever possible. The final decision would be made by a judge, at a care hearing in the family court.

'Was there anything else?' Eileen asked, clearly hoping there wasn't.

'Her behaviour is as stated.' I'd told her everything that had happened, just as I had Jill, but Eileen didn't seem to have much in the way of response to any of the reports of self-harm, violent tantrums or anything else. I could feel my heart sinking as I realized that it was unlikely Jodie was going to get the kind of support I'd hoped for from her. 'Let's hope we can make a difference,' I finished.

The next morning, I was woken by Jodie stamping down the stairs at 5 a.m. I was getting used to the disturbed nights – she was calling out for me a couple of times a night and seemed to be suffering from nightmares – and the invariable early starts. I'd had a feeling this would be a pattern with Jodie: in general, the more disturbed children are, the more troubled their nights are and the earlier they rise in the morning. Sometimes that can be because foster children have been used to the responsibility of looking after younger siblings and have quite often had to get their parents up in the morning and make the family breakfast. In other cases, it is because they are on constant alert and consequently unable to sleep much at a time because their survival mechanism is always switched on. So it was no surprise that Jodie was up and about at dawn.

I leapt out of the bed and hurriedly followed; the last thing I wanted was Jodie left alone in the kitchen. I managed to persuade her to go back to bed, but each time I thought I'd settled her, she'd be off again minutes later. By the third time I was fully awake, and there was no point going back to bed. I sat in the living room, trying to read, with one ear alert to what Jodie was up to.

A couple of hours later I heard Paula get up, followed shortly after by Lucy and then Adrian.

I had started preparing breakfast, when I suddenly heard Jodie shouting. Rushing upstairs, I found Paula standing in the bathroom doorway wearing only a towel, while Jodie sat on the landing, glaring at her menacingly.

'Whatever's going on?' I asked.

'I'm trying to get past, but she keeps kicking me,' replied Paula, obviously frustrated and vulnerable.

At this, Jodie started screaming and banging the floor with her fists and feet. I waited for her to calm down, then went over and gently lifted her to her feet and guided her towards the stairs.

'Come on, Jodie, why don't you help me make you some breakfast? You must be hungry by now.'

She resisted at first, but eventually followed me downstairs, presumably feeling that she'd won this battle, and Paula was allowed to continue getting ready in peace.

Downstairs, Jodie agreed to lay the table, while I boiled the kettle and set out four cups. She'd already been extremely trying this morning, but as I watched her lay the table I was reminded of how difficult her life was. Even in performing this simple task, Jodie's limitations were obvious. She couldn't grip the cutlery, because her motor skills were so poor; instead, she clamped the pile to her chest. Predictably enough, on her way to the table she dropped one of the spoons. She grunted in frustration, then dropped the rest of the cutlery on the table, making a loud clang. She picked up the stray spoon from the floor, licked it on both sides, then wiped it on her sleeve, and proceeded to set the places.

It was no surprise that she was so clumsy. Poor motor skills and bad coordination are all part of developmental delay. I was no expert on the matter, but I knew that a lack of stimulation of an infant's brain could have a severe impact on its growth and development. Even being given a rattle to hold helps a baby learn about how the world works and teaches the muscles and brain to respond, so that it can master its environment. Later on, reading books and playing with jigsaws and puzzles help the brain continue to grow and learn. While I didn't want to leap to conclusions about what had happened to Jodie in the past, I couldn't help wondering if neglect and a lack of stimulation had contributed to her acute malco-ordination and clumsiness. It certainly wouldn't be the first time I'd seen it, though never this pronounced.

'Well done, Jodie,' I said, with exaggerated enthusiasm. 'You've been a big help'.

She barely responded to my praise, and that too was unusual. It was odd to meet a child who didn't enjoy approval. She seemed very shut off and far away, and nothing I said seemed to reach her. I'd been expecting something of the sort but the extent of it was beginning to puzzle and worry me.

I poured Jodie some Rice Krispies, and finished making the tea. Paula and Lucy came down together and sat at the table. Jodie's mood switched immediately, as it seemed to when the other children came into the room. I could see her becoming tense, and her eyes narrowing with anger. She looked up at Paula with an unpleasant grimace, then started poking her in the ribs.

'Stop that, Jodie!' I said, but she persisted. Paula tried to fend her off, and then lost her temper, and poked her back. Jodie started screaming, making the most of the minor assault.

'Paula, you mustn't do that!' I said, angry with her for losing control. 'Now, the pair of you behave!'

'Sorry, Mum,' said Paula.

77

'And apologize to Jodie, please,' I said, feeling slightly guilty. I knew Paula would feel this was unfair, with good cause, but it was in all of our interests to make it clear to Jodie that you didn't poke, and you apologized after doing something wrong.

'Sorry, Jodie,' Paula muttered, without looking up. Jodie was still clutching her side melodramatically, so I decided there was little chance of coaxing an apology out of her, and left it at that.

'Thank you, Paula. That was the adult thing to do.'

The children left for school, and Jodie helped me to clear the table and load the dishwasher, thankfully without any mishaps. Then we sat down in the living room and I tried to interest her in some games. I decided now might be a good time to broach the subject of her contact. She would be seeing her parents twice a week for an hour at a contact centre, with a social worker present all the time. Meetings with natural parents are generally arranged some time in advance, but my policy was to remind the children only on the day, as mention of it could often unsettle them. In my experience, children tended to play up just before contact so I made the time available for this emotional upheaval as short as possible for all our sakes.

'Jodie,' I said brightly, 'you'll have your bath later this afternoon, because you're going to see your parents tonight.'

She looked at me blankly. Had she understood? She carried on playing, mashing stickle bricks together. After a moment, she asked, 'Am I going in a van?'

'No, the escort will pick you up here in a car, just like when you were at your previous carers. They'll take you to meet your parents, and then bring you back here.'

'Not going in a van. Hate them. Blimmin' vans,' she replied, becoming more animated.

'That's right, Jodie, the escort will pick you up in a car. I know your dad's looking forward to seeing you. That will be nice, won't it?' Apparently, however, I'd lost her attention, and she returned to her playing, with a puzzled expression on her face. It was hard to tell what she made of the prospect of seeing her mother and father again.

Jodie was difficult for the rest of the day, as I'd expected. She had two more tantrums before lunch, and caused me a minor panic when she knocked a picture off the wall, smashing the glass, then tried to pick it up. In the afternoon, I kept her occupied with a singalong video in the lounge, while I prepared dinner. At four o'clock Adrian came in warily, and was relieved not to be greeted with a kick from Jodie. He joined me in the kitchen, and told me about his day. It felt like a long time since we'd had the chance to have a chat in peace without screaming, tantrums or violent fits, even though Jodie had been with us less than a week. It was lovely to have a few

79

moments with my son and I knew how important it was to snatch any opportunity to spend time with my own family in the often demanding first weeks of a new placement.

Adrian went to take his bag up to his room, and I was pleased to hear him go into the lounge first, to say hello to Jodie. However, my moment of pleasure was short-lived, as I suddenly heard him shout, 'Oh God! Mum, come in here!'

I rushed into the hallway, as Adrian marched upstairs. In the lounge, I found Jodie sitting on the sofa with her legs in the air and one hand in her knickers, masturbating.

'Jodie, stop that!' I said firmly.

'Why?' she barked.

'If you want to do that, you go to your room and do it. It's private. Is that clear? Now, either go upstairs or sit properly please, good girl.'

She glared at me for a few seconds, and I prepared myself for another tantrum, but eventually she pulled her skirt down and sat up straight.

I was puzzled and disturbed by this new incidence, of this time highly sexualized behaviour. I knew that it was not unusual for very young children to masturbate, even if it wasn't generally talked about; but by the time a child was eight years old he or she usually had a sense that this was not something to be done in public, even when the child had learning difficulties. Was Jodie intending to be observed? Given that we were always in and out of the lounge, she must

80

have known she'd be seen. Was she trying to shock us, or was it something entirely unconscious? An act of self-comfort, or a physical habit as harmless as sucking her thumb? I didn't know the answer, but anything that came within the framework of sexualized behaviour had to be noted down. I made a mental note to log it in the diary, and raise it with Eileen the next time we spoke.

When the girls arrived home from school they were both greeted with a vicious thump, and I wearily told Jodie off. She had another full-scale tantrum, and I again had to restrain her. Eventually, she calmed down, and I finished making the evening meal, which was spaghetti bolognaise. We sat down to eat, and I cut up Jodie's spaghetti for her.

'Want burger,' she demanded, pulling a face.

'We'll have a burger another night. I've done this for now.'

She picked up her plate and hurled it against the wall. It hit the wall with a crack and the plate fell in pieces to the ground. There was a vivid splash of dark bolognese mixed with strings of spaghetti on the wall. It began sliding downwards, before dropping on to the floor. We all looked at it in silence for a moment and then I felt the children gaze at me in shock.

Anger and frustration rushed through me. I had put up with Jodie's bad behaviour all day and was worn out with it and her. Now she had thrown a perfectly good meal away, caused a terrible mess and upset us all, for no good reason that I could see.

'Go to your room!' I snapped. 'I've had quite enough of this for one day!'

She struggled down from her seat, and as she left the table, punched Lucy in the back of the head, hard, with a closed fist. She stormed out of the room, slamming the door with such force that a piece of plaster fell from the ceiling. Lucy didn't say anything, but I could see the tears welling in her eyes. I hugged her.

'I'm sorry,' I said, mortified that I could have caused my children such pain. 'I think I've made a mistake. I shouldn't have accepted her. This is too difficult for all of us. I'll speak to the social worker first thing in the morning.'

At a little after six the doorbell rang, and a dishevelled young man introduced himself as Jodie's escort for contact. Jodie bounded down the stairs and left in a cheerful mood, waving goodbye as she walked up the garden path. Was she completely unrepentant, I wondered? Was she even aware of how bad her behaviour had been, or the sad atmosphere which now pervaded the house?

It was the first moment of real peace in almost a week. The children were upstairs doing their homework. I sat in the living room with the television on, although I wasn't paying attention. Instead my mind was in turmoil. Life with Jodie was not only far from easy, it was well-nigh impossible, and for the first time I was beginning to feel as though I might not be able to reach her. Jodie was the most disturbed, demanding child I'd ever come across; she was so cold and unresponsive, with no desire to be liked. It was not possible to find a way to mediate with her because she had no interest in meeting me halfway. It seemed as if she didn't want to change but was content to remain in her far-off state, shut into her own world, expressing herself through tantrums and violence. In my experience, human relationships are all about give and take and mutual needs for affection and approval being met. If one party has absolutely no need of anything the other party has to offer, then where can the compromise come? That's how it was with Jodie. I had never known a child so shut off, or so unseeking of warmth and affection. It seemed that the task I had set myself of caring for Jodie and somehow breaking through the huge barrier of emotional coldness around her had magnified itself a hundred times. I was in a no-win situation. I couldn't have Jodie stay, because it was unfair on my children; her behaviour was just too disruptive. I couldn't bear to see their home life and their security undermined and destroyed when they had just as much need of love and stability as Jodie, even if it was less pronounced.

On the other hand, I knew what sending Jodie back now would mean. Not only would it be yet another rejection, and another black mark against her name, turning her into an object of fascinated horror – 'Six carers in four months! Just think how awful she must be!' – but it would also condemn her to a children's home. I knew that a children's home was not the right environment for Jodie, and also that it would probably mean that her last chance of living in a normal family was gone for good. If I didn't keep her, then no one else would take her in. And what was the point of being a foster carer if you couldn't help the most troubled children?

As I sat and worried, I heard three pairs of feet coming down the stairs. Lucy and Paula entered and sat either side of me, while Adrian disappeared to make us a cup of tea. I was touched; the children had come to comfort me about my failure. Adrian returned with a tray of drinks. 'There you go, Mum,' he said.

'Thanks, love.'

Adrian looked at the girls, then cleared his throat. 'Mum, we've been thinking,' he said, and paused.

'Oh yes?' I replied, expecting another request to extend their coming-in time.

'Yes. We want Jodie to stay, for a while at least. We think we should wait, and see how it goes.'

I couldn't say anything for a moment while I absorbed this, taken aback by their generosity. Life had been pretty miserable for the last week, and home, far from being a refuge of safety and contentment, had become a place where vicious kicks, punches and sudden attacks, along with spine-curdling yelling, high-pitched screaming and disturbed nights, were just par for the course. Were my children really prepared to put up with this indefinitely, when I had offered to hand Jodie back and restore calm and quiet to our home? Yet again, I was stunned by their extraordinary kindness and maturity when it came to the children we fostered. I looked over to Lucy and Paula. 'Are you sure?' I asked anxiously. I didn't want them to regret this. 'Is this really what you want? She'll probably get worse rather than better in the short term.'

'We all want her to stay,' said Lucy firmly. 'We know she'll get better. And if not we can always kick her out next time!' She grinned mischievously.

I felt a surge of relief, as well as immense admiration for my children. I know I'm biased, and I'm sure other parents feel the same about their kids, but at moments like these I couldn't help but swell with pride.

It was after eight by the time Jodie returned from seeing her parents, and she was in high spirits. So were we. We'd had almost three hours' respite, and we had a new sense of purpose. Jodie proudly showed us the dolls and sweets her father had given her. She also pointedly told me twice he had bought her burger and chips. I smiled. I was used to being played off against the parents of my foster children. No doubt the parents got the same kind of thing themselves. Apart from her boasting, Jodie had nothing else to say about her contact with her parents.

It was well past her bedtime, so with my usual mixture of coercion and repetition I took her up to the bathroom, then saw her into bed. She didn't want the new dolls, but instead chose a large panda she had brought with her, and snuggled into it. I read her a short story, then said goodnight. I left the light on, came out and closed the door. I was feeling optimistic. Now Jodie had seen her parents, she might start to settle, with the two halves of her life running side by side. I sat in the lounge, and picked up the book I'd been trying to read for a fortnight. It was a comic satire, and it made me laugh out loud. At 9.30 Paula called from the landing that she was ready for me to tuck her in; it was a ritual she wasn't too old for, as long as her friends didn't find out.

As I went in, I noticed her rag-doll pyjama case wasn't on the bed. 'Where's Betsy?' I asked.

She looked at me, with her eyes large and imploring. 'Don't be upset, Mum, but I think there's been an accident.'

'What sort of accident?'

She nodded at the wardrobe. I went over and slid the door open. Lying at the bottom was Betsy, with her head ripped off, and stuffing falling out of her neck.

86

'This isn't an accident, is it, pet?' I picked up the dismembered parts. 'Why didn't you tell me sooner?'

'I didn't want more upset, Mum. It's only a toy. Really. It doesn't matter.'

I sat on the bed, reminded once again of how much the family had to put up with. 'I'm sorry, love. I watched her like a hawk today. The only time I didn't was when I was in the loo. I'll try and find another one, but in future you must tell me. I know you feel sorry for her but if there's any chance of us helping her, she's going to have to learn. OK?'

She agreed, and we had a big hug, then I left her reading and continued my night-time rounds. I knocked on Lucy's door, and waited for her shout of 'Come in!' She was in her pyjamas, propped on the pillows.

I sensed immediately that something was wrong. 'Not you as well?' I said.

She opened her bedside cabinet, and took out her makeup box. I looked at the congealed mess of black mascara, blue eye shadow and beige foundation.

'It's my fault,' she said quickly. 'I shouldn't have left it on the bed.'

'Of course you should! You have every right to leave your things out in your room. I'll speak to her first thing in the morning.' I repeated what I'd told Paula – that I'd replace it, but she had to tell me immediately if it happened again, so that

I could deal with it at the time. It seemed that Jodie hadn't taken my explanation about privacy very much to heart.

She took my hand and gave it a squeeze. 'Cathy, was I this naughty when I first arrived? I don't remember.'

'No. You had your moments but I wouldn't have expected any different. You'd had a lot of moves but you soon settled. What we're seeing in Jodie is severely disturbed behaviour.'

She looked away. 'I know I shouldn't say this, but sometimes she gives me the creeps. When she stares at me, it's so cold I think she could kill me.'

'It's OK. I understand. She hasn't had much love and I'm hoping we can change that. Now off to sleep. You've got your science exam tomorrow, haven't you?'

She grinned sheepishly. 'I will, and thanks for looking after me. I do love you, you know that, don't you?'

It was the first time she'd said it, and ironically it had taken the hatred of a disturbed child to cement our relationship. 'I love you too, sweet. You're a good girl. Jodie couldn't have a better example.'

CHAPTER 8

JULIE

Jodie had been living with us a little over a week when her eighth birthday arrived. I'd got so used to thinking of her as eight already because that's how the Social Services had always referred to her, but in fact she was on the tail end of seven years old when she arrived. Jodie celebrated her birthday with her parents at the next contact session and spent her actual birthday with us.

When she got back from her birthday celebration with her parents, Jodie was loaded down with more bags of big, cheap, glittery toys of the kind that would last five minutes, and hold her interest for half that time. But if the amount was anything to go by, Jodie was certainly used to getting plenty of what she wanted. Even so, just as with the new things she had brought back from her previous contact sessions, the novelties and toys didn't hold much charm for her. It seemed she liked getting them, but after a moment or two they had no worth or meaning.

I asked Jodie what she would like to do for her birthday and she announced that she would like to go bowling, which surprised me. Bowling didn't seem to be something that a child with such bad coordination would enjoy much, but it was her birthday and if that was what she wanted, then that was what we would do. Bowling it was. As Jodie wasn't at school, there were no friends to ask along, so it was Jodie, Paula, Lucy, Adrian and me.

First, we opened her presents at home. I'd put a lot of thought into what to get her. I could tell she liked dolls' things, and she seemed to treasure her life-size doll, Julie, so I bought her a doll's car seat, just like the real thing, and a doll's high chair. She unwrapped her presents without the excitement I would usually have expected in a child, examined them and then pushed them to one side without any further comment. I felt vaguely hurt, and rather mystified. It wasn't that she didn't like them – it was just as though nothing had any value for her, and I couldn't understand why. But I quickly put the anti-climax of the gifts behind us, and we all left for bowling.

As I'd suspected, Jodie couldn't bowl to save her life, but she seemed to have a good time anyway, although she did her usual stomping about, hands on hips, ordering everyone around. But there were no tantrums, either in the bowling alley or later in McDonald's, which was where she wanted to go for dinner. But then, as it was her birthday, we were all obediently doing what she wanted and she rewarded us by not throwing a screaming fit or landing a punch or two. We all went home, satisfied that Jodie's birthday had gone as well as it possibly could.

One morning, after Jodie had been with us for a fortnight and the day after a contact session with her parents, I left her playing in her room until everyone had gone to school. She wasn't happy about this, but I needed to establish some sort of working routine, and a peaceful breakfast would be a good start. Once the others had left for school, I went up and told Jodie she could get dressed, and asked her what she wanted for breakfast.

'Nothing. Hate you,' she snarled and poked out her tongue. 'Bugger off.'

'That's a pity,' I said, ignoring the swear word, 'because I like you, and I'm looking forward to our day together.'

She stared at me as though I'd finally lost it. 'Why? Why do you like me?'

'Because underneath that angry Jodie is a kind and happy Jodie waiting to come out. Now get dressed and come down for breakfast.'

And she did. Without arguing. I gave her lots of praise and mentally awarded us both a gold star.

The tutor was coming to give Jodie her lessons but she wasn't due until 1.30, so in the morning we went shopping to replace Paula's pyjama case and Lucy's makeup. In the car, I explained to Jodie where we were going and why. She didn't comment, and I wasn't looking for a confession, so I restated our rules regarding other people's bedrooms and property and left it at that. I found what I was looking for in the department store, then took the escalator to the top floor, and headed for the café. We both had a piece of apple cake, and sat by the window, looking down on the street below. We could have been any normal mother and daughter on a day out, and I wondered, not for the first time, what had happened to knock Jodie's life so far off course. She seemed much more deeply damaged than Gary had led me to expect in the case history he'd given at the pre-placement meeting. Whenever I wondered what had happened to her, I put a mental stop on myself. Not only was it unprofessional to make assumptions but I knew that it was far too early to see any patterns in her behaviour. As it was, Jodie kept me so busy that it was impossible to stand back and see the bigger picture. At least I would get a couple of hours to catch up on paper-work while she was with her tutor that afternoon.

We finished our drinks, then had a look around the shops on the first floor. I could see Jodie was flagging, so we decided to call it a day, and walked over to the lifts. I showed Jodie how to push the button, and explained to her how the lift worked. By the time it arrived, there were a number of people waiting, but we were the first in line. We walked in, and stood at the back. Jodie held my hand, but as the doors started to close she pulled my arm and started shouting. 'No! Make it stop! Don't want to!'

I quickly leaned in between two women and pushed the button to reopen the doors, apologizing as I led Jodie out. I bent down and put my hands on her shoulders. 'What's the matter, Jodie? There's nothing to be scared of.'

'Don't want to,' she moaned. 'I'm not going in there!'

'That's OK, we don't have to if you don't want to. We'll just take the escalator instead.'

We walked over to the escalator, and Jodie gripped my hand as we descended. 'I'll take my dad in there,' she said, her face crumpling.

'What, in the lift?'

She nodded. 'I'll scare him. See how he likes it. I'll show him.'

'Why do you want to scare him, Jodie?'

But she just shrugged. She had closed down again, and the door that had briefly opened on her past had slammed shut.

Jodie recovered quickly from her fright, and by the time we returned home I was feeling positive again. I praised her over and over, telling her what a nice time I'd had, and how much I had enjoyed her company. She said she was hungry, so I left her playing with Julie, her life-size doll, and went into the kitchen. She wanted peanut butter in her sandwich, and I spread it thinly. I was determined to do something about her weight. I set the plate on the breakfast bar and poured a glass of squash, then started towards the lounge to tell her it was ready.

Something made me hesitate before going in. Perhaps it was the quiet. I couldn't hear the usual babble that accompanied everything Jodie did. I looked round the half-open door, and froze. She was still playing with Julie, but had pulled the doll's dress up, and was licking between its naked legs. She was making low, grunting noises as if from pleasure, and seemed totally oblivious to my presence. I walked in and Jodie looked up.

'That looks a strange game, Jodie,' I said evenly. 'What are you doing?' I knew that showing any alarm or surprise was not the way to go, and telling her off would be counter-productive. Besides, I needed to know if she understood what she was doing.

She glanced down between the doll's legs, then up again at me. There was no embarrassment. 'Kissing,' she said, with a grin. 'She likes kissing, she does.'

'Isn't it an odd place to kiss her? We usually kiss each other on the cheek.'

She looked surprised. 'But you haven't got a man. Mans kiss here' – she pointed to Julie's naked crotch – 'and girls here.' She jabbed her forefinger at her cheek.

I went over and sat on the floor beside her. I needed to stay calm, so that Jodie would too, and to keep her talking for as long as I could. I had to find out what she'd seen, deal with it, and inform the social worker. She wouldn't be the first child to have watched an adult video, or slept in the parents' bedroom with no partition – I hoped that this was all it was, Jodie acting out something she had seen when she wasn't supposed to. I would log it down in my notebook, though, in case any other kind of picture emerged. I tried to remain professional: calm but direct.

'Jodie, can you tell me how you know men kiss there?'

She shrugged. 'Just know. Girls like it and men do it. Mummies, daddies and girls.'

'And were you pretending Julie was a mummy or a girl?'

'Don't know. A lady.'

'OK, so if Julie was the lady, who were you pretending to be?'

'The man!' She frowned, impatient at my slowness.

'Any man? Or were you thinking of one?'

She hesitated, screwing up her brow. 'Don't know. A daddy. A big big daddy.'

I couldn't read anything into this. All men were daddies to her, as they are to many young children. I needed to steer her round to describing what she had seen, and where, but before I could get any further she suddenly jumped up and started kicking the doll viciously.

'It's her fault!' she shouted, her eyes blazing. 'It's her fault! I told her no! Now look what you've done! I told you to keep your big mouth shut!'

I flinched as the doll's plastic head clattered against the radiator. She was shouting at Julie as if repeating something that she'd heard. I took her arm, picked up the doll, and led the three of us to the sofa. 'Come on, sweet, calm down. There's no point in hurting Julie.'

She cradled the doll in her lap, and stroked her head, whispering words of comfort, trying to make her better. 'Don't worry,' she said. 'You're safe with me. Sshh. Sshh. It was wrong of the man, wasn't it?'

'Yes,' I said, not sure if she was talking to the doll or me. 'What the man did seemed very wrong.' I paused. 'Jodie, sometimes we see things that we don't understand. It looks like people are hurting each other and it can make us very unhappy. Did you see a man kissing a woman there?' I pointed to the doll's legs. 'What we call our private parts?'

'Yes.'

'Where did you see this? On television?'

'In the bedroom and the car,' she replied clearly.

'The car? I don't understand. Was there a television in the car?'

She shook her head.

'But you saw this in a bedroom and a car?'

She nodded.

'Whose car was it?'

'The man's. It was a big van.'

96

I paused. 'Was it a film, Jodie, or was it real?'

She screwed up her eyes, as though blotting out the image. Her reply was barely audible. 'Real. He was there. The girl and the daddy.'

'And who was the girl? Do you know her name?'

She crushed the doll's face into her chest. 'Jodie. Me. Jodie's bedroom. Daddy's car.'

'Your daddy?'

'Yes.'

CHAPTER 9

DISCLOSURE

We sat quietly for some time. I had my arm around Jodie, and she had hers around Julie. My heart was thumping and my mouth was dry. This was the very worst confirmation of my suspicions. The little pieces of evidence had all been pointing this way but I had forced myself not to jump to conclusions and I'd been hoping against hope that what I feared would not be the case. I knew that Jodie had now given me the key to all her suffering, hurt, self-loathing and despair.

I had to continue asking her questions and make the most of this moment when she was willing to talk, but I was holding back. I didn't want to hear the answers, didn't want to know the extent of what had happened to this poor child – but my professional, practical side told me that what she said now would be crucial in determining her future, not only in terms of whether she would return to her parents, but also with a view to a possible prosecution. As part of my foster-care training, I'd attended sessions on aspects of sexual abuse. I had learned that the first disclosure is vital, as children rarely lie, and what they said should be recorded verbatim so that it could be used in court. It was important that I handled it properly. My training had told me that I must not lead her, but had to question her in such a way that would let her tell me in her own words what had happened. Unfortunately, I had not been told much more than this and I had certainly never been in a situation like this before. But I had learned how to deal gently with children who revealed experiences of violence and neglect, and I knew that I would have to draw on that now and hope that it was the right way to help Jodie open up.

I looked down at the doll. She had used it to represent herself, and it was no coincidence that she'd given it a name similar to her own. Children sometimes use role play to dramatize things that they can't express verbally about themselves.

'Jodie,' I said, quietly. 'You've been very brave telling me this. I know how difficult it is. Now I want you to try and tell me everything you remember so that I can help you. OK?'

She nodded.

'Good girl.' I paused and took a breath. I needed to be careful. I couldn't lead her otherwise it would invalidate any evidence which might later be used in court. 'When I came into the room just now you were pretending Julie was you and you were your daddy.' The term stuck in my throat. 'If we do that again do you think you can show me what happened? I know it's difficult, pet.'

She nodded again and I gave her a hug, then took the doll from her arms and lay her on the sofa between us. I put on her pants, and covered them with the dress. If this was to be any use, she needed to show me step by step what had happened, as it would have to stand up under cross-examination.

'OK. So Julie is now Jodie. Where is she? In the car, bedroom, kitchen, garden? You tell me.'

'Not the garden, silly,' she grinned. 'The bedroom.'

'Right, so whose bedroom is it?'

'Mine. Jodie's bedroom. At home.'

'And what is Jodie wearing?'

'Her pyjamas.'

'So we'll pretend these are her pyjamas.' I pointed to the doll's pants. 'Is Jodie in bed or hasn't she got in yet?'

'In bed,' she stated categorically.

'And is the light on or off?'

'Off.'

'Now tell me, is Jodie asleep or awake?'

'Sleep.' She screwed up her eyes to demonstrate.

'OK, good girl. So Jodie is asleep in her bed. Now what happens?'

We both looked at the doll. She thought for a moment, then stood and went over to the door. 'I'm coming in,' she growled, broadening her shoulders and stamping across the floor, in her interpretation of an adult male.

'You're coming into Jodie's bedroom? Who are you?'

'The daddy. My daddy. I'm in Jodie's bedroom now.'

She stomped up to the doll, then hesitated and looked at me.

'Do you want me to move?' I asked.

'Over there.' She pointed to the far corner of the room, by the door.

I walked into the corner and stood as unobtrusively as I could. I was trying to make sure I remembered every detail, as I would need to write it all down later, as accurately as possible. I watched as she leaned over the doll, lifted up its dress, then roughly pulled down the pants and took them off. There was no self-consciousness, as she parted the doll's legs, and nuzzled her head deep between the open thighs. She made low grunting noises as she had before, then flattened herself on top of the doll, her head overlapping, face down into the sofa. Her bottom began rising and falling in a rhythmic jerk, and she breathed louder and louder. Her head came up and she let out a long groan before lying completely still. It was an accurate portrayal of sexual intercourse. I felt sick to the pit of my stomach.

The room was quiet. I looked at the raped doll, and tried to hide my revulsion and desperate pity for this poor little girl. No eight-year-old should be able to do this, or know of such things, or have suffered them. I could hardly bear the thought of what she had been through, and was filled with terrible rage towards the animal who'd done this to his own daughter. My eyes stung with tears of anger and sadness, but I blinked them back.

I took a deep breath. This wasn't a time for my emotions. I needed to be calm and dispassionate for Jodie's sake. She wasn't embarrassed, but climbed off Julie and came over to me. 'Did I do well?' she asked, unfazed.

I smiled weakly. 'You're a brave girl, Jodie.'

But it hadn't taken bravery. Jodie had shown no self-consciousness or hesitation; it was almost as if this had been part of what Jodie regarded as normal life. I took her hand and led her to the sofa, where we sat side by side, both looking at Julie. I was aware that there were some discrepancies I needed to clarify. I gave her hand a little squeeze.

'You did very well, Jodie. There are just a few things I'm not sure about. I want you to try and think back and answer my questions. If you don't know or can't remember, say so. Don't guess or make it up, all right?'

She nodded.

I kept hold of her hand, and turned sideways to look at her. Her expression was completely blank. 'Just now, you were pretending to be your daddy, right?'

She nodded again.

'And the real Jodie was asleep in bed with the lights off?'

Another nod.

'If you were asleep, how do you know he came

into the bedroom like you showed me? He might have crept in on tiptoe, or even crawled across the floor. You were asleep with your eyes closed, weren't you?'

She thought for a moment.

'If you don't know, or can't remember, say so,' I reminded her.

'I can,' she said. 'I was sleep sometimes, and sometimes I was awake.'

'I understand. Do you remember what he was wearing?'

'Jeans and top,' she said without hesitation. 'He always wears them.'

'Did he keep them on or did he take anything off?'

'He took the zip off.'

I assumed she meant he undid the zip, but again I needed to clarify. 'Can you show me what you mean?'

She stood, undid the top button of her jeans and pulled down the zip.

'I see. And did he stay like that while he was on top of you?'

'No. More.' She dropped her jeans to her ankles, and was about to pull down her pants.

'OK. Leave them on, just tell me.'

'His pants down with his jeans,' she said.

'Round his ankles?'

'Yes.'

'I understand. Pull your jeans up again, good girl.' I helped her to do up the button, and settled her beside me on the sofa.

'Was Daddy naughty, Cathy?' she asked. Her brow creased as she thought about this.

'Yes he was, Jodie. Very naughty.' I'm not supposed to make value judgements about the parents, but there was no question in my mind that Jodie had to know immediately that this was very wrong and that she was in no way to blame.

'Naughty Daddy,' she said, and thumped her fist hard on her knee. 'He hurt me. I want to hurt him. See how he likes it.'

I put my arm around her, and drew her to me. I wished I had it in my power to draw out her hurt and heal her. 'It's all right, Jodie. You're safe with me now. It won't happen again, I promise.'

'OK, Cathy,' she said, far too easily appeased. I knew that this placid acceptance and lack of emotion meant that we had come nowhere near the heart of her suffering.

'Jodie, you said just now he hurt you. Can you tell me how?' It was a dreadful question, but I knew it was one she would be asked later by the Child Protection Officer, and it was important to get her initial answer on record.

'He made my tummy sore, here.' She pushed her hand between the top of her legs. 'And he wet himself and it tasted horrible.'

'Tasted? Did he put something in your mouth?'

She screwed up her face and made a spitting motion. 'When we was in the car, he weed in my mouth.'

I turned away to hide my reaction. I was burning

104

with anger and humiliation, the humiliation which Jodie should have felt, but didn't. I wasn't about to tell her it wasn't wee. There was no point, and the naïve terminology, using the only point of reference she had, not only made it all the more pitiful, but also underlined its authenticity. I had no doubt she was telling the truth.

I turned to look at her again. 'One last thing, Jodie, I need to know. Did this happen once or lots of times?'

'Lots, Cathy. Naughty Daddy. Cathy, why are you crying?'

I couldn't help myself any longer. I was weeping. 'Because I've heard something sad, sweet.'

'Why is it sad?'

The fact that she didn't understand the horrendous nature of what had happened to her made it even worse. 'Because this is a very bad thing, Jodie, and it should never happen to anybody.'

'Yes. Naughty Daddy,' she said again. 'Can I have my lunch now?'

CHAPTER 10

REPORTING

I considered cancelling the tutor, but she was probably already on her way. Besides, Jodie was looking forward to seeing her, and I needed the time to phone Jill and tell her what had happened, without being overheard.

My mind was reeling from the disclosures. I couldn't help replaying them over and over in my mind, hearing and seeing the awful truth as portrayed through the words and actions of an innocent eight-year-old girl. It was hard to get the frightful images she'd evoked out of my mind, and as I went about the homely, normal actions of making lunch the horror of what I had just learned overlaid everything I did. It felt as though an awful poison had been released into the atmosphere, and I couldn't shake the sense of dread and revulsion that engulfed me.

Jodie, on the other hand, seemed to have recovered quickly, and devoured her sandwiches, crisps and yoghurt, then asked for more.

'You've had enough,' I said, ignoring the protests that followed.

In the conservatory, I cleared the small table

that would act as a desk, and laid out some paper and pencils ready for Nicola's arrival. Jodie followed me round, excited at the prospect of seeing her tutor again. When the doorbell rang she flew to answer it, but then remembered my warning, and waited for me to join her.

'Good girl,' I said, and she gave me a hug.

I'd met Nicola briefly at the pre-placement meeting, and I'd been immediately impressed. Her calm, firm approach was exactly what Jodie needed. Jodie clearly shared my enthusiasm, as she greeted Nicola like a long-lost friend. Nicola seemed pleased to see her too, and she chatted pleasantly to Jodie as she took off her coat and gathered her things together.

We went through to the conservatory, where Jodie clambered into her seat, and started scribbling furiously on the paper I'd laid out. In a good impersonation of Mary Poppins, Nicola delved into her large upholstered bag, and brought out a huge assortment of workbooks, sheets and brightly coloured teaching aids. Jodie was mesmerized.

'We'll get started now,' Nicola said efficiently. 'I usually take a break halfway through. Perhaps we could discuss her progress then?'

'That's fine. I'll bring some drinks and snacks for half time.' I checked she had all she needed, then left them to it, grateful to have been relieved of the responsibility, if only for a couple of hours.

Upstairs, I closed my bedroom door so I wouldn't be overheard, then perched on the bed with the phone at my side. I ran through what I was going to say. I hadn't had time to write up my log notes yet, but it was all still clear in my head, and depressingly vivid. I keyed in the numbers, and the secretary answered.

'Jill, please. It's Cathy.'

'I'll put you through.'

A click, then Jill's voice. 'Hello Cathy, is everything all right?'

'No. It's not. Jodie's been sexually abused. I'm sure of it. She couldn't make up this lot.' I quickly ran through the disclosures, explaining how Jodie had used the doll to tell me, and repeating what she'd said almost word for word.

Jill was silent for a second, and then asked, 'How are you, Cathy? No one had any idea.'

No idea? Knowing what I now knew, it was hard to believe that no one could have guessed what was going on – but I had to give the Social Services the benefit of the doubt. Obviously if anyone had suspected what was happening, Jodie would have been removed earlier. But how could they have missed all the signs, and for so long? Perhaps they'd focused on the obvious physical abuse of knocks and burns and broken bones, rather than a deeper and more vicious evil.

Now that I didn't have to control my emotions in front of Jodie, I could feel the shock and upset welling up in me. My eyes pricked and my vision blurred as hot tears filled them. I felt such an awful mixture of impotent fury and utter sadness on Jodie's behalf. Nevertheless, I couldn't let myself fall to pieces. I had to be strong, for Jodie's sake. I took a deep breath. 'I'm upset, obviously. But at least it's out in the open. And it does explain why she's so disturbed. In fact, it explains a lot of things – it's no wonder she wants to hurt herself and has shut herself off from the world. And, Jill, it sounds like it's been going on for years. She was quite matter-of-fact in the way she described it, as if it was normal.'

There was another pause. I knew Jill was affected by what I had told her. Revelations of sexual abuse are something that anyone in children's social work will encounter, but they never lose their power to shock and horrify, and Jodie's story was particularly appalling. The idea that a small child could have been undergoing this kind of ordeal over a period of years was almost too awful to contemplate.

After a moment's silence, Jill swung into action. 'Right, I'll contact Eileen as soon as we've finished. We'll have to look at contact ASAP. I'll need your notes. Can you write them up while the tutor's there and email me over a copy?'

'I'll do my best.'

'Jodie obviously trusts you, Cathy, more than she's trusted anyone before. She's been in care for four months and said nothing. What I don't understand is where was the mother while all this was going on.'

'I know. From the way Jodie told it, it's hard to imagine that her mother didn't have any idea. But I just don't know. She wasn't mentioned.'

'Would Jodie answer a direct question if you asked?'

'I'm not sure. She told me this, but it was as a result of playing with the doll. I think it was triggered by being in the lift.'

'The lift?'

'Yes. When we went shopping, she was scared in the lift, so much so that I had to stop it and take the escalator. It was like she equated the fear to being scared with her father, and I think that may have been the catalyst for the disclosure. Do you want me to ask about her mother?'

'Yes. But don't push it. It might all come out now she's started, or it might take time. See what you can find out and get as much information as you can – obviously, as gently as possible.' I heard Jill draw her breath in sharply. 'For Christ's sake, she's been on the at-risk register since birth and there's been nothing! Someone's head is on the block for this.'

Jill was angry, understandably, just as I was. Although her role was mainly supervisory, Jill cared deeply for the children we fostered. You couldn't do this kind of work without becoming emotionally involved.

'You know, Jill,' I added, 'she talks a lot of stuff and nonsense with all her imaginary friends. Sometimes it's hard to get a word of sense out of her. But I've never seen her so clear and focused as when she was describing this. It was like she was a different person.'

'Thank goodness she's with you. Let me get things moving and speak to you later. If there's anything else call me straight away.'

'OK.'

I replaced the receiver and leaned back, daunted by the responsibility. Now Jodie had opened up, there was no way I could terminate the placement, whatever she threw at me. Without realizing it, Jodie had invested a lot of trust by telling me. I couldn't let her feel that her trust had been misplaced. I stood up and went downstairs. As I passed the lounge I could hear Nicola reading a series of short words, which Jodie was repeating in her childish voice; she sounded like a four-year-old.

I continued along the hall to the front room, took the foster carer's log out of my desk, and started writing up my notes. I wrote quickly, trying to get everything down as accurately as possible, and I'd covered a page and a half when the phone rang. I answered immediately, expecting Jill or Eileen.

'Hello?' I said. There was no reply.

'Hello?' I said again.

Still nothing. Yet the line was open, someone was on the other end. I listened, and thought I heard a rustle as though someone had jolted the receiver. Perhaps it was a child trying to get through, hesitant, wondering if they had the right number. Perhaps it was my friend Pat, who now lived in South Africa, and phoned once a month – there was often a problem with the connection. I tried once more. 'Hello?'

The line went dead. I hung up, then dialled 1471. The automated voice spoke, 'You were called today at 2.20 p.m. We do not have the caller's number.'

I stood for a moment pondering, then returned to my desk. Could it have been Jodie's parents? In theory, they shouldn't have had any of my personal details, but years of fostering had made me naturally suspicious. I finished writing up my notes, then began typing them on to a Word document. A few minutes later I heard Jodie bounding down the hall.

'Cathy! It's break time. Where's me trainers? We're going to the park.'

'The garden,' corrected Nicola, from the back room.

I clicked 'Save' then went into the hall and helped her into her trainers and coat. She rushed through to the conservatory and I opened the door to let her out. Nicola joined me at the French windows, and we stood watching Jodie's unco-ordinated efforts to set the swing in motion.

'Poor kid,' Nicola said, then she turned to me. 'Cathy, she said something rather worrying earlier and I think you should know.' I met her gaze. 'It was while we were working on the letter T.

112

One of the words I gave her was T for trousers. I showed her a picture of a pair of trousers, and she got very annoyed and wouldn't look at it. Then she said, "My daddy takes his trousers off. He's naughty, isn't he?"'

'I understand where that's come from,' I said, and I briefly explained the nature of Jodie's allegations, without giving specific details; confidentiality has to be respected, even with the tutor. 'I've alerted her social worker,' I added. 'I take it nothing like that's been said before?'

'Not to me, but there was that episode at Hilary and Dave's. I expect they told you.'

'No.'

'Oh. Well, I'm not sure exactly what happened, but Dave told the social worker that at times Jodie behaved as though she fancied him. She was flirting, and going into his bedroom when Hilary wasn't there. I understand they called an end to the placement when she tried to touch him through his trousers.'

'No, I wasn't told,' I said, my voice tight, 'and I should have been. I've got a son of seventeen. It's very bad social work practice.'

I knew from experience that dealing with Social Services meant coping with an endless series of petty mistakes and failings. The sheer size of the huge machine, and the number of cogs involved, meant that errors were constantly being made. I was used to that, and I could deal with it. I understood that human error happens and that, with so many cases to process, mistakes are made. Nevertheless, I wanted to trust that when something important happened, something that had immediate relevance to a child's state of mind or health, or the vital decisions being made on that child's behalf, then people would take care and be extra sure that things were done correctly.

Looking back, I could see obvious instances of sexualized behaviour before today's revelation: I had seen Jodie with her hands down her knickers, furiously masturbating in public like no normal eight-year-old child would; I'd seen her trying to climb into bed with Adrian and occasionally sidle up to him, try to sit next to him or grin and bat her eyelids at him. Flirting was the word for it, if I'd thought about it properly. The problem was that Jodie took up so much of my time, energy and mental strength that I rarely had the opportunity to stand back and observe her objectively and analyse her behaviour. It was obvious now that she was treating Adrian in a sexual manner because her experiences at the hands of her father had taught her to view all males as sexual beings first and foremost. Everything was beginning to fall into place. Now I realized that this was part of a pattern, and that others had noticed it too.

If there had been evidence before of sexualized behaviour, why hadn't anyone begun to come to the obvious conclusion – that someone was sexually abusing Jodie? And why on earth had I not been told about her behaviour towards her previous carer?

I bit back my anger. None of this was Nicola's fault and I didn't want to dump my frustrations on her.

After fifteen minutes we called Jodie in from the garden. I helped her off with her trainers, then returned to the front room and continued typing from my log, while Nicola and Jodie returned to their session. Once I'd finished, I emailed the file to Jill. Perfect timing! I'd just turned off the PC, as Jodie marched into the room.

'We're done! Come and see me work!'

I went through and admired the letter and number work, then arranged the next session for Thursday, and Jodie and I saw Nicola out. As soon as she'd gone the phone started ringing, and it didn't stop for the rest of the afternoon. Jill told me the team leader had convened an emergency strategy meeting, with the time and venue to be announced shortly. She would let me know when there was any more information.

Next, Eileen called me. I was glad to hear from her, but I didn't get quite the response I'd been hoping for. Somehow, she didn't seem to be too shocked or horrified by what the child in her charge had suffered.

'I've heard what's happened,' she said in her flat way. 'Has Jodie said any more since?'

'Not much more, but she did make a comment to her tutor today,' I said, and told her what Jodie had said to Nicola. I reminded myself that social workers often have to retain a bit of distance and put up walls between themselves and their cases, in order to protect themselves from getting too involved emotionally and becoming unable to do their job properly. Nevertheless, I couldn't help feeling that Eileen just didn't seem very bothered, or to empathize with Jodie at all.

'Right,' said Eileen with a sigh, as she noted down what I'd said. It almost seemed as though the most depressing aspect of all this for Eileen was the amount of extra work it would involve for her.

I took a deep breath and asked about Jodie's relationship with the previous carer, Dave.

'It'll be on the file if there is anything,' she said, using the same excuse as last time.

I felt like saying, 'Well, read the bloody file then!' but settled instead for a repeat of the more diplomatic, 'I'd be grateful if you could give me any relevant background information. It's even more important now.'

I put the phone down, frustrated. Really, this wasn't something I should have had to tell her. Why hadn't Jodie's social worker familiarized herself with the case by now? She obviously still hadn't read the file – neither had she been to visit Jodie yet. They barely knew each other and good social work practice said that she should be establishing a relationship with the child for whom she was legally responsible. Nor had she offered to come round now, to offer her support to Jodie and demonstrate her concern.

Thank goodness for Jill. She seemed to appreciate the gravity of the situation and phoned again to tell me that the strategy meeting had been convened for later the same morning. Because Jodie wasn't in school, and it was too short notice to find a babysitter, Jill said she would go in my place, and let me know the outcome.

Sally, the guardian ad litum appointed by the court to represent Jodie's interests, phoned next. I'd liked Sally right from the start: she showed exactly the right mix of professionalism and concern that reassured me that the right steps would be taken for Jodie. She called to hear from me in person the details of what had happened to Jodie – and she said how sorry she was, and how dreadful that the abuse had not been discovered before. She had to be objective, of course, but it was clear that Jodie's case had touched her, and I appreciated her showing that. Once again, I repeated the details of Jodie's disclosures. Sally thanked me for all I was doing, and gave me her home telephone number in case anything else should emerge.

Finally, the phone stopped ringing. I put the kettle on, and tried to settle Jodie with play dough, but she was having none of it. She was high on the frenzy of activity, rightly believing that it related to her. Luckily, Paula and Lucy arrived home from school, and they distracted her long enough to allow me to collect my thoughts.

A little while later, the phone rang again. It was Jill.

'Hi, Cathy. I'm just calling to let you know the outcome of the strategy meeting. Contact with both of Jodie's parents has been suspended with immediate effect, until further notice. Can you tell Jodie please?'

'So she's not seeing her mum either?' I asked, surprised.

'No. Until they know more, they're playing safe.'

'All right. I'll explain to her. Goodness knows how she'll take it.'

'As we said earlier, it would be great if you could try and find out where the mother was while the abuse was taking place.'

'I'll try.'

'Between you, me and the gatepost, this looks like one hell of a balls-up by Social Services. All hell's broken loose while they try and find out how this could have happened.'

I hung up and looked at the clock; it was already 5.30, and I hadn't even thought about dinner yet. I wearily went through to the conservatory, where Paula and Lucy were doing a good job helping Jodie model the dough. I decided to deal with the contact first, as I didn't want her to feel in any way responsible for not seeing her parents.

'I need to have a chat,' I said to the girls. 'I'll explain later.' They took my meaning and left. 'Thanks for your help,' I called after them.

118

'I'll explain later,' Jodie repeated. I heard the girls laugh.

I squatted down beside her and began talking to her about being safe, keeping safe, and how safe she felt with me.

Obligingly she said, 'I wasn't safe with my daddy, was I, Cathy?'

'No you weren't, pet. And because of that, Eileen feels it would be better if you didn't see either of your parents for a while, until it's all sorted out.'

'OK, Cathy,' she said, not in the least perturbed. 'I'll tell her.' Then she stood up, and started a conversation with herself, in which she told Jodie she wasn't seeing Mummy or Daddy because she had to be safe.

That was too easy, I thought. It's not normal. After all, she'd been with them for eight years. I'd dealt with many children who'd been neglected or even abused, and no matter what they'd been through, they always had some emotional connection with their parents. I'd never seen a reaction like this before. I moved on to the second matter of Mum's presence during the abuse. Jodie sat down again, and picked up a lump of multicoloured dough.

'Jodie, you know what you were telling me earlier? Can you remember where your mummy was while your daddy was in your bedroom?'

'It's a cat!' she exclaimed, pulling the dough into an elongated pear shape.

'Is it? That's nice.' I leaned closer. 'Jodie, when

your daddy was in your bedroom doing naughty things, where was your mummy?'

She shrugged and curled her tongue over her top lip in concentration.

'Was she in the house, Jodie, or out? Did you tell her what he was doing?'

'I told her,' she said, thumping the dough with the palm of her hand. 'I told her. I said I want a cat. Get me one now.' Then she was off, in search of Toscha. I didn't pursue it. I'd have to wait until she was ready.

CHAPTER 11

COOKING AND CLEANING

In the middle of the night I was woken by the most terrifying screams. I didn't have time for my dressing gown and slippers. I hurried out of bed and rushed on to the landing, dizzy from standing too quickly. I flung open Jodie's bedroom door. She was on the floor thrashing from side to side, screaming at the top of her voice, gripped in a paroxysm of fear.

'Jodie!' I shouted, trying to break through her nightmare. 'Jodie, it's Cathy!' But her screams drowned out my cry.

I dropped to my knees and took hold of her hands. Her face was screwed shut, and she was clawing at her eyes, trying to gouge them out. I pinned one arm under my knee, and the other above her head. She was fighting for all she was worth, and her strength was incredible, as though the demons had risen up to do battle against her.

'Jodie! Open your eyes. It's Cathy. You're safe with me.'

Her teeth gnashed and her feet drummed the floor. I held on, and kept talking. 'Jodie! You're safe in your room. It's a nightmare. Nothing can harm you here.'

The screams peaked, then died, and her body went limp. I heard a gush of water, then a stain appeared on her pyjamas. Her eyes flickered open, and her head slowly turned. She looked up at me, fixed and staring, then turned her head and vomited. It was like the end of a seizure.

'All right, Jodie. It's OK. Everything's going to be all right.'

She murmured, and her eyes started to focus. I relaxed my grip, and cradled her against me. The smell of vomit and urine made my stomach heave. 'You're safe, Jodie. Nothing can harm you here. I'll take care of you. Don't worry, pet.' I gently rocked her.

She whimpered, then wrapped her arms tightly around my waist. 'I don't want it in my mouth. Tell him. Tell him it makes me sick, Cathy.'

'It won't happen again, pet. I promise. You're safe.'

'I told her to make him stop. I did. But she wouldn't listen.'

'Who, Jodie? Who did you tell?' She started to cry again. 'It's OK. Don't worry. You can tell me when you're ready. Only when you're ready, pet.'

I held her until she was completely calm, then brought her to her feet, and led her to the bathroom. I cleaned us both, then helped her into a clean pair of pyjamas. She was silent and exhausted. I steered her round the landing and tucked her into bed, then sat on the floor next to her, stroking her hair.

Eventually, she fell asleep. I left the light on as I crept out of her room and gently closed the door. I returned to my bedroom for a clean nightdress, my dressing gown and slippers, then went downstairs. It was 3 a.m. Jodie's screams must have woken the others, but they seemed to have turned over and gone back to sleep.

In the kitchen I filled a bucket with hot water, added some disinfectant and left our nightclothes to soak. There was little point in returning to bed yet. I wouldn't be able to sleep – I was too full of Jodie's suffering, and I half expected her to wake again any minute. I hadn't seen anything like this before in any child I'd looked after, and it had left me stunned and drained. I leaned heavily against the work surface, and watched the clock on the oven tick over another minute. Toscha purred around my legs, uncertain if it was time for breakfast. I poured her a saucer of milk, then made myself a mug of tea.

My thoughts went to the packet of cigarettes on top of the broom cupboard. I'd put them there when I was giving up, six months ago. I had managed to quit by only having one when it was essential, and making them difficult to reach. I dragged the breakfast stool into place and climbed up. I felt a stab of guilt as I opened the packet and slid one out. The matches were in the child-proof cupboard under the sink; I had thrown all the lighters away. I unlocked the back door and stepped outside. I'd never smoked in the house.

The night was cold and clear. I couldn't see the moon, but the deep black sky was a blanket of twinkling stars. The cold air was a relief from the heavy atmosphere which now pervaded the house. The match flared in the darkness, as though highlighting my transgression. I held it to the tip and inhaled. I felt that old familiar rush, at once intoxicating and reassuring, then another surge of guilt, but I inhaled again, concentrating on the ritual, allowing myself to think of nothing else. By the time I'd finished, I wasn't sure if I felt better or worse.

Returning inside, I put the matches back in the cupboard, and secreted the cigarettes in a more accessible drawer. It was still quiet upstairs, so I went into the lounge and switched on the television. There was ice hockey on Channel Five. I turned the volume down and gazed absently, while my thoughts travelled faster than the puck. Whatever had that child suffered? I could only begin to guess. And who was this 'her' whom she had told? Her mum? An aunt? A teacher at school? I was amazed that nothing had been picked up before. Jodie had been on the at-risk register since birth, so she should have been visited by social workers every couple of months. I couldn't believe that none of them noticed anything untoward in her relationship with her father, as it sounded like the abuse had been going on for years. Surely her mother must have known – but that was another avenue that I couldn't bear to go down yet. At some point I must have dropped off, for suddenly the ice rink had been transformed into a weather map, and dark rain clouds were covering most of southern England. The clock in the corner of the screen said it was nearly 6.30, and the house was still silent. Perhaps telling me about the abuse had proved cathartic for Jodie; perhaps she'd be less disturbed as a result. I crept upstairs, and took the opportunity for a long, relaxing shower. As the hot water drummed on to my neck and shoulders, I felt the tension dissipate, and prepared myself for a new day.

As I dressed, I felt rejuvenated and ready for action. I hung up the towels, and heard Jodie stir. Within minutes she was off, screaming abuse and trashing her room. I went in and tried to resettle her. When this failed, I told her off, and when that failed, I ended up having to remove the television as a punishment.

Fearful of the damage she might do if left unattended, I allowed her downstairs to breakfast with Lucy and Paula, which turned out to be a massive error of judgement. From the moment she sat down, she tormented the girls by poking and kicking, digging her spoon into their breakfasts, and generally making herself disagreeable. Paula left most of her Weetabix, in a bid to escape, while Lucy finally gave her a tap on the hand and flounced off to finish her toast in her bedroom.

By the time Adrian appeared, my nerves were in tatters, and my morning serenity had all but vanished.

'What you staring at?' she demanded as he sat down. Jodie seemed to have a particular fear of being looked at, and was never happy if she felt she was being observed, getting upset with whoever was looking at her. I'd noticed when she arrived that she avoided eye contact and preferred to look at people's chests when they were talking to her. Similarly, she'd never been able to relax, always jumping if someone walked into the room as if she was on constant alert and ready to take flight if she had to. I hadn't really thought about it before, but now, in the light of what she'd told me, everything took on a sinister significance.

Adrian shifted awkwardly and concentrated on his breakfast.

I saw her grin, that ghoulish contortion of her face, then quick as a flash she scooped up a handful of porridge, and hurled it at him.

'Jodie! Stop that!' I cried, and took her bowl away. 'That was naughty. Now I've got to clean his blazer. Look at the mess you've made.'

She sneered. 'That's what you're here for. To clean and cook. Get on with it, bitch.'

Adrian couldn't believe what he'd heard, and neither could I.

'I beg your pardon?' I said. She looked as if she was about to repeat it so I interrupted. 'Don't you dare say that. If you think I've got nothing better to do than clean up after you, you're very much mistaken. You've lost your television today, and if there's any more it'll be for the rest of the week.'

I washed her hands, sponged down Adrian's blazer, then cleared away the breakfast things. I didn't speak to Jodie or make eye contact with her. I wanted her to feel my disapproval. I appreciated that she had suffered a great deal in her life, but the only hope for her future was for her to try and understand how to function in a normal family and in society. She had to learn what behaviour was acceptable and what kind of treatment of others was entirely wrong.

Only when I'd loaded the dishwasher and seen Adrian, Lucy and Paula off to school did I make the peace. 'No more swearing or throwing things around. Do you understand? It's naughty, and you're not a naughty girl.'

'No. I'm sorry, Cathy,' she said, temporarily chastened.

'OK. Would you like me to read you a story now?'

'Yes please, Cathy.'

I gave her a hug, and we went into the lounge, where she picked up half a dozen books and dumped them on my lap. We sat side by side on the sofa, and Jodie asked for another hug. I put my arms around her, and thought now might be a good time to ask her about her mum, as she was subdued and reasonably cooperative.

'Before I start, Jodie, I want to ask you something

127

about last night. You remember you were upset and I came into your room?' She looked at me blankly, which was nothing unusual, so I decided to continue. 'You said you told someone about what Daddy was doing? You said you told her to make him stop.' She was still looking at me, and her brow furrowed in concentration as she tried to remember. 'Jodie, who was it that you told? Can you remember? I know it was a woman because you said "her".'

She pulled slightly away, and took the top book off the pile. 'Free 'ickle pigs. I told the free 'ickle pigs, and they blew my house down.'

I smiled inwardly at this quite witty diversion. 'No, you didn't. Now be sensible. It's important.'

'Can't remember. Can't. Really, I can't, Cathy.'

'OK darling, let's read.'

That afternoon, I phoned Jill, and told her I hadn't had any success. 'She genuinely doesn't seem to remember. I'll have to wait until she's ready.'

'OK. You're doing everything you can, Cathy. This is not unheard of. In some cases, when a child is emotionally traumatized, the brain can shut down to protect the child from the horrendous memories. Once the child feels safe again, they may be able to release a bit more, but only to the extent that the brain feels able to cope with it.'

It sounds like a mechanism I could do with, I thought to myself. I finished my conversation with Jill feeling a little comforted. I could only hope that this was a turning point for Jodie. Now that she'd been able to reveal what had happened to her, perhaps she would begin to get better.

I couldn't have been more wrong.

CHAPTER 12

MONSTERS

It was weeks before Jodie felt safe enough to reveal any more, and during that time her behaviour, far from improving, deteriorated still further. She became increasingly violent, not only towards me and the other children, but also towards herself. For some reason, she frequently became distressed at the dinner table. In the middle of a meal, she would suddenly start clawing at her face, or tearing at her hair. At other times, she would scratch and pinch her arms, leaving marks and bruises. I would quickly restrain her, of course, wrapping her in my arms until she'd calmed down.

She was also defecating again. After the first couple of instances, she had calmed down and stopped messing herself, but now it started up again and was worse than before. Now she was simply smearing shit all over herself and then, if I didn't get to her quickly enough, over the house. There was no apparent pattern or motive, but she did seem to understand that messing up fabrics would lead to a more severe telling-off than smearing impermeable surfaces (such as the walls or banister) and she appeared to make a point of avoiding getting it on the sofa and curtains. As usual, it was impossible to understand Jodie's motives, or even whether she was really aware of what she was doing.

As a result of her activities, the house constantly smelled of disinfectant. One evening as I prepared for bed, I saw that the skin on my hands had become chapped and red, and my fingertips were puckered from all the detergents. This habit of Jodie's was unpleasant for everyone in the house, to say the least, even though we probably have an unusually heightened tolerance of poor hygiene, having dealt with a number of foster children with similar problems. I don't think I'll ever forget the day I looked round one teenage girl's bedroom, trying to find the source of a persistent nasty smell. When I peered behind her wardrobe, I found a stash of used sanitary towels, dating back to when she had first arrived six months before.

Despite the violence, the insults, the excrement, the lack of sleep and numerous other traumas, the children were remarkably patient with Jodie, as they now knew the reason for her behaviour.

Shortly after the first disclosures, I sat down with them one evening and told them about the abuse, and warned them about some of the additional difficult behaviour we might expect. It was import-ant to tell them because Jodie was as likely to disclose to them as to me, so they needed to be prepared. Besides, they were already hearing

131

things that she had started saying. Just as she had with Nicola, she was beginning to drop casual references about what had happened to her into conversations. I had to tell them what she was talking about.

With Paula being only thirteen, there were certain physical aspects of the abuse that I had to explain to her in detail: when Jodie mentioned her father weeing in her mouth, for example, they had to know she meant oral sex. Not only was this embarrassing for all of us, but I was once again reminded of the potentially negative effect fostering might be having on my children. How healthy was it for Paula to learn about sex in this context? Was there a risk that it might harm her relationships in the future?

The children were, as I'd expected, shocked and horrified. I wished that I hadn't had to bring all this into their worlds as well, and it was awful to see them struck dumb as they absorbed the implications of what I was saying. The fact that Jodie's father had done this to her was clearly a difficult and near impossible concept for them to cope with. They were already used to hearing about the difficult backgrounds of other children I'd fostered – it was often important for their own protection that they knew what had happened – but this was beyond all of that.

'As you know, this is strictly confidential,' I reminded them, and they nodded at me, their faces serious. They'd always understood that anything they learned in the house had to stay there and was not to be repeated to anyone. I trusted them completely.

After we had this chat, the children became even more tolerant of Jodie's behaviour. They tried to spend more time playing with Jodie, and remain sympathetic even when she was screaming at them to 'Get out of my fucking house!', or lunging at them with a kick. Nonetheless, their patience had limits, and when Jodie interrupted one meal by graphically describing how blood had dripped from her finger when her mother had purposely cut it, Lucy lost patience. 'Gross!' she exclaimed, then she picked up her plate, and took her dinner into the living room.

One summer's afternoon, when Jodie had been with us for about four months, Jill came round for one of our regular meetings. Although, being a link worker, she had no statutory obligation to visit us (unlike Jodie's social worker), good practice dictated that she should come round every four to six weeks to see how things were going, offer a bit of support and check my log notes.

As it was a glorious sunny day, we decided to take Jodie to the park. Despite having been up most of the night with nightmares and general distress, as she often was, Jodie was full of energy, and restless to get out into the sunshine. I, on the other hand, was simply worn out.

'So, how's she doing?' asked Jill, as we walked

through the park's immaculately tended flower garden. Jodie was marching a few metres ahead, anxious to get to the playground, and apparently oblivious to the dazzling array of colours and scents around her.

'She's getting worse,' I replied. 'She's having more and more of those hysterical screaming fits, for no apparent reason, and once she recovers she seems barely aware of what's happened. That's why Nicola didn't stay for the tutoring this morning; about once a week Jodie's simply unmanageable, so we have to give up and cancel the session.'

'And how's she sleeping?'

'Not wonderfully. She wakes up at five, sometimes earlier. She had been learning to stay in her room and play quietly. But over the last few weeks she's started having dreadful nightmares, which seem to be more like hallucinations. They're completely real to her, and sometimes they seem to continue after she's woken up. It's awful, you wake up to her screaming, and find her writhing on the floor, then she's like that off and on for the rest of the night. It's got to the point where I keep a chair outside her room on the landing, so once I've settled her the first time I just sit there waiting. If I'm lucky I get to doze for a few minutes, until she starts up again!'

'You must be absolutely shattered.'

We arrived at the playground, where Jodie jumped on a swing and started working herself higher and higher.

'Careful, Jodie,' I warned, then stood with Jill on the grass verge, where Jodie could see me watching. She had no sense of danger or instinct to protect herself, and would swing out of control, then fall off, if allowed to.

'How did the hearing test go?' Jill asked. I had taken Jodie for a test the previous week, as there had been occasions when she didn't seem to hear what was going on around her.

'I think it's OK. We're waiting for the doctor's letter but the nurse seemed to think there was nothing wrong with her.'

'So she is shut down?' asked Jill, referring to the way some badly abused children seem to switch off their senses, as a way of protecting themselves. If you can't see, hear or feel anything, it might not be happening. When they shut down in this way, these children become less aware of what's going on around them, and less conscious of things that we usually take for granted, like noticing the pleasant taste of food, or recognizing that the water in the bath is too hot.

'I think so,' I replied. 'There are certainly signs. Hardly anything gives her any pleasure, and she doesn't seem to be sensitive to temperature: even when it was really cold, I had to fight with her every day to stop her wearing just a T-shirt and shorts. There are days when she is on a relatively even keel, I suppose, though I couldn't describe even those as good days. If we manage to get through a day without a fullscale tantrum, we've done extremely well. That's very rare.'

Jill looked at me sympathetically. 'You're working tremendously hard, I know that. You're doing a brilliant job, you really are.'

I smiled weakly. Compliments were nice, but what I really wanted was a good night's sleep. I was constantly exhausted, and although my patience was just about lasting out I felt at the end of my tether.

We started walking back, pleased that the outing had so far passed without incident. The sun was still bright, but I was keen to capitalize on Jodie's good behaviour. If we could get home without any drama, it would allow me to praise and reward her, and we could set a positive precedent for how a day out should go. Jill and I each took one of Jodie's hands, as we ambled back through the park.

'I must admit I'm concerned about the absence of any improvement,' I said, using deliberately vague language so that Jodie wouldn't realize that we were talking about her. 'The disturbances are getting worse, especially at night.'

'And have any of the disclosures dealt with the maternal presence as we discussed?'

'No. She tells me about those events time and time again, but there's hardly any new information coming out. Frankly I'm worried sick, things seem to be getting worse rather than better. Is there no practical advice you can give me?' I tried to keep the edge of desperation from my voice.

'No more than you're already doing,' Jill said sympathetically. 'And to be honest there's a limit to what you should be expected to cope with. It's quite possible that the emotional trauma is so severe that only a therapeutic unit can put it right. I tell you what, I'll have a look and see what's available. I won't do anything, I'll just have a look.'

As we reached the corner of my street, I allowed Jodie to run ahead, while Jill and I walked in silence. I had been hoping for some practical advice, but the level of Jodie's disturbance seemed to be outside Jill's experience too. I was disappointed, but I vowed to press on. I saw Jodie had stopped further up, and was crouching with her back to me, intently focused on something in the gutter. 'Jodie,' I called. 'What are you doing? Come here.'

She turned around, grinning, then held up a dead pigeon, proudly displaying it like a trophy. The bird's head slumped sideways, and its breast had been torn open, so that its bloody insides were exposed. Jodie stared at it, fascinated.

'Jodie! Put that down, right now!' I said firmly. She stared at me, then slowly turned away, poking at the pigeon's bloody flesh, and dropped it back in the gutter.

'Yuck,' Jill said.

I cupped Jodie's elbows in my hands from behind and steered her, arms outstretched, towards the house. Jill got straight in her car without coming in, as she had another meeting to go to. I manoeuvred Jodie in through the front door and straight to the kitchen sink. She looked up at me as I filled the bowl with hot water and soap.

'We had a nice time at the park, didn't we, Cathy?'

Her face was flushed, happier than I'd seen her in weeks. I smiled back. I couldn't be angry; after all she hadn't really done anything wrong. But I was concerned at the ghoulish fascination the dead bird had inspired.

The next morning it was clear early on that something was different. Jodie wasn't screaming at five o'clock, nor six, nor seven. I had time to shower, dress and dry my hair. I made the children's packed lunches, and even drank a cup of coffee in peace. Then I started to worry.

I crept up the stairs, tiptoed to Jodie's door, and listened. There was silence. She wasn't even talking to herself, which she usually did continuously, even in her calmer moments. I knocked and went in. She was lying on top of the duvet, flat on her back, with her eyes wide open, staring at the ceiling. She was so still that for a moment I feared she could be dead.

'Jodie?' I shook her shoulder. 'Jodie?' She gave a small twitch at the corner of her eye. 'Jodie? What's the matter? Are you ill?'

She didn't move. Her arms and legs were held straight, so stiff it was like they were encased in concrete. I knew this wasn't a fit, or at least not like any fit I'd ever seen. I placed my palm on her forehead. It was warm, but not feverish.

'Jodie? Can you hear me?'

I shook her again, this time more robustly. 'Jodie, look at me. Tell me what's wrong. It's Cathy. Jodie? Can you hear me?'

She blinked, then slowly turned to look at me. Her pupils were dilated, and there were large dark rings around her eyes. When she spoke, it was in a flat monotone. 'He came here last night. You said he wouldn't, but he did. I know, I know who it was.'

I knelt down, and held her hand tight. 'No sweet, no one came here. You've remembered something and it seems real.'

'I didn't tell. I didn't tell because she saw. She saw, Cathy. She saw, and didn't stop him.'

'Someone saw Daddy do naughty things to you?'

She nodded.

'Who, sweet? Who was it?'

She stared straight at me, eyes wide with terror, her cheeks deathly pale. I could see the pulse throbbing in her neck.

'Mummy. Mummy saw. I said make him stop but she didn't. She laughed and watched. They all did.'

I turned cold. 'They? There were others there?'

'Uncle John, and Ken, and Aunt Bell. They took pictures when Uncle Mike did it.'

139

'Uncle Mike?'

Her face was blank, she was looking at me and talking, but it was as though she was in a daze.

'He lay on me, same as Daddy. I didn't want to. It hurt. Daddy held me when it was Uncle Mike's turn. I was shouting and screaming, so Daddy put his thing in my mouth. Aunt Bell said, "That'll shut her up." And they all laughed.' She was shaking with fear.

I tried to hide my horror and concentrate on what I was hearing. I needed to make sure I remembered all the names and details, to get as much evidence as I could while she was talking. I didn't know when or if she would open up again. I stroked her forehead, and whispered words of comfort.

'Jodie, you're safe now. The doors are locked and bolted. We have a very good alarm. No one can get in. What they did was the most dreadful thing any adult can do to a child. They are very wicked people, Jodie.'

She nodded, but without conviction. 'They gave me lots of sweets and toys.' She glanced at the overflowing toy boxes.

'Did they buy all these?' I asked. She nodded again. So that's what they were – not presents, not things designed to bring pleasure; they were bribes, to buy silence and compliance. No wonder they meant nothing to her. 'Jodie, good adults don't buy children presents because they've done bad things to them. Was it to stop you telling?'

140

'It was our secret. They said if I told, horrible things would happen. I'd be taken to a dark cave and a monster would come and chew off my arms. Will he, Cathy?' Her voice rose fearfully. 'Will he come here and bite my arms off?'

'No, absolutely not. The only monsters are those people, and they won't come anywhere near you, ever again. I promise, Jodie.'

She thought about this, and then a sad smile crossed her lips. 'Aunt Bell was nice. She didn't do things. She only watched.'

I shuddered at this twisted logic. 'That's just as bad, Jodie. She watched you being hurt and didn't help. She should have stopped them. That's what I would have done. Where were they when they were watching?'

'In my bedroom.'

'And the car? You once said something about a car? Who was in the car, Jodie?'

'Mummy and Daddy. Mummy took the pictures of Daddy and me. It's a very big car. We was in the back. It was dark. I don't like the dark. The camera made it light up. Will he be told off, Cathy?'

'I sincerely hope so, sweet. All of them. I'll tell your social worker, and she'll tell the police. The police will want to talk to us, but don't worry, I'll be with you.'

I was still holding her hand and stroking her forehead, reluctant to let go. It was well after seven, and I should have been waking the others for

141

school. 'Is there anything else you want to tell me now? You've been very brave and it's important you tell me if there is.'

She shook her head. I cuddled her for some time, then gently eased her into bed, and tried to focus my mind.

'Cathy?' she said suddenly.

'Yes, sweet?'

'Did your daddy do those things to you?'

'No. Absolutely not,' I said. 'Never in a million years. He's a good, kind man. Most adults are.'

'And Paula and Lucy's daddy?'

'No. Paula's daddy never hurt her. Lucy's daddy hit her, which is why she's here. But he didn't hurt her like that.'

'Was it my fault, Cathy? I didn't want to. Mummy said I was lucky. She said it was because he liked me so much. She said I should belt up and enjoy it. She said I was Daddy's girl.'

'She was wrong, Jodie. Parents cuddle their children to show their love. They don't hurt them. And it wasn't your fault, Jodie. Don't you ever believe that.' I gave her another hug, then she asked for the television, and for the first time since arriving she seemed content to stay in bed while the others got up.

I left her room and stood for a moment on the landing, trying to compose myself. I was ice cold and trembling with rage. I could see Jodie being held down by her father. I could see the others watching. I could hear their laughter. It was little wonder she was in the state she was. I knew now where her anger had come from, and I now shared it. I had not wanted to believe it could be any worse than Jodie's father subjecting her to the vile acts she had described, but now, to my horror, I realized that it was much, much worse than anyone had suspected. She had been the victim of the most awful kind of abuse I could imagine, where not just one of her parents subjected her to the most degrading treatment any child could suffer but where both of them were complicit, and so were other adults. I could feel the nausea churning in me as I realized that it was not only her parents, in their position of precious care and trust, but many others who had conspired to turn Jodie's world into a nightmare of suffering and perversion; they had reversed everything that should be good in a child's life, turning it into something so deeply wicked and evil that I couldn't find the words to describe what I thought of it.

No wonder the poor child had cut off the world around her. No wonder she had no sense of being able to relate to other people, when all she had experienced was cruelty and pain. No wonder she tried to beat herself, maim herself and smeared herself with filth – what else had she ever known?

Somehow I made breakfast, and saw Adrian, Lucy and Paula off to school. As soon as they were gone, I phoned Jill and told her everything. 'It's worse than we thought,' I said. 'Much worse.'

As I reported what Jodie had said, I could sense Jill taking in the scale of what had happened. She breathed in sharply as I told her that Jodie had been abused by a circle of complicit adults, photographed and watched and jeered at.

'Oh my God, Cathy. I can't believe what that child has been through. This should be enough to start a police prosecution,' she said. 'I know it must have been awful to hear all this from her, but you've done a great job.'

I didn't feel like I'd done a good job. I felt as if I'd been party to Jodie's suffering. I felt ashamed to be an adult.

'Do we know how long it's been going on?' she asked.

'I think quite a while. She asked if my father did it to me, and was surprised he didn't. The way she describes it, it sounds like it was the norm, part of everyday life, and it's only now she's realizing it's wrong.' I paused. 'Jill, at what age can a child be raped?'

'Any age. There are cases as young as six months.'

I cringed.

'Cathy, this has all the hallmarks of a paedophile ring. Was she ever shown the photographs?'

'Not as far as I'm aware. She didn't say.'

'OK, write it all down when you have a chance. Eileen's on annual leave . . .'

'Again?'

'Yes, so I'll speak to Dave Mumby. They'll want a forensic medical and a police memorandum interview. I'll get back to you. How are you coping, Cathy?'

'A damn sight better than Jodie. Bastards!'

CHAPTER 13

INTEGRATION

There's a joke among foster carers that goes like this: How many social workers does it take to change a light bulb? Thirteen. One to find the bulb, and the other twelve to hold a meeting to discuss how best to change it. It's not much of a joke, admittedly, but it does encapsulate how we often feel about the inability of Social Services to take action when it's most needed.

Following Jodie's latest disclosures, Dave Mumby wanted to set up a meeting, but not until Eileen could be present, which wouldn't be until well into the following week, as she was indeed on annual leave. As Jodie's social worker, Eileen had a statutory obligation to visit Jodie in placement every six weeks, and yet the two had still never met. Although Eileen phoned every now and then to get a report on Jodie's progress, I got the impression that it was more to save herself the trouble of having to visit us than any real interest in the case. Perhaps she had a very busy workload – but then, so did all social workers – or maybe she was better than most at not getting too personally involved in a case. Whatever it was, it not only saddened me that Jodie didn't have a social worker to take an interest in her and champion her cause, but it was also highly unprofessional. I wondered if Dave Mumby, her team manager, knew.

Jill reported back to me that the nature of the meeting meant that I wouldn't have to attend, and she would represent us both. In the meantime, she said, Dave had asked if I could focus my attention on finding Jodie a school, as her parents had made a formal complaint about her lack of education. Jodie had left her previous school when she was taken into care, and the speed of her various moves, then her behaviour, had precluded finding her a new one.

I was flabbergasted. Jodie's parents would now know what they were accused of. When a child makes an accusation, the parents are always informed of the nature of the allegation. Moreover, when all contact between Jodie and her parents was abruptly stopped, the reasons would have been given. I was doubly amazed that Dave was acting upon this as a priority, while delaying the meeting.

Jill suggested that I try Harvestbank, which was a local primary school with a good record for taking children with learning and behavioural difficulties. Jodie already had a Statement of Educational Needs, which is a document outlining the child's particular needs, completed after he or she has been assessed by an educational psychologist. Jodie's needs were severe enough that her statement authorized funding to pay for a full-time assistant in whichever school accepted her. This meant, in theory at least, that a school might have an additional incentive to take her, if they were short on funds.

I phoned Harvestbank, and spoke to the deputy head. She was a pleasant lady, who explained very nicely that they had more than their quota of special needs children, and were stretched to the limit. She suggested I try again in six months' time. I thanked her, and hung up.

Opening the Yellow Pages, I highlighted all the primary schools within reasonable travelling distance, and began making the calls. The next four schools gave me the same response: each of them was over their quota, and there was a waiting list. So much for the sweetener of extra funding. I set the phone down, and took a deep breath. I wondered if I should approach the school Adrian and Paula had gone to. It only had a small special needs department, but they knew me and my family, and I had had a good relationship with the staff. I took another deep breath, and dialled the number.

The secretary remembered me, which was nice, and she put me through to the headmaster, Mr Rudman. We exchanged a few pleasantries on the passing of time, and he asked me how Adrian and Paula were doing. I said they were doing well, and buttered him up by telling him what fond memories they had of the school.

'I'm still fostering,' I said, and then explained about Jodie, adding that although she had behavioural problems I had found them manageable. I made light of the rapid succession of foster carers, and said his was the first school that had come to mind; a little white lie, but in aid of a good cause.

'I'll see the statement,' he said, 'although you appreciate I'm not offering a place. It will depend on the level of provision, and whether we can best meet her needs.'

I thanked him effusively, then phoned Jill to arrange for the statement to be faxed over. Buoyed by this, and in dire need of some exercise after nearly an hour on the phone, I rescued Jodie from the congealed heap of paper, glue and paint which had kept her occupied.

'It's a dog!' she exclaimed.

'That's lovely. Now we're going for a walk to the post office.'

I helped her wash her hands, then brushed her hair, and changed her top. By the time we left the house, she looked quite presentable, in a smart yellow T-shirt which I knew was one of her favourites.

There was a pleasant breeze as we walked up the street, but Jodie was anxious, and grabbed my hand as a car drove past.

'Cathy,' she said.

'Yes, Jodie.'

'Is my dad hurting my mum?'

'I hope not, Jodie,' I replied, uncertain quite what she was asking.

'He is,' she responded. 'Poor Mummy.'

We carried on walking, and I watched Jodie as she frowned, apparently still troubled by this idea. Eventually, she looked up at me.

'I don't want him hurting her,' she said, then jutted out her chin, and clenched her fists. 'I'll kill him.'

Again, I wasn't sure what to say. Did she feel guilty about leaving her mother to deal with her father alone? Should I correct her anger, or encourage her to face these issues? It might not have been very professional, but my personal feeling was that she had every right to feel angry, and every reason to want to kill him. I decided to address the possible guilt. 'If he hurts her, Jodie, I think she should leave him, and tell the police. But she's an adult and she can make that decision for herself.'

I hoped she understood what I was trying to say – but then, I wasn't even sure what she was telling me. Was she hinting at domestic violence? Perhaps she had seen her father hitting her mother. Or perhaps she had witnessed them having sex and assumed it must hurt her mother as much as it hurt her.

I changed the subject to something lighter as we reached the high street. We walked past the various shop fronts with their colourful signs and enticing displays, and I remembered how excited I'd felt as a little girl, being taken out shopping by my parents. I could still remember my initial thrill at the strange sights in the fishmonger's window, and the mysterious smells at the shoe-mender's. I looked sadly at Jodie, who was staring straight ahead, alert for danger, and oblivious to the sensory pleasures around her. The world was not a place she could enjoy like any normal child; it lacked excitement and stimulation for her. She had been deadened to everything because of what she had suffered. It was heartbreaking.

I did what I had to do at the post office, and because she had queued patiently by my side I bought Jodie a packet of Smarties as a reward. As we walked back down the high street, I noticed she had gone quiet again.

'What shall we do when we get home, Jodie?' I asked.

She was silent, and I could see her face had set.

'Is something the matter, Jodie?'

'What were they starin' at?' she muttered. 'Don't stare at me.'

'Who, Jodie? In the post office?' I asked. She didn't contradict me, so I continued. 'But no one was staring at you, sweet. They were probably just looking at you because you look so smart in your lovely T-shirt.'

She didn't respond, so I decided to leave it. You could never really persuade Jodie of anything, or have any kind of discussion with her. Caring for Jodie was rather about coping with her needs, and trying to distract her before she could get too upset. We walked a little further, as a middle-aged man in a suit came the other way.

'What's he fuckin' starin' at?' Jodie muttered as he approached. As far as I could see, the man didn't seem to be looking at us at all.

'Jodie, don't be rude.'

As the man got closer, she said it again, louder this time: 'What's he blimmin' starin' at?'

He must have heard this time. I smiled at the man apologetically, and he looked away, embarrassed.

'Jodie, that was rude. You've no reason to worry, no one was staring at you.'

'I'll show 'em,' she muttered. 'No one'll stare at me. I'll kill 'em all!'

Jodie's mood didn't improve once we got home, but for some respite I let her watch *Mary Poppins*, which was her favourite video, while I did some chores. I put on a load of washing, and began emptying the dishwasher, all the while wondering about Jodie's strange behaviour. I had noticed before that she seemed to have a particular anxiety about being stared at; this was one reason why mealtimes had become so unbearable, as she would constantly bark 'What you starin' at?' to anyone looking even vaguely in her direction. I had suspected that this anxiety might have been linked to the abuse, but now, as the extent of it was revealed, her phobia became even more understandable: if there had been a number of people present, watching Jodie, it was no wonder if she had a horror of being looked at.

After about half an hour I'd finished what I needed to do and joined Jodie in the living room, bringing with me a carton of Ribena. She was staring blankly at the screen, while Bert serenaded Mary as they strolled through the magical chalk landscape. After a while, she turned and looked at me, and then came and sat next to me on the sofa.

'You know, you've got really little eyes,' she said.

'Have I?' I said, surprised. If anything, I had always felt my eyes were one of my better features and I was rather proud of them.

'Yeah, really piggy little eyes. Like a little pig. Oink! Oink!' She grinned, as if expecting me to join in the hilarious joke.

'That's not a very nice thing to say, Jodie. Don't be rude. We don't make personal remarks in this house.'

'But you have. Stupid little eyes. That's why you can't even see where you're going. Stupid!'

This was a strange thing to say, and it sounded like something Jodie must have heard before, an insult that had been thrown at her, and that she was now mimicking. Apart from being inaccurate, it had a level of detail and logic which Jodie wouldn't have been able to come up with. Was this something Jodie had been told at home? Before I could pursue this, the phone rang. Oh no,

I thought, it will be the school calling to tell me there isn't a place after all. Only a rejection would have come so quickly. I smiled and tried to sound bright. 'Hello,' I answered.

'Hello, is that Margaret Brown of Bowham Close?'

I looked anxiously at Jodie. It was my address but Margaret Brown was the name of Jodie's mother.

'No, it's not. Who's this?'

'Oh, I'm sorry. My mistake. I'm calling from Ear, Nose and Throat at St John's Hospital. About Jodie Brown?'

'Yes. This is Cathy Glass, Jodie's carer.'

'Sorry, I've just found the note on file. The doctor's letter is in the post, together with a prescription for some ear drops. Doctor wants a follow-up appointment for Jodie in a month.'

I made the appointment, noted it in my diary, and hung up. I wasn't happy. I had given specific instructions to the hospital that my details should be kept confidential and, to avoid confusion, should be kept separate from Jodie's parents'. It was clear this hadn't happened. This time they had called me asking for Margaret, but next time they might just as easily call Margaret asking for Cathy Glass. All she would then need to do would be to ask the receptionist to confirm her latest address, and she and her husband would be led straight to my door. Then, Jodie and I would have bigger things to worry about than my piggy little eyes.

CHAPTER 14

THE PARK

Eileen returned from her holiday, and Dave was finally able to convene his strategy meeting. Jill attended in my place, and things suddenly started to happen. I was told to make a number of appointments for Jodie. First, she would have to be assessed by a child psychologist, to help the Social Services decide how best to proceed with her case. She would also have to have what's called a 'memorandum interview'. This is a videotaped interview with a police Child Protection Officer, which in this case would be the starting point for a criminal prosecution of Jodie's father and, hopefully, the other abusers too. Jodie would also have to see a police doctor for a forensic medical – an intimate gynaecological examination – to verify her claims.

I immediately started to worry about the forensic medical. It was traumatic enough for an adult to be examined in this way, but for an abused child it could be seen as another assault. I had given Jodie my promise that nothing of that kind would happen to her again, and I was frightened that she would think I'd broken my word and lose her trust in me.

In the meantime, our days had settled into something of a routine. On Mondays, Wednesdays and Fridays, Jodie's tutor would come in the morning, and then in the afternoon we would go out, usually to the park. On Tuesdays and Thursdays we went shopping, although Jodie and I had somewhat differing views about this. Jodie enjoyed shopping more than anything, whereas for me it was perfunctory. Jodie seemed to relish causing a scene in public, aware that there was little I could do in response. These tantrums were designed to bully me into buying her something, but I could never give in, as this would set a precedent by rewarding bad behaviour. However, Jodie had clearly used this technique successfully for years, so I wasn't expecting her to unlearn it any time soon.

The sessions with Nicola were improving, in terms of Jodie's behaviour, but she was making little progress in her education. In my view, this lack of progress was only partly attributable to Jodie's learning difficulties and delayed development and more likely a result of her emotional state. A further problem was that Jodie seemed to have no interest in learning; she could never see the point of any of Nicola's exercises, and it was very difficult to motivate her, as she apparently had no desire to win approval.

My worries increased one afternoon when I did finally receive a call from Mr Rudman's secretary: he was dreadfully sorry, but he didn't feel able to offer Jodie a place.

'Back to the drawing board,' I said to Nicola, and spent the second half of her session on the phone, trying to interest another head teacher, but without success.

'The trouble is,' Nicola said, 'she really needs a special school, but unless her statement can be changed to say this, there's no chance.'

'How long would it take to get it changed?'

'Anything up to a year.'

We agreed that this wasn't an option, so after Nicola left I set out more paper, paint and glue, and spent another hour working through the Yellow Pages. It was demoralizing work, but by the end of it I'd found another head who was willing to look at her statement. The school, Elmacre Primary, was five miles away, through the city traffic, but at least they had a vacancy.

The most enjoyable times I spent with Jodie tended to be our visits to the park. Jodie was less anxious in open spaces, presumably because there were fewer people around. She enjoyed playing on the swings, and I was slowly encouraging her to engage with the world around her, by pointing out pretty flowers and trees, and telling her the names of distinctive birds.

We often bumped into people I knew, and I hoped this kind of friendly contact would be helpful for Jodie. I'd lived in the same area for twenty years, so we would often run into someone I knew on any trip out. I would introduce Jodie, as I do with all the children I foster, but instead of saying 'Hi', or smiling shyly, she'd stick out her chin, screw up her eyes, and cackle like a witch. She had recently developed this cackle, and I wondered if it was a defence mechanism, to stop people getting close. If so, it was certainly effective; only the resolute would try and pursue a conversation. Fortunately, most people knew I fostered, so no one was too offended.

Despite my various schemes to broaden her horizons – which had included the zoo, the cinema and a local museum – Jodie seemed only to enjoy the park, specifically the park playground. As soon as we reached the gate, she would rush in, and head straight for the swings. She rarely played with other children, or even acknowledged they were there. This was hardly surprising, as she barely interacted with me. Instead, she would swing up and down, muttering or singing to herself, until it was time to leave. She was the same when we tried to play sociable games at home; she preferred to play by herself, in her own little world.

On the few occasions she did initiate contact with other children, it was usually out of curiosity. She would see a smaller child doing something interesting, or wearing something that caught her eye, so she would walk over and stand in front of them, and stare at their chest; she still had a complete aversion to eye contact. Understandably, the other children would find this quite intimidating, although this didn't seem to be Jodie's intention. Nonetheless, it often led to a scene, with the child running to its mother to complain about 'that girl'.

On one occasion, we were in the playground, and a young father came in with his two daughters. There's an area in the playground for very young children, as these two were, so that was where they went to play. For some reason, this piqued Jodie's interest, so she followed them over and stood there watching as they clambered over the castle-shaped climbing frame. I was a few metres away, keeping an eye on her. At one point, one of the girls was coming down the slide, and Jodie went over to watch, and stood a bit too close to the bottom so that she was in the little girl's way. The girls, father marched across, put his hands on Jodie's shoulders and said, 'Come on now, out of the way.'

I thought this was a little over the top, but I came over quickly and apologized to him. 'Sorry about that. Come on Jodie, come and play on the swings.'

We turned and walked away, and as we did the man shouted after us, 'You want to learn to keep your daughter under control.'

This was definitely uncalled for, but I didn't respond, and Jodie and I carried on playing. A few minutes later a smartly dressed, middle-aged lady came into the playground, and headed purposefully towards us.

'Excuse me,' she said to me, 'this is Jodie, isn't

it?' She leaned down towards Jodie and smiled. 'Hello, Jodie, it's lovely to see you again.' Jodie looked at her, and carried on swinging lazily. She held out her hand to me. 'Hi, sorry, I'm Fiona. I used to be Jodie's teacher.'

I shook her hand. 'Hello there, I'm Cathy. I'm Jodie's foster carer.' I usually wouldn't mention that I was a foster carer, for fear of embarrassing the child, but in this case it seemed safe to assume that Jodie's teacher would know she had been taken into care. 'How long did you teach Jodie for?'

'A year,' Fiona replied. She smiled at Jodie. Jodie looked back at her, blankly. Did she even recognize her? I wondered.

'I must say,' Fiona continued, 'it's nice to see Jodie looking so well, and so clean. It looks like you're doing an excellent job.'

'Oh, thank you,' I replied. 'Yes, we're plodding along, aren't we, sweet?'

Jodie nodded her head, not really understanding.

'How long has she been with you?' asked Fiona.

'A few months now. She had a number of carers before me, but it looks like she's settled now.'

'Oh good. I'm sure that's just what she needs. Well, I'll let you get on and enjoy your afternoon. Jodie, it was really lovely to see you, and nice to meet you, Cathy.'

She left, and I stood on the grass verge, watching Jodie play. The father of the young girls started walking towards me, and my anxiety level rose.

160

'Excuse me,' he said. 'I don't want to bother you. I just wanted to apologize for my tone.'

'Oh, right,' I said, relieved. 'Well, it doesn't matter.'

'I overheard you say you were a foster carer, but I'd just assumed she was your daughter.'

'Not to worry. Sorry we were in the way.'

He smiled apologetically, and walked back to his girls.

As we walked home, I marvelled at the double standards. As a foster parent, you often have to deal with strangers who are quick to blame you for a child's difficult behaviour. If they find out you're fostering, however, they suddenly take a very different view. But why do they feel the need to criticize in the first place? Being a parent of any kind is difficult enough, without having to deal with strangers' condemnation.

A few days later, I received a call from the headmaster of Elmacre: he said he was very sorry, but they couldn't offer Jodie a place. My spirits sank, but he then explained that he had a colleague at a different school who might be able to offer a place. The colleague was Adam West, of Abbey Green School, and he had now been given my details and would shortly be in touch. I thanked him effusively, and with a grin on my face relayed the good news to Jodie.

'Not going,' she replied. 'Hate school. Hate you. Hate everything.' She stuck out her tongue, and stamped down the hall.

CHAPTER 15

PAST AND PRESENT

I was woken at around 2 a.m. by screams from Jodie's room. I pulled on my dressing gown, and staggered along the corridor, feeling like I'd only just gone to sleep. I gave the door the usual quick knock, and went straight in. Jodie was lying in bed, holding the duvet over her head, clutching it tightly with her fingers. I sat on the edge of the bed, and Jodie stopped screaming. 'What's the matter, love?' I asked.

'It's the eyes!' she moaned, terrified.

'What eyes, sweet? Come out from under there so I can give you a hug.'

'No! They're everywhere. The eyes in the walls, staring at me.'

I put my hand on the duvet where her feet were, to try and comfort her. 'Jodie, love, I know you're scared, but it's your imagination. There are no eyes here. No one's watching you. Please give me a hug.'

'They're here!' she shouted back. 'I can see them, coming at me! I'm not stupid. Make them stop, Cathy!'

'Jodie, shush,' I said firmly. 'Now come out from

162

under there, and I'll show you. There's nothing there, I promise. I'm here with you, and I wouldn't let anything happen to you, would I? I'm here to protect you, that's my job, isn't that right?'

She fell silent for a second, and then loosened her grip on the duvet. I eased it down, and she clambered up and hugged me.

'Now look, Jodie. You see, there's nothing there.' I walked over to the wall, and rubbed my hand across it. 'See? There's no one here.' I sat back down on the bed. Jodie's cheeks were red, and her forehead was hot and sweaty. She was genuinely scared; whatever these visions were, they were very real to her. What had started as straightforward nightmares had gradually developed into something closer to hallucinations. Increasingly now, when I went in to her room to comfort her, I would find her in a strange state that seemed somewhere between sleeping and waking; sometimes it would seem as if she were awake but still trapped inside her nightmare. I couldn't tell if she was truly aware of what was happening but it seemed that whatever she was seeing was taking on a greater reality.

'Will you read me a story?' she asked.

'Yes, OK, but then you have to go to sleep, all right?'

'All right.'

I read her the story, and put her to bed, but at four o'clock she was screaming again. I went back and resettled her, but an hour later she started up again. There was no chance of getting her back to sleep now, which meant there was no chance of me sleeping, so I went downstairs for a cup of coffee and a much-needed cigarette. I stood on the patio in my dressing gown and slippers. It was still dark and I knew the sun wouldn't be up for another half hour. I smiled to myself, as I wondered how many other mums knew exactly what time the sun came up.

It was a cold autumnal day. Summer had now passed us by and Jodie had been living with us for over six months. It was hard to remember a time before Jodie now, or a life that was lived without this intensity. Jodie and her problems occupied me constantly, and there was little in my life that wasn't filled with looking after her and her needs. Now that the weather had turned cold, it was becoming quite a challenge to persuade Jodie to wear suitable clothes. Later that day, we left the house to go shopping, but as I went to close the door I realized I'd forgotten my own gloves. I left Jodie on the doorstep, while I popped inside to retrieve them. Suddenly the door slammed and Jodie was running up the hall towards me.

'Whatever's the matter?'

'My dad. He's outside!'

'What? Where is he?' I felt a rush of fear. It was far from unlikely that Jodie's parents had been able to track me down, if the usual mistakes and errors had been made. I had a particular dread of seeing Jodie's father; I wasn't scared for myself – I didn't feel that I was in great danger from him – but I was terrified that Jodie's safe place in my home could be contaminated and threatened if she ever laid eyes on her father while she was here. And what was more, I never wanted to set eyes on him myself. The very thought of him made me feel physically sick. 'Where did you see him, Jodie?'

'In his van. Driving up the street.'

'Go in the living room and stay put.' I walked outside, drawing the door to behind me. I looked out from the doorstep but couldn't see a van. I walked up the path and on to the pavement, peering up and down the street. I knew from what Jodie had said before that her father drove a white van, but I couldn't see any vans at all. I looked up and down but there were definitely no white vans. I looked once more and then, seeing nothing, I went back inside, relieved.

'It's OK, Jodie, there's no van. He's not there. He doesn't know where we live, so I'm sure it wasn't him. It must be someone else's van.' I gave her a hug. 'Shall we go to the shops now, or do you want to wait a bit?'

'I'll come,' she said passively.

I reassured her again and, holding her close, led the way to the car. As we drove into town I watched her in the rear-view mirror, as she anxiously kept watch in every direction, presumably looking for vans.

I parked in the multi-storey and bought a ticket for two hours. As we entered the shopping mall, we were immediately transported into a fairyland of illuminated trees, sparkling foil garlands and a giant Father Christmas booming 'Ho ho ho!' I felt a surge of panic, as I compared the stores' festive preparations with my own. I'd done nothing yet, and as I counted up the weeks I realized we were only six away from Christmas Eve. I picked up a basket, and we made our way round the department store.

Jodie was as ever an enthusiastic if not discerning shopper, and she happily grabbed any gaily packaged parcel that came within reach. While we shopped, I talked to her about Christmas and told her about the little traditions that she could expect with us, like decorating the house and the tree, the family service at our church on Christmas Eve, and the pillowcases we all hang on our doors before going to bed. I told her about the glass of sherry and the mince pie that we leave out for Santa, along with carrots for the reindeer. Jodie listened with mild interest but contributed nothing of her own experiences. She didn't even mention her last Christmas with her parents, which is usually very poignant for children in care. Instead she grasped the material aspect of the festival and started telling me a long list of all the presents she wanted this year, which was, in a nutshell, anything brightly coloured – preferably pink and sparkly.

'What did you get last Christmas?' I asked, interrupting her.

'Shoes,' she said. 'Black ones for school. But they wasn't wrapped.'

'And what did you do on Christmas Day? Did you play games?'

She nodded. 'We went up the pub and played darts. Mum had lots of beer and fell over so we had to go home. They went to sleep, so I put a pizza in the oven and after that they felt better.'

I sighed. What a miserable Christmas – and to think that Jodie had assumed responsibility for her parents like that, particularly with her problems! I'd quickly guessed that she had taken a big portion of running the home on to her seven-year-old shoulders. For all her malcoordination and poor motor skills, she'd told me once how to mix a baby's bottle and she knew how to cook fish fingers in the oven. But if her Christmas was joyless, it was no worse than others I'd heard of from my foster children who'd never known the excitement and pleasure of waking up on Christmas morning to bursting pillowcases and presents under the tree. 'Well, Christmas will be very different this year, Jodie, and I know you're going to enjoy it.'

'Will I, Cathy?' she said, and her face lit up.

'Yes. I promise.' As we carried on shopping, I resolved that she would have the best Christmas I could possibly give her – it would be one way that I could try and restore a piece of her childhood to her. I couldn't wait to see her pleasure on the day itself, even if it was over a month away.

I found presents for my nieces and nephews, then spotted a pair of Winnie the Pooh slippers which would go into Paula's sack. Not wishing to have the surprise ruined, I discreetly placed them at the bottom of the basket, and distracted Jodie while I paid. I did the same with the other stocking fillers, including a Tweenies jigsaw for Jodie, and some fancy hair conditioner that Lucy had mentioned. I would be doing all my shopping with Jodie this year, so it would have to be furtive and piecemeal, but it would be worth it.

When we arrived home, Lucy and Paula had just beaten us in. They were in the hallway, removing their coats and unloading their school-bags.

'We've been to Christmas,' Jodie shouted excitedly.

'Shopping,' I added. 'I've made a start.'

'Yes, shopping,' Jodie repeated. 'And my daddy was naughty, he took his clothes off and weed on me.'

The girls laughed uncomfortably. Neither of them knew what to say.

'Jodie,' I said, 'we went shopping this afternoon. What your daddy did happened more than a year ago. Don't link the two. It's confusing.'

But she often did this, running past and present together in a continuum of now. Right from the start she had had no conception of time, but her inability to distinguish between past, present and future seemed to be getting worse.

'Do you want to play a game?' asked Paula.

Jodie stared blankly back.

Paula persisted. 'Let's all do a jigsaw together!'

'What about Barbie?' asked Lucy. 'I'd love to play with your Barbie dolls.'

'No!' snapped Jodie. 'My dolls! Cathy, can I watch a video?'

'Wouldn't you rather play with the girls, Jodie?' I asked. 'I'm sure that would be much more fun, and I know the girls would like to hear all about your day at the shops.'

Jodie sighed, exhausted by my unreasonable demands. 'Please, Cathy,' she pleaded. 'I been good?'

I reluctantly agreed, and let her take one of her Early Years videos upstairs. The girls went up to their rooms, and I could see they were a little hurt. Of course, they had no particular desire to play Barbie dolls with Jodie, but no one likes being rejected. Paula and Lucy had been trying to spend more time with Jodie, and to become her friends, but she was impossible to break through to. Most children, no matter how bad their behaviour, do essentially want to be liked, and to feel the approval of those around them. Jodie, on the other hand, simply couldn't have cared less. When the girls wanted to play with her, she wasn't pleased or flattered, and it didn't even occur to her that she might hurt their feelings. She was completely oblivious.

Her relationship with Adrian was even more distant. Because of the nature of the abuse she had suffered, Jodie regarded all males in sexual terms, and would try to flirt with them, or rub provocatively up against them. There was nothing deliberate about this, it was simply the kind of behaviour which had characterized her relationships with men in the past, and it was going to take an awfully long time to reverse this pattern. As a result, Adrian found her very difficult, and tended to just stay out of her way.

As I began peeling the potatoes for dinner, I heard loud thumps coming from upstairs. I was about to climb the stairs, ready to go up and deal with yet another scene, when I realized what the noise was. Jodie's video contained song and dance routines for the children to join in with. Jodie was simply dancing along to her video.

As I returned to the kitchen, I felt immensely sad. Given the choice between playing with my daughters or watching a video on her own, Jodie had had no hesitation in choosing the video. It wasn't even that she didn't like the girls; if she had the option of being alone or of spending time with anyone, Jodie would always choose to be alone. Her history had taught her that the company of others could only bring pain and rejection, and this lesson had isolated her from the world.

My fear was the effect that this awful legacy was likely to have on the rest of her life. Jodie's hostility, defensiveness and delayed development meant that she really had nothing going for her. She wasn't pretty, bright or talented. She wasn't kind, warm or vulnerable. She was still overweight, despite my efforts, although her weight had stabilized. She was rude, unpleasant, aggressive, violent, and she had absolutely no desire to be liked by anyone. It was a mixture that was bound to alienate her and she had no tools to win other people over, nothing at her disposal to make others wish to be around her, or to win her affection.

As far as I could tell, not one person had ever taken an interest in Jodie in her entire life, except those that had wanted to hurt her. Not one person had ever loved her. But as I listened to her clumsy, arrhythmic stomping coming from upstairs, I felt more drawn to her than ever. Surely it wasn't too late for her? She was only eight years old, for goodness' sake. Could her entire life really be mapped out?

I hoped fervently that there was time to heal her broken personality, and I longed to put her back together again so that she could have another chance at the childhood that had been so cruelly taken from her. I was determined to try my very best for this child and if love, attention, kindness and hard work could do anything, I would not stop until she was better.

CHAPTER 16

THE SPIDER'S WEB

It was a beautiful, crisp winter morning in early December; the sun was a soft golden ball in a clear sky. Jodie's usually pale cheeks were glowing red from the cold and the exertion of riding her bike. Every so often she stopped to flip back her scarf, part of a set I'd bought: a lilac hat, scarf and gloves with a fluffy trim. Only prolonged coercion had stopped her from wearing them in bed. Finally I'd done something right!

I set a brisk pace as we approached the park gates, and my mind was racing. I was anxious, and for once my worries were not entirely down to Jodie. The previous day we had visited Abbey Green School, and met the headmaster, Adam West. Although the visit had gone well, Mr West had said that he wouldn't be able to offer Jodie a place until funding had been approved, which might take three months. Jodie would have to continue with Nicola, her tutor, in the meantime, but this clearly wasn't meeting her needs. Jodie desperately needed not only education, but also the routine of school, and the company of other children.

I paused by the entrance to the park, and called Jodie back. Strung between two shrubs was a large spider's web, still in the shade, sparkling white with dew.

'Look at this, Jodie! A spider's web. Isn't it beautiful?' I said. 'Like one of those decorations we saw in the shops.'

'Beautiful,' she repeated. 'Really beautiful.'

'And can you hear that rustling in the undergrowth? I bet that's a bird.' We stood very quietly and listened. Moments later we were rewarded, as a large blackbird with a fiery orange beak quickly hopped across the path. Jodie's face beamed.

'Beautiful. Really beautiful,' she said again, and I knew the phrase would be repeated for the rest of the day.

We made four laps of the park, then headed back. I always felt better after a walk, and for Jodie the energy release was essential, otherwise she'd be hyperactive for the rest of the day. She waited at the park gates, and we crossed the road together, then she sprinted ahead to the top of our road. Arriving at the gate, she heaved her bike up the step. To a stranger watching her who didn't know anything of her past, she could have been any normal child arriving home, cheeks flushed from the cold air, looking forward to the warmth of home and the comfort of a hot drink. Just for a moment, I pretended to be that person, so that I could briefly enjoy the pleasure of seeing Jodie as she could be, if all of our efforts paid off.

We took off our coats, and I wheeled her bike through to the conservatory. I heated some milk and made us both a mug of hot chocolate. We sat either side of the kitchen table. I passed Jodie the biscuit tin and she dived in, grinning.

'One,' I said. 'You had a cooked breakfast.' I took a sip of my drink and set it down. She followed suit.

I took a deep breath. Now was the moment that I had to broach the subject that had been on my mind all morning. The innocence of our park trip was about to be sullied with the darkness of the adult world that Jodie had been so brutally exposed to. 'Jodie,' I said.

She met my gaze, the blue-grey eyes blank as usual.

'I need to explain something. Can you listen carefully?'

She nodded.

'When we've finished our drinks, we're going out in the car. Do you remember Eileen?'

She wouldn't remember her, of course, even though Eileen had finally made her first visit. A few weeks before, she had come round to introduce herself. Jodie was unlikely to recall it and I could hardly blame her, as it had been a flying visit, to say the least. After a few uncomfortable minutes, Eileen had made her excuses and gone on her way. She clearly wasn't at ease with Jodie.

Jodie looked blank at my question, so I carried on. 'Eileen's your social worker, you remember?

Well, Eileen wants you to have something called a medical, where a doctor will examine you, but there's nothing to worry about. I'll be with you.'

In an ideal world Eileen would have come around herself to explain to Jodie what was going to happen, but I'd given up expecting anything like that.

'Will you, Cathy? That's nice.' She dunked her biscuit, then began licking off the melted chocolate.

'The doctor will have a look at you, to make sure you're OK. Do you remember that you had a medical when you first came into care? It will be like that, but this will be a bit more thorough.'

'Will I have to take me clothes off, Cathy?' she said, more interested in the biscuit than the conversation.

'Yes. But it will be a nice lady doctor. She's used to children, so there's nothing to worry about. She's going to look at your body, particularly where Daddy and Uncle Mike hurt you. You know, what we call our private parts.'

I waited for a reaction: fear, horror or outright refusal, but there was nothing. She finished her drink, wiped the back of her hand across her mouth and stood up, leaving me wondering if she'd fully understood.

'If you think of any questions,' I added, 'tell me and I'll explain.'

Strapped in the back seat, she resumed chattering about anything and everything, including medicals in general. Had I ever had a medical? Had Lucy and Paula? Did they have to take their clothes off and show their private parts? Did Adrian? I stopped that line of questioning, and switched on the radio. A bouncy pop song came on.

'My mum likes this song,' she said. 'She likes the boy singer. We listen to it in the pub.'

'You used to listen to it in the pub,' I corrected her. As usual, Jodie seemed unable to distinguish between then and now but I was trying to point out the difference whenever she muddled them up, in the hope that she would begin to put what was finished behind her. I worried that she was still existing emotionally in the bad place she had come from, and if that was the case she was unlikely to begin her recovery. 'We don't go to the pub now. That was in the past.'

'Why, Cathy? Why can't we go to the pub?'

'I don't think it's the right place to take children. I prefer the park for an outing.'

'My mum thinks it's right, so does my daddy, and my auntie Bell.'

'I dare say.'

'Cathy, is my mummy having a medical and showing her private parts?'

'No. Not as far as I know.'

She paused, as though weighing this up. Then her voice piped up again. 'She should. My daddy does naughty things to her as well.'

I glanced in the mirror. It was a throwaway comment, but loaded with connotations, as

176

many disclosures are. 'How do you know that, Jodie?'

She shrugged. 'Don't know. Just do.'

She had shut down again, and I knew there was no point in pursuing it. I was sure that she meant that she had seen her father and mother having sex and it was no surprise that she couldn't distinguish between that and what happened to her. When she said it was 'naughty', did that mean she was starting to accept that what had happened to her was wrong? Or was she just repeating back what I had said to her? It was so hard to know with Jodie how much she understood and accepted.

The rest of the journey passed with Jodie singing along to songs on the radio, many of them near word perfect. I always found this unreasonably irritating: how could she remember these daft lyrics, but not her ABC?

The medical centre was housed in a purpose-built bungalow and offered a range of paediatric services. I'd been there before with other foster children for general health checks, but never for a forensic medical; I couldn't help feeling very apprehensive because I had a fair idea of what was in store for her. I knew that the police didn't do this very readily with young children who are likely victims of abuse, because it can seem like another form of assault. I had talked it over with Jill earlier and she had reassured me that if Jodie put up any resistance or seemed distressed, the doctors would stop immediately. There was no question of forcing her to go through with it.

It was always a struggle to find a parking space, but I spotted a gap at the kerb, and anxiously tried to parallel park, while a van waited impatiently behind.

'You been here before?' Jodie asked, releasing her seatbelt.

'Yes. For eyesight and hearing tests.'

'Did they look at your private parts?'

'No, sweet. Stay put, and I'll let you out.'

I went round and opened her door. She jumped on to the pavement and I took her hand. I had no idea which department we wanted and the entrance board didn't seem to cover private parts. I approached the receptionist.

'Jodie Brown,' I said. 'We've a forensic medical booked for twelve-thirty.'

She glanced at the appointment list. 'Oh yes. We're waiting for the police doctor. Take a seat over there. She shouldn't be long.'

I steered Jodie to a small recess with four plastic chairs, and a box of well-used toys and books. A door led off, with a sign that read 'Consulting Room One', and a small metal plate marked 'Vacant'. Jodie brought me a pop-up book of Cinderella. I had just opened it and begun to read, when a smartly dressed woman walked over. She was in her late fifties, with bright red lipstick and horn-rimmed glasses.

'Cathy?' she smiled. 'I'm Linda Marshall, the police doctor. And you must be Jodie?'

She wasn't what I was expecting at all, and from the look on Jodie's face I gathered she wasn't what she was expecting either. With her red plaid suit, sheer black stockings and high stilettos, she wouldn't have looked out of place at a department store beauty counter.

'Sorry to keep you waiting,' she said. 'How are you?'

'Fine, thanks,' I answered for us both.

Jodie eyed her suspiciously. 'Are you a doctor?' she barked.

'Yes,' she whispered conspiratorially. 'But children tell me I don't look like one. Shall we go in?'

Jodie immediately dropped my hand and took hold of the doctor's. I followed them into the consulting room. There, a young woman in a white medic's coat was sitting behind a small desk, looking much more like the kind of doctor we had expected. She came round the desk and shook my hand.

'Hello there, I'm Dr Pratchet,' she said. 'I'll be carrying out the examination today, with the help of Dr Marshall here. Do sit down.'

I took the only available chair and looked around. A long reclining couch with leg rests dominated one side of the room. At its foot was a large spot lamp on an adjustable metal stem, which was switched off for the moment. I shuddered, aware of what was in store.

Dr Pratchet returned to her desk, and Linda Marshall perched on the edge of the couch. Jodie went straight for the toy box in the corner, which she upturned, spilling its contents across the floor. I shot her a warning glance.

'I'd like to ask you a few questions first,' Dr Pratchet said. 'You're all right playing there for a few minutes, aren't you, Jodie?'

Jodie grinned at me, holding out a toy she'd found. 'Look, Cathy!'

'Yes, it's a jack-in-a-box, like the one at home. Put it back when you've finished, good girl.'

The doctor opened an A4 folder, and pulled out a bundle of papers. 'Jodie's eight and a half now? And she's been with you since the third of April?'

I could tell that the doctor was well aware of the contents of Jodie's file and knew exactly why we were there. 'Yes, that's right.'

'How is she generally? Eating? Sleeping? Behaviour?'

I gave her a brief summary of Jodie's state: that she ate well but her nights and general behaviour were becoming increasingly difficult.

'And does she understand why she's here?'

'I've explained she's going to have a medical, and you will need to look at her private parts to make sure she's OK.'

She nodded, and I assumed she approved of my explanation. 'Apart from what Jodie's said, have you noticed any other indicators? Soreness, a rash, discharge?'

Foster carers can't afford to be squeamish. 'No, but she does soil herself a lot. It's not deliberate, as it used to be. It's more that she doesn't seem to quite make it to the toilet in time. Or if she does, she's not very good at cleaning herself up. I'm often changing her and washing her so it wouldn't necessarily be obvious.'

'Quite,' Linda Marshall agreed.

Dr Pratchet made a note and then looked up at Jodie. 'OK, we're going to start by measuring and weighing you, Jodie. Do you think you could jump on those scales?'

'Jump' was not the best choice of word, as Jodie took it literally. With a resounding leap, she threw herself on to the platform. The sprung metal plate clanged and shuddered.

'Gently,' I said redundantly.

Linda read out the results and Dr Pratchet noted them down. 'Good girl. Now, can you climb on to this couch for me? It's a bit high; do you need some help?'

Jodie, oblivious to what lay in wait and eager to demonstrate her agility, scrambled up. She sat with her chubby legs dangling over the edge, grinning at me proudly. I watched as Dr Pratchet opened her desk drawer and removed a stethoscope and a wooden spatula. Looping the stethoscope around her neck, she tucked the spatula into her coat pocket. I shuffled my chair back to allow her to pass. I could feel my anxiety level rising fast.

'I'm going to have a look in your mouth first, Jodie,' she said. 'Say aaah.'

Jodie opened her mouth wide. Dr Pratchet

placed the spatula on her tongue, and the two women peered in. I could guess what they were looking for. If Jodie had been forced into oral sex, there was a chance she might have contracted a sexually transmitted disease in her mouth, but I hadn't seen any sores or white thrush spots when I'd helped brush her teeth.

'Excellent,' said Dr Pratchet. 'Well done.'

Jodie closed her mouth, and grinned at me. I smiled back reassuringly.

'Now, can I listen to your chest?'

Linda gently lifted up Jodie's jumper, waiting for Jodie to give permission by raising her arms, and Dr Pratchet listened with her stethoscope. I felt reassured: they certainly knew how to put a child at ease. I relaxed a little.

'Excellent,' she said again. 'You're doing very well. Aren't you a big girl?'

Jodie beamed, as though she'd just won a medal, but I was aware we were approaching the next stage of the medical, and I was praying for Jodie's continued cooperation. The doctors wouldn't force her to go through with it, but without this evidence there would be little chance of a prosecution.

'Can you lie down on the couch for me?' asked Linda, patting the bed.

Jodie flopped back in her cumbersome way and cackled loudly.

'We need to have you further this end,' said Linda, and eased her down, so that her legs hung over the edge. Dr Pratchet switched on the lamp.

'Would you like to come and hold her hand?' Linda asked, looking over at me.

I manoeuvred my chair so that I was sitting beside Jodie's head, and held her hand. I was pleased to be doing something. Dr Pratchet passed Linda a blanket, and she covered Jodie's body.

'I'm going to slip off your trousers and pants,' she said, and discreetly removed them under the blanket. 'Good girl. Now let your legs go floppy, and I'll put them in the right position.'

She raised Jodie's knees. It was an ungainly, vulnerable position, but with the blanket covering her she at least retained some dignity.

Linda joined Dr Pratchet at the foot of the couch, and both women put on rubber gloves and began the examination. I stroked Jodie's forehead and held her hand tight. Her cheeks flushed, and she bit her bottom lip.

'Won't be long,' I said, 'then we can go home.'

The women began discussing what they saw. I recognized the word 'lesion', but none of the other terms were familiar. Their tone was flat and professional, revealing nothing.

'It hurts,' said Jodie. I squeezed her hand, willing them to hurry up.

Dr Pratchet suddenly straightened. 'All done. You've been a very brave girl. You can get dressed now.'

I breathed a sigh of relief and helped Jodie sit

up and dress, while the two women shed their gloves into the bin.

'We'll send the report to the social worker,' said Linda. 'You can reassure Jodie she's quite normal.'

This was all we would be told for now. The social worker would eventually pass on to me anything I needed to know. Jill had said that this could take anything from ten days to a month. I thanked them warmly, took Jodie's hand, and we walked out into the winter afternoon sunshine.

'You were very brave,' I told her. 'You won't have to go through that again. It's over now.'

'I wished it was a man,' she said, giving a little hop beside me.

'What? Doing the examination?' I was surprised. Surely a man performing that kind of procedure was the last thing Jodie would want, after what she'd been through. 'Why?'

'Ladies hurt more than men, 'cos they haven't got a willy.'

I stopped and turned to her as the significance of her words sank in. 'What do you mean? What ladies? How do they hurt you?'

Her brow furrowed, as she searched through her limited vocabulary to try and explain. 'My mum and Aunt Bell, they had to use things because they haven't got willies.'

'Use things? What, on your private parts?'

'Yes. Like the doctors. They poked things inside me.'

I froze. Oh please, no. How much more could this child have endured? 'What things, Jodie?'

'Spoons, like the one the doctor put in my mouth. Only it was silver.'

'Are you saying that Mum and Aunt Bell put a metal spoon in your private parts?'

She nodded. 'It was cold. Daddy warmed it in his hands first. He was kind sometimes, wasn't he, Cathy?'

It was too much. I could no longer hide my anger with the people who'd done this to her. 'No, Jodie, he wasn't. He was wicked. They're animals. All of them. I hope they rot in hell!'

CHAPTER 17

NOSY COW

I sat at my desk writing, logging in my diary the vile details of Jodie's sexual degradation. I felt sick to my core. The active involvement of Jodie's mother in the abuse was such an appalling inversion of the maternal role and every-thing we feel mothers should be. We foster carers were supposed to be non-judgemental but there is a cut-off point and, for me, this was it. I could hardly bear to record Jodie's childish conclusion that, because her father had warmed the object used to defile her, this act of kindness made him less culpable.

As soon as Jill received my emailed report, she phoned. 'Jesus,' she said. 'It's a wonder the poor child's functioning at all with all this.'

'She isn't really. And she's functioning less with every new disclosure.' As I said it, I realized the truth. On a day-to-day basis, there were ups and downs, bad days and better days; but if I stood back for a moment and considered it all carefully, I could see that in reality it was a steady decline. Jodie was getting worse. 'I'm out of my depth, Jill.'

Jill could hear the rising panic in my voice. She said soothingly, 'OK, don't worry. You're seeing the psychologist next week, aren't you?'

'Monday.'

'Why don't you ask her for some strategies to help? I know that's not why she's there, but she might be able to offer something. It's worth a try.'

'Thanks, Jill. That's a good idea.' I felt a small vestige of comfort. 'I'll see what she says.'

Jill was right. The psychologist had been appointed by the court to assess Jodie as part of the ongoing care proceedings, and it wasn't her role to advise me, or to offer therapy for Jodie. Still, it was a glimmer of hope – surely she would have some idea of what I might do.

The bureaucratic wheels were grinding slowly on, as Jodie's case worked its way through the system. Jodie had been brought into care under an Interim Care Order, which meant that the court would decide at a later date whether to return her to her family, or to issue a Full Care Order. The psychologist would meet Jodie a number of times before filing her report, as this was a crucial part of the court's decision-making process.

The court had set dates for two 'direction hearings' in January and March, which would be followed by a 'final court hearing' in May. The purpose of the direction hearings was to allow the judge to consider the evidence that had been presented so far, so that he or she could take interim decisions in the child's interests, without having to wait for the final court proceedings to be resolved. Throughout the process, the guardian ad litum would meet with all the parties and provide the judge with an objective assessment, making recommendations in the best interests of the child. In practice, judges tend to be guided by the guardian ad litum, and usually follow his or her recommendations.

If a Full Care Order was granted at the final hearing, the local authority would become Jodie's de facto guardian, and Social Services would place her either with a longterm foster family, or into a residential care home, or, if she was very lucky, they might find a family to adopt her. However, given Jodie's age, aggression and learning difficulties, this last option was extremely unlikely.

Before the first meeting with the psychologist, Jodie was scheduled for the police memorandum interview. This interview, as well as being part of the care proceedings, would also be used in the police investigation, with a view to prosecuting Jodie's parents and any other abusers. Jodie would be interviewed by specially trained police officers from the Child Protection Unit, and I hoped that she would be as forthcoming with them as she had been with me.

We arrived for our appointment with the Child Protection Officers in good time, which gave Jodie a chance to peer into the police cars parked outside the station. I pressed the buzzer for entry, then gave our names to the PC on reception. He came out from behind the desk and showed us through to a special suite. As we walked in, I felt reassured: the suite was clearly designed to set a child at ease. The room was brightly furnished, with a big red sofa, lots of toys and colourful *Lion King*-themed wallpaper. Two WPCs in civilian clothes stood and introduced themselves.

'Hello, you must be Jodie,' one said brightly. 'My name's Kelly, and this is Harriet.'

Jodie grinned while I shook their hands.

'Coffee?' Harriet asked.

'Yes please.'

'And squash for Jodie?'

'Thank you,' I said.

Harriet left the room while Jodie brought a jigsaw from a toy box and the three of us began assembling it. Harriet returned with the drinks and a packet of biscuits. We sat for a while, as the WPCs tried to engage Jodie's attention, asking her about her hobbies, her favourite television programmes and so on. Jodie, however, remained oblivious to their chat, preferring to sit in the corner exploring the toy boxes. After a while, Kelly got on her hands and knees and tried to join in with Jodie's games, but this too was only partially successful. I didn't think Jodie was being deliberately hostile, it was just that she didn't see the need to interact, even though I had explained the importance of our visit both that morning and the night before.

Explaining to Jodie what was going to happen had been a delicate process. I had tried to make it clear that some nice, kind people would be asking her questions about the things she had told me had happened to her, but there was not much more I could add without being in danger of prejudicing any eventual court case. I couldn't say, 'You must tell the police the naughty things that Daddy did to you,' in case I was in any way putting ideas into Jodie's head. All I could do was ask her to tell the truth. If it came out in the interview that I had put any detail in her head, then it could be used by the opposing barrister in an effort to disprove Jodie's claims.

I hoped that Jodie had understood how important it was to be frank and honest with the officers but, as ever, it was hard to tell what she had absorbed. I crossed my fingers that she was in a compliant mood, as she had been in the medical, and hoped she would enjoy being the centre of attention. Many foster children are like this: before they come into care they've often been neglected and ignored, so when they are given lots of attention and a host of professionals involved in the case is brought into their lives they can sometimes become little stars. On occasions, Jodie could thrive on being at the centre of things, so I hoped that this would work in her favour today.

Another ten minutes passed, then Kelly suggested we make a start. She touched Jodie's arm softly and said, 'We're going to go through to what's called an interview room in a minute. I know Cathy's told you all about it. It's just through there.' She pointed to the door.

Jodie looked up. 'Is Cathy coming?'

'Yes, to begin with, and then she'll come back and wait in here, and we'll have a chat in there. Now, while we have our chat, a very nice man is going to video us, so we can remember everything we talked about later on. Does that sound OK to you?'

Perhaps Jodie had lost interest in the toys for suddenly, very obligingly, and to my great relief, she stood up and took hold of Kelly's hand. 'Come on then,' she said. 'I want to be in the video.'

I followed them out of the door and into the next room, where a young policeman, also in civilian clothes, greeted us.

'Hello, Jodie,' he said. 'I'm John. I work the camera. Do you want to come and have a look?'

The interview room was small and bare, with three plastic chairs, a central light, and a blackout blind over the only window. I was surprised how austere it was; I'd imagined it would be more child-friendly.

John showed Jodie and me where the camera was mounted, and where he would be standing, hidden from view by a screen. 'We're going to make a video of you, and record what you're saying. Is that OK, Jodie?'

I remembered the photo I'd taken of Jodie when she'd first arrived at my home, and how she'd tried to take off her clothes. Would she be upset now at this strange man wanting to video her? She hadn't been bothered when I'd explained it to her earlier, and so far at least she seemed unfazed, as she nodded her assent.

'Can you sit in this chair?' Kelly said, helping her up, while John discreetly moved behind the screen.

'Cathy's going to wait in the room next door now, while you stay with us, all right?' Harriet said.

Jodie wriggled in her chair and gave a little wave, and I left the room. As her carer, I was not allowed to be present during the interview, in case it affected her testimony. Memorandum interviews have to be done under controlled conditions, in order for them to be admissible as evidence in court.

I returned to the bright, cheerful suite, which seemed such a contrast to the small, dark interview room. I sat down, but I found I couldn't relax, so I decided to pop outside for a cigarette. The wind was piercing, and I took shelter in a doorway, furtively puffing while I worried about what was going on in the interview room. What Jodie said now was crucial because without her evidence on tape there would be little chance of a prosecution. At her age and with her learning difficulties, there was no way she could go into a witness box to testify. The adversarial nature of our legal system, even in child abuse cases, would mean that she could be cross-examined by a barrister. There was no way she would be able to cope with that, and what child of less than ten who had been through what she had could? As a result, it was little wonder so few cases came to court, let alone ended with a successful prosecution of the abusers. I smoked only half the cigarette, then stubbed it out, and felt only half-guilty. I pressed the buzzer to re-enter the station, then made my own way to the suite. I paced, then sat, and paced again. Twenty minutes passed, then the door opened and Kelly stuck her head round.

'We're giving it another ten minutes, then we're going to call it a day. We've not had much luck, I'm afraid.'

I nodded, my heart sinking, as Kelly returned to the interview. I wandered over to the window, which looked out over the courtyard at the rear. I watched as a patrol car pulled in, and two uniformed officers climbed out, sharing a joke. As a foster carer, I often have dealings with the police, not only with child protection issues, but also with runaway teenagers, or those who've committed offences. Theirs was a difficult job, and I'd always had the utmost respect for the police, particularly the Youth Offending Team, who have to have the patience of saints.

A sense of depression engulfed me. I could imagine that if Jodie hadn't opened up by now, she was unlikely to. I knew what she was like when she didn't want to talk. There was no forcing the issue – she was as immovable as a mountain. She had just a few short minutes left to tell the police what they needed to hear if there was any hope of punishing the people who had made her suffer so terribly.

While I waited, I wondered, not for the first time, about Jodie's brother and sister. Had they been made to suffer in the way that Jodie had? I hoped not, but it was unlikely that I would ever find out. I was only given information that was strictly relevant to Jodie and all I knew was that her siblings were with other carers now. My hope was that, because they were so much younger than Jodie, they might have escaped what Jodie had gone through.

A short while later I heard Jodie's voice outside the door. It opened and she bounced in. 'We did the video,' she grinned. 'It was really good.' She rushed over to the toy box.

I looked up hopefully at Harriet and Kelly, who shook their heads. Harriet motioned for me to join her, while Kelly helped Jodie into her coat.

'She wouldn't talk, I'm afraid,' said Harriet. 'She kept telling us how she wanted to rip her father's head off, but she wouldn't say why, or give any details. We won't try again while she's so young, but we'll keep the file open for the future. Hopefully one day she will be ready.'

'Thank you,' I said, unable to hide my disappointment. 'I'm sorry she wasn't more cooperative, but it isn't altogether surprising.'

'No. Certainly not, not with everything that's gone on. I dealt with that family years ago. God knows why she was left there so long.'

I was intrigued but the police woman didn't say any more and confidentiality would not allow her to. Clearly the police had been involved with the family at some level but it could have been for anything from parking offences to petty crime or drug dealing. Nevertheless, I had the feeling that Harriet had formed the impression that something had been going on in the house . . . but I would never know for sure.

I buttoned up Jodie's coat, and the two WPCs saw us out. As soon as we turned the corner, Jodie's good mood disappeared.

'Cathy, is the monster going to come? Is it going to come and do what they said?' Her questions were breathless and anxious. 'I think that monster's coming. He's under my bed and he wants to chew up my hands while I'm asleep.'

'No, sweetheart, it's not, I promise. Why do you think that?'

'My dad and Uncle Mike said if I ever told anyone, it was going to come.' The anxiety in her voice rose higher until she was ranting. 'It's going to chew my arms and legs off! That's what's going to happen!'

'No, sweet,' I said, trying to pacify her. 'It's not going to come. You did your very best with the police, I know that. You were a good girl and nothing is going to hurt you. You're safe with me, you know that, don't you? There's no monster.'

As I tried to calm her, I realized that it was this fear that had stopped her from talking to the police. Instantly my anger flared at the power the abusers still had over her. She was unwittingly protecting them because the terror they had planted in her was so strong that it overrode everything else.

'You're safe with me, Jodie,' I said, as we headed for home. 'I promise.'

That night, when I turned on the ten o'clock news, the screen was dominated by a rock star, arrested as part of a worldwide investigation into child pornography on the Internet. The police had seized his computer and found images of children on the hard disk.

I seethed with anger. How did these perverts think the photographs were obtained? For every image downloaded, a child had been abused, and a life and personality destroyed. The end result was children like Jodie, fractured and hurt almost beyond repair. As far as I was concerned, the person buying this filth was just as responsible as the abuser, and I had no sympathy for his fall from grace, or for the claim that he was researching a book.

Our appointment with the psychologist was set for Monday afternoon. Although this was our first meeting with Dr Burrows together, Jodie had seen her once before, while she was with her second carers. For some reason, she seemed reluctant to see her again.

'But Dr Burrows will be able to help you,' I explained. 'Everyone wants to help you, Jodie, but first we have to tell Dr Burrows what we know. You need to say what happened so that people can make it all better.'

'None of her damn business,' she snarled. 'Nosy cow.'

'What isn't her business?' I asked. But she wouldn't be drawn. I suspected her parents had warned her against this kind of thing, and against cooperating, fearing that a psychologist would be a particular threat to their shameful secret.

They needn't have worried. From the moment we arrived, Jodie was hostile and uncommunicative. She wouldn't answer any questions, not even on innocuous subjects like her favourite toys, or what she liked to eat. The only answers she did give were monosyllabic or gibberish.

Dr Burrows was professional and business-like, and clearly knew how to connect with children, but she was making no progress with Jodie. After a while, she gave up trying to ask straightforward questions and tried a different approach. She brought out a pad of paper and some coloured pencils.

'Jodie, would you be able to do some drawings for me? I'd like to see some pictures – how about drawing me a picture of your mum and dad at home?'

This did seem to soften Jodie a little, and she took up a pencil and began to draw in her clumsy, malcoordinated way. We watched as she scrawled out a picture. I'm not a psychologist but I was at a loss to see how her pictures could be of any use. They were childish pin-men drawings, with over-sized heads, and no detail. Jodie, however, clearly felt that she had done more than enough, as all further questions from the doctor were met with, 'Don't know. Piss off.'

At last the hour's session drew to a close. It felt as if it had been a bit futile, and I took the opportunity to ask the doctor if she could suggest anything to help me cope with Jodie's needs.

'Her main need is primary care,' she replied. 'I can see you're performing that admirably. She'll respond to continuity and firm boundaries. I'm very pleased she's placed with you. You're doing an excellent job.'

Compliments are all well and good, but what I had actually asked for was advice. I felt exasperated and very isolated. I wasn't trained for this – I was just muddling through in the dark, beset by fatigue, confusion and the sense of being hopelessly out of my depth. The tools and training I had just weren't sufficient for Jodie's needs, I realized now. The doctor was clearly excellent but she didn't seem able to grasp that I couldn't divorce Jodie's primary care from her mental welfare. I dealt every day not just with feeding her, amusing her and keeping her clean, but also with tantrums, violence, nightmares, waking visions, hallucinations and abject terror. Those things couldn't be fitted nicely into a one-hour slot. I lived with them day and night.

As we left, I felt more alone than I had in my life.

Before I knew it, Christmas was only ten days away, but my excitement of a few weeks ago was now hard to muster. It was going to be a low-key affair this year. I'd already bought and wrapped most of the presents, and decorated the house, but my heart wasn't in it. I tried to put on a brave face for the sake of the children, but I'd scaled down the usual arrangements. I was simply too exhausted to cope with a full-scale celebration. My parents were coming for Christmas Day, along with my brother and his family. I usually had a small party for friends and neighbours on Christmas Eve, but it wasn't going to be feasible this year. I explained to them that I had rather a lot going on at the moment, and I'd have them round when things were calmer. I hoped no one was offended.

In quieter moments, when I had time to reflect, I could see that I was becoming too involved in Jodie and her suffering. I was getting sucked into the abyss of her emotional turmoil, and although I was aware of it I couldn't seem to shake it off. She occupied my thoughts continuously. When I tried to read a book, I would find myself turning the page without having followed any of the plot. It was the same with the radio or television. I was constantly preoccupied by Jodie, and my own state of mind was suffering. Her distorted perception was colouring mine. It felt as though the evil that had corrupted Jodie's world was creeping out and corrupting my home as well. There seemed to be a poison in the air, and Jodie was its innocent transmitter. I decided I needed a break to put things back in perspective. I called Jill.

I explained to her that I was becoming physically and mentally exhausted. 'Jill, I'm not kidding, I need a break. Just some time to regroup and get my strength back, and think of something else for a bit. My own children could do with a bit of my time and attention as well. Could you look into arranging respite, please? Any weekend in January will be fine.'

'Of course,' she replied. 'You deserve a holiday. More than that, you need one, if you're going to be able to stay the course. I'll look into it this afternoon. The only problem is, Cathy, I'll have to find carers who are up to it. They'll need to be very experienced, with no younger or similar-aged children. I can think of one couple in Surrey. I'll see if they're free.'

'Thank you. I'd be grateful.' I put the phone down, my spirits lifting just a little.

CHAPTER 18

FIRE

The next day, Jill phoned to arrange her last visit before Christmas. We chatted for a while. Jill asked me if Jodie ever mentioned her brother and sister.

'Occasionally,' I replied, 'in the context of something she's telling me about home.'

'She doesn't ask to see them?'

'No, she doesn't.' And it suddenly occurred to me how unusual this was. The bond between siblings in care is often strengthened by separation, so even if the children aren't seeing their parents, Social Services usually make sure that contact is arranged between the brothers and sisters. 'Are there any plans for them to keep in touch?' I asked.

'Not at present. There were concerns about Jodie's treatment of them. I think they had reason to believe that she could be a bit heavy handed with them, which is why they all went to separate carers.'

I could imagine that. Jodie often lashed out when she was frustrated. 'What about Christmas cards and presents?' I asked.

'We can certainly pass them on, if she wants to send them.'

That afternoon, I asked Jodie if she wanted to go Christmas shopping to buy presents for her brother and sister.

'No,' she said. 'Don't want to.'

'How about sending a card? I'll help you write it if you like.'

'No. Hate them.'

'Why do you hate them, Jodie?'

She thought for a moment. 'Mum liked them more than me. She took them away when Dad came into my bedroom.'

'OK, pet, I think I understand.' I wasn't sure exactly what she was telling me but it was quite possible that the younger ones had been protected in some way from what Jodie went through. No wonder she would resent them. Perhaps she'd even hit out at them because she was jealous of their escape and wanted to punish them. It was conjecture, of course, but I hoped for the other children's sakes that they had been left alone.

Not only was Jodie cut off from her parents, she was also isolated from her siblings. With no grandparents in the picture, and abusers for aunts and uncles, this meant we were the only family she had. I thought of my own children, and the extended family who wouldn't hesitate to step in and look after them if anything happened to me. This wasn't such an issue now, but it had been a real concern in the past. My husband had left when Adrian was Jodie's age, and in darker moments I had welcomed the safety net of knowing that were I to fall under a bus they would be loved and cared for just the same. Jodie, on the other hand, had no one in the world but us.

Instead of shopping, Jodie wanted to do some painting, so I covered the table with paper, and set out the paints, brushes and a pot of water. I tied Jodie's apron around her, and left her for a few minutes to work on her masterpiece. When I came back to check on her, I was impressed. Jodie had produced a number of pictures which actually looked like something.

'Do you like them, Cathy?' Jodie asked proudly.

'I really do. These are excellent, Jodie. Can you describe them for me? Tell me what they are?'

'All right. This one is a house.'

'That's very nice. And those are the windows, aren't they?'

'Yes, windows. This one's a car. And this one's my dog, stupid old dog.'

I jolted to attention. At the pre-placement meeting, I had been told that Jodie had set fire to her dog, and had nearly burned her house down in the process. It was this incident that had finally led to her and her siblings being taken into care. 'I see,' I replied. 'Can you tell me more about the picture?'

'Yes I can. This is our dog, Sam. He's a big brown dog, always woofing.'

'And why did you say he was stupid, Jodie?'

'I don't know,' she replied impatiently.

'There must be a reason why he's stupid. You can tell me.'

'He's all ugly and burnt. He's horrible.'

'Oh dear. How did he get burnt?' I asked, trying to keep my voice light and relaxed. We were still standing side by side, looking at the pictures, and I was anxious not to put pressure on her. Jodie shook her brush in the water, then tested it on the paper. Finding it was still not clean, she dipped and shook it again.

'Jodie, can you tell me how Sam got burnt? I promise I won't be angry.'

'Jodie did it,' she muttered. 'I put all the bog roll on him, then used Mum's lighter. He was jumping and jumping, and woofing, and started running around, and everything was burning.'

'Where were your mum and dad when you did this?'

'They were at Uncle Mike's.'

'Were you on your own?'

'No, Ben and Chessie was there.' Jodie's sister's name was Chelsea, but she had trouble pronouncing it. 'I was looking after them.'

'So what happened next?'

'I picked up Chessie, and took her and Ben in the garden, and the stupid dog came and started rolling in the dirt. It looked all ugly, with its hair hanging off, and it stinks. And it made a lot of noise. I went in the hall and dialled 999, and the firemen came and put it out.'

'That was sensible, calling the firemen. You saved Chelsea and Ben.'

'Yeah,' she said, grabbing a fresh sheet of paper.

'Jodie, can you tell me why you wanted to hurt your dog?'

'Wasn't my dog,' she snapped. 'Daddy's dog. I told you.'

'Oh, right. Can you tell me why you wanted to hurt your daddy's dog?'

Her brow furrowed in concentration. Gradually, her face hardened, and her fist clenched around the brush. 'I hate him. I hate them, and I wanted to burn the house down and get out. It's a horrible house.' She thumped the table. 'And I want my daddy arrested. He's horrible, he sat on my face. They should arrest him, kill him!'

'But why set fire to the dog, Jodie? Why not burn the curtains or the sofa if you wanted to burn the house down and get out?'

'You are silly. I get smacked if I mess up the settee. Can I have a biscuit now, Cathy?'

While I got her a biscuit, I wondered if Jodie had set the dog alight as a way of punishing her father by hurting something he loved. Or perhaps, despite all her learning difficulties and developmental delays, Jodie had worked out a way to get herself out of that house. The frightening thought was that if she hadn't done what she did, she might still be there, undergoing that vile degradation day after day.

★　★　★

In the days that followed, Jodie became increasingly distant. I renewed my efforts to draw her into the heart of our family, but she remained fiercely resistant, acting as if she needed no one and could manage alone. I'd seen this kind of behaviour before – self-sufficiency is not unusual in abused or neglected children, as they've often had to be resilient in order to survive – but Jodie took it to a new level. Any expression of care or concern from us was met with outright rejection, or sneered ridicule. She wanted no part of the daily support or interaction that made up family life, and erected barriers to emphasize her separateness. One afternoon, Paula and Lucy joined us for a shopping trip, but Jodie refused to walk with us, instead she walked six paces in front or behind, and barely spoke a word. The next day, I took Jodie to the cinema to see *Lilo and Stitch*, and she pointedly sat two seats apart from me. She only rejoined me when the lights went down, as she was scared of the dark. She'd never been to the cinema before and she didn't show much excitement either before or afterwards. It was another sign of how dulled and desensitized she was. She basked in her loneliness, and I was completely at a loss to know how to break through.

My only hope was that Christmas would strengthen our relationship. After all, there's nothing more family oriented than Christmas.

CHAPTER 19

SPECIAL LITTLE GIRL

Nicola came to give Jodie her last lesson before Christmas, and the following day the girls' school and Adrian's college both broke up. Suddenly, the five of us were together all day. However, I use the term 'together' loosely, for although we were under the same roof, togetherness was avoided, and not only by Jodie. Adrian, Paula and Lucy spent most of their time in their rooms, and when they did come down they were met with a kick, a punch or a volley of 'What you doing? Get out. It's my house now' and so on. Her attitude to the others had not softened much in her time with us. Illogically, the more attention I gave her, the more jealous she was of the others.

I explained to Jodie over and over again that we all lived together, as a family, but she wasn't open to reason. Even so, although she didn't want the family, it seemed that she did want me. Her possessiveness had been consolidated by the weeks when there had been just the two of us during the day, and I was starting to resent it. She demanded my constant attention, and I saw that she was doing what no other child had done before: undermining the fabric of our family. Normally, I would have dealt with this by trying to put some distance between us, but this was virtually impossible with Jodie, because of the high level of her needs.

Jodie's hostility and aggression had a powerful effect on everyone in the house and created an unpleasant atmosphere. Even when she was up in her room, we could feel it in the house, like a malevolent presence. At dinner, on the occasions when we did all eat together, I would have to carry the conversation, as the children had become inhibited by Jodie's endless snapping and kept quiet. We were even looking at each other less, because if any of us looked in Jodie's direction this was liable to set her off. One glance could quickly lead to a tantrum, and no one wanted to be responsible, however indirectly, for ruining yet another meal.

We were also communicating with each other less, as the nature of Jodie's abuse meant that we were limited to a very narrow range of conversation. We couldn't, for instance, discuss Lucy's new boyfriend, even though he was pretty much the only thing on her mind. In fact, men of all ages had become effectively taboo in our house; we were even wary of discussing pop stars on TV.

With the girls at home, I became acutely aware of the physical distance that Jodie had created between herself and the rest of the family. In the first few months after her arrival, Jodie had needed lots of hugs and comfort, but recently she had cut out almost all physical contact, even when she woke screaming in the night. I was always hugging and kissing the girls, and to a lesser degree Adrian, and this made it immediately apparent how isolated Jodie had become. I tried to remedy this, of course, but when I tried to hug her before she went up to bed, or asked her to sit next to me on the sofa, she would make a joke of being disgusted, and either shake her head or simply run away.

I was always upset when she did this, because it was clear that she was terribly sad and lonely, and I wanted nothing more than to show her the affection and love that my children took for granted. I'm no psychologist, but my guess was that the legacy of abuse had tarnished physical contact in her mind, and made it uncomfortable and frightening. It was an awful catch-22: Jodie needed affection more than anyone I'd ever known, but the means by which affection is communicated would only contribute to her anxiety.

Sally, the guardian ad litum, came to visit and asked to spend some time alone with Jodie. I left the two of them in the lounge, and took the opportunity to spend some time with Lucy and Paula, while Adrian was out with his friends. Jodie had been disruptive and aggressive all morning, and I found Paula sitting despondently on her bed. 'I wish I was back at school,' she admitted. 'I'm dreading Christmas. She'll ruin it.'

'No she won't. We won't let her. And we may find it's just what she needs to open her heart. I know it's difficult, but she can't keep this up for ever.'

'Can't she? She's done a good job so far. I daren't even bring my friends home because of how she is.'

I was taken aback. My usually sociable daughter was now too embarrassed to bring friends home. I went over and hugged her. 'I'm sorry. I didn't realize. How about you arrange a sleepover when she's away on respite? Videos, midnight feast, the lot?'

She brightened a little. 'OK, Mum. I'm sorry.'

'No need to apologize. I understand.'

I went into Lucy's room, but the second I mentioned Jodie's name she turned on me.

'It's all we ever talk about. Jodie, bloody Jodie. I'm sick to death of her. I wish she'd never come. You won't change her, Cathy, whatever you do. Surely you can see that by now? She's evil. She needs a bloody priest, not a carer.'

I wondered if Sally had noticed the tension in the house, for as she was about to leave she paused in the hall and placed her hand on my arm. 'Cathy, you're doing a really good job, but make sure you and your family don't suffer. These children can play havoc with your emotions. Remember, her damage isn't your responsibility. You can only do so much.'

I found Sally's words comforting. It was nice to

hear someone say something positive and to recognize what was going on. I respected Sally – she managed to combine professionalism with an ability to empathize that made me feel she understood.

Later that afternoon, Eileen phoned. 'Hello, Cathy,' she said, in her flat, plodding way. 'We've got a bit of a problem.'

'Oh yes?' I replied, unperturbed. I was used to social workers telling me 'we' had problems. It usually meant that something unpleasant was coming my way.

'When we sent a copy of the doctor's letter to Jodie's parents, someone forgot to blank out your details, so I'm afraid they sent them your name and address.' As usual, she didn't sound very sorry at all. I was furious. I'd been worrying about the Ear, Nose and Throat department being indiscreet, but meanwhile the Social Services had been handing out my details. I thought back to the silent phone call I'd received when Nicola had been with us; could that have been Jodie's parents?

'I see,' I said. 'That's really going to make Jodie feel safe! I can't say I'm surprised, though. When did it happen?'

'I'm not sure exactly. We only found out when Jodie's mother phoned today, demanding contact. She threatened to come to your house if we didn't arrange it. Obviously, we told her that was unacceptable, but I thought you should know.'

'Thanks,' I said tersely. 'And what did she say? Is she still planning on coming round?'

'I don't think so. She only mentioned it once. But don't worry, if she does come round we'll apply for an injunction straight away.'

Yes, I thought, but an injunction's only a piece of paper. I'd had angry parents turning up on my doorstep before, and I knew waving a scrap of paper at them wouldn't have had much of an effect. If a child is on a Voluntary Care Order, or we're working towards rehabilitating the child so that he or she can go back home and the parents are cooperating, then there's no problem in them knowing where the child and I live. Indeed, sometimes contact takes place in my house. But that clearly wasn't the case here, far from it. It was blindingly obvious that the highest level of care should have been taken to protect my details and that hadn't happened.

Eileen was impervious to my frustration, and there wasn't much I could do about the situation now. An injunction was as useful as locking the stable door after the horse had bolted.

'Right,' I said stiffly. 'Thanks for letting me know.' And ended the call.

I was angry, of course, but, as I'd said to Eileen, I wasn't terribly surprised. While the care proceedings are in progress, there are a huge number of documents flying around, between the parents, solicitors, social workers, the guardian ad litum and others. The present system relies on someone in the office at Social Services remembering to blank out the confidential details from every document, so it's inevitable that there will be mistakes. In my experience, about 50 per cent of parents are given my address at some point, which in my view is unacceptable.

As a result, when there is a breach of confidentiality, we as a family have to take special precautions. My children always look through the spyhole before answering the door, and if it's someone they don't recognize, they don't open it; instead, they fetch me. Foster children don't answer the door at all. On top of this, we have an expensive alarm system, a Chubb lock, and I always look up and down the road before leaving the house. After a while it becomes second nature, and we have all learned that we simply have to accept the risks. Thank goodness that, apart from some nasty verbal confrontations, none of us has been placed in real danger.

My patience with Eileen, however, was stretched to the limit a few days later. For reasons known only to themselves, Social Services decided to call a meeting to discuss Jodie's mother's threat to come round, and they wanted Jill and me to attend. We marvelled that they had the time, so close to Christmas. And what were we going to discuss in any case? No one could take back the information now that it had been released; taking out an injunction forbidding Jodie's parents to come near my property would have been pointless; the only other option was to move Jodie to new carers, which was clearly in no one's interests – especially not Jodie's. And who would take her anyway, with her complex needs, and at such short notice?

The meeting went as I had expected. We discussed all the possible options, before deciding on the sensible course: namely, to do nothing. I was relieved to get out of there and was just shaking my head at the monumental waste of time we had all been through when Eileen caught up with me in the corridor.

'Cathy, just before you go, can I give you this? It's a Christmas present for Jodie. Her father asked me to pass it on to her.'

I stared at her, astonished, as she held out a well-used Tesco carrier bag.

'I'm not sure it's really appropriate, Eileen,' I said, with forced diplomacy and reminding myself of my professionalism. 'Contact has been suspended, and present-giving is usually classified as contact, particularly in a case like this. Jodie feels very hostile towards her parents at the moment, understandably.'

'Oh, right,' she replied, mulling this over. 'Do you want me to give it back then?' As she said this, she pulled the unwrapped present out of the bag, presumably to show me how harmless it was, and that I was being overcautious. It was a bright pink, long-sleeved T-shirt, with 'Daddy's Little Girl' printed on the front in big sparkly letters.

Eileen looked at it, then held it up. 'So you don't think Jodie would like it?' she said.

I was almost lost for words as I looked at her holding up a T-shirt that was just about the most bitterly ironic thing I'd ever seen.

'Eileen,' I said, slowly and deliberately, 'Jodie has been sexually abused by her father, probably for most of her life. I don't think a T-shirt calling her daddy's little girl is very appropriate, do you? If I gave her this, Jodie would be terrified by the sight of it.'

The penny dropped. 'Oh, yes. Right, I take your point. We'll give it back then. Have a lovely Christmas!'

By the time I reached my car, I was still shaking my head in astonishment.

CHAPTER 20

CHRISTMAS

I was determined to make sure Jodie enjoyed Christmas, and started to feel part of the family. I knew from sad experience that foster children have often missed out on Christmas in the past. In fact, because they're at home for at least two whole days, and their parents tend to drink more, it can be the worst time of year for many children.

I remembered my previous placement, Callum, a sweet-natured ten-year-old. Callum had lived with his mother, who was a non-functioning alcoholic. That meant that she was incapable of leading a normal life, she was too locked into the prison of her alcohol dependency. The Christmas before Callum came to me, his father had sent him a cheque, which his mother had subsequently taken and spent on drink. On Christmas Day, she'd woken up after midday with a hangover, and then tried to make Christmas dinner. She hadn't done any shopping, so she'd peeled the breadcrumbs off some chicken nuggets, and tried to pass it off to Callum as roast turkey.

Despite her drink problem, Callum's mother

216

hadn't been violent or abusive towards him, but her alcoholism had been such that Callum had had to look after her, rather than vice versa. For the previous three years, he hadn't had a single Christmas or birthday present. The Christmas he spent with us, I bought him a skateboard, helmet and kneepads, and when he opened them he ran out of the room, because he didn't want us to see him cry.

On Christmas morning, Jodie was up before six as usual, but she seemed to regard it as just another day. The previous night, we had all hung pillowcases on our doors, and these were now full of presents. I led Jodie downstairs and showed her that the glass of sherry, mince pie and carrots had all disappeared, which meant that Father Christmas had come to visit in the night.

'That's nice, Cathy,' she replied, as if humouring me. Throughout the morning, even as we opened up the presents under the tree, Jodie remained fairly flat, but she did seem to have some understanding of the importance of the day. She behaved well and generally joined in with the family. As I watched her, I hoped that, even though she wasn't showing much enthusiasm, the goodwill of the day was having some impact, and that she would remember it fondly in the future.

In the afternoon my parents arrived, along with my brother Tom, his wife Chloe and their six-year-old, Ewan. Suddenly the house was full of noise and excitement, and I realized how cut off we had all become from our normal lives. For one thing, I hadn't had any adult company for more than a week. Jodie had met all of my family before, when they had come round to visit me in the usual run of things, and they always included the children I fostered, treating them like members of the family. Nonetheless she seemed a little startled when they all arrived at once, and she remained inhibited for most of the day.

After I'd made a round of drinks, we all gathered together in the lounge, ready to exchange presents. My family had brought some for us, and we had kept theirs under the tree, ready and waiting. We were all excited, but I could see that this was another ritual which was new to Jodie. As the presents were handed out, she stared at the others, taking cues on how to behave. She watched Ewan as he opened a present, and then she followed suit. She looked at it blankly, and I had to coax her to show excitement.

'That's lovely, Jodie, isn't it? You can play with that this afternoon. Will you say thank you?'

She did as she was told, but without any of the excitement and shining eyes that Christmas usually brought to children. Throughout the day, she didn't seem ungrateful for what she was given, and she did seem to like some of her gifts, but it was sad to see her having to mimic the enthusiasm and happiness that came naturally to the others.

After dinner we sat around and played games, as we slowly recovered from the meal. The girls worked hard to include Jodie, but she grew irritable, perhaps worn out by the excitement of the day. She went through the motions of playing the various games, but didn't seem to derive any pleasure from them. When she didn't win she became angry, and slammed her fist on the arm of the sofa. When she did win she was flat; she couldn't take any pleasure from it, and couldn't celebrate gregariously with the others. When we cheered for her, she joined in, but it seemed hollow.

Some time later she seemed to become frustrated and started holding her nose. I ignored it at first, suspecting that she was simply seeking attention, but when she persisted I eventually asked what was wrong.

'My nose hurts,' she said, her voice muffled by her hand.

'Oh dear,' I replied. 'Can I take a look?' She removed her hand, but squirmed away when I tried to touch her face. 'I can't see anything wrong. Is there anything I can do?'

'It hurts!' she moaned.

'Why does it hurt, Jodie? Have you done something to it?'

'It hurts.' She was getting louder, and did seem to be in pain.

'OK, well, come with me, and we'll put a cold flannel on it.' I took her into the bathroom and put the wet flannel to her face. 'Can you tell me what you did, Jodie, to make it hurt?'

'It was him. He whacked me in the face.'

'Who, Jodie?'

'Daddy! He thumped me,' she wailed, sounding like she was about to cry.

I had been sitting next to her in the living room, so I knew that nothing had actually happened. However, even though the pain seemed to be imagined, in the sense that she obviously hadn't been injured today, it was totally real to her. It sounded like she was remembering being hurt in the past, and was transposing the memory on to the present. We stood in the bathroom for a while, until she'd calmed down, then we went back to the lounge to rejoin the others.

At eight o'clock we stood on the doorstep and waved as my parents and my brother's family drove off home. I closed the front door. I was relieved that Christmas was over, even though it had gone as well as I could have hoped. Jodie had been somewhat overawed by the occasion and the large gathering, but she had behaved reasonably, and I hoped that some of the warmth of the season had got through to her. While it hadn't proved a breakthrough, and hadn't touched Jodie emotionally in the way that Callum had been touched, I hoped that Christmas would now mean something good to Jodie, and that she'd had a small taste of what other children enjoyed every year.

CHAPTER 21

A NEW YEAR

As the New Year approached, my spirits rose. A new year offers a new start, and anything seems possible on the first of January. Giving up smoking, however, was not on my list of resolutions, and I was now sneaking outside upwards of seven times a day, deluding myself that I would quit again when things were calmer. But when on earth would that be?

Despite my hopes, Jodie showed no improvement as the New Year passed. Her behaviour continued to be difficult and hostile, and her nights were increasingly disturbed by nightmares and hallucinations. She was having more incidences of remembered pain now, and these became linked to disclosures; Jodie would complain that her arm hurt, and this would lead to the memory of her mother hitting her with an ashtray, or her father scalding her with hot water. In all of these cases Jodie's pain seemed to be completely genuine, despite my attempts to explain to her that the injuries she was describing had happened months, sometimes years, ago.

Although I didn't think she was fabricating the

remembered pain, I was becoming increasingly aware that she was lying in other situations. Often, she was so convincing that I found myself questioning what I'd seen, and doubting the evidence of my own eyes. If I caught her red-handed in the middle of some misdemeanour, she would so emphatically deny that it was happening that I had to stop and reassess what I was looking at. She had sometimes told lies when she first arrived, but I had assumed that she had been reverting to past experience, telling lies to avoid punishment, so it had been somewhat understandable. Now, however, she must have known that she didn't have to worry, that there was never any risk of her being physically or emotionally punished. Why, then, did she feel it necessary to deny her actions so vehemently?

She also started making false accusations, making up stories about the other children, even when I was in the room and had obviously seen that nothing had happened. She would claim Lucy or Paula had kicked, pinched or bitten her, which was clearly ludicrous. If anything, they were scared of her, quite understandably. When I pointed out to her that I had been in the room the whole time, and had seen that no one had gone near her, she flared up.

'She did. She did! Why don't you ever believe me?'

She was so passionate and convincing, I was often tempted to reconsider, and had to remind myself of what I'd seen.

At other times I caught her deliberately hurting herself. It wasn't like the time she had cut herself so chillingly. Now it seemed more as though it was done in anger, in a fit of fury or passion, when she would thump herself, pinch herself, thud her head against something or pull her hair. Then she blamed it on one of her imaginary friends. Some friend, I thought. I would have to patiently tell her that actually she was the one who was doing it, as no one else had touched her. This self-harming was one of the most disturbing aspects of Jodie's behaviour, and the pinches, scratches and thumps she inflicted some-times produced marks, which she then used to convince herself even further that someone had been attacking her.

Even more worryingly, a week into the New Year the different voices she sometimes used began to suddenly take on identities of their own. Adrian's mobile phone went missing, and after a lengthy search I eventually found it in Jodie's toy box, which was on a shelf in the conservatory. Jodie hadn't stolen anything before, but she did have problems respecting other people's property, and I had been trying to teach her that we couldn't just help ourselves to what we wanted, that we had to ask the owner first.

'It wasn't me, honestly,' she repeated, looking me straight in the eyes and speaking in a babyish voice. 'It really wasn't. I'm not big enough to reach.'

Adrian and I both looked at the shelf, on which Jodie had just placed the toy box with ease.

'Of course you are,' said Adrian. 'It's just above your waist.'

'No,' she insisted, heightening her baby voice. 'It was her.' She pointed to the space beside her. 'It was Jodie.'

'You're Jodie,' I said wearily.

'No. I'm Amy. I'm only two, and I can't reach.' She rubbed her eyes, and pouted like a toddler. I told her again that she mustn't take Adrian's mobile, and left it at that.

A day later, the separation of her personality took on another, more sinister form. She was up at 5.30 in the morning, so I went in to settle her. She was sitting on the bed playing with her music box, and clapping loudly.

'Quietly, Jodie,' I said. 'Find something to do that's quiet if you've had enough sleep.'

She spun round to face me. Her features were hard and distorted. 'No,' she shouted, in a gruff masculine voice. 'Get out or I'll rip you to pieces. Get out! Bitch!'

I instinctively took a step back. 'Jodie! Don't use that word. Now calm down. Find something to do quietly. I mean it. Now.'

She stood and brought herself to her full height. She advanced towards me, with her hands clawed, baring her teeth. 'I'm not Jodie,' she growled. 'I'm Reg. Get out or I'll fucking kill you.'

I wasn't going to tackle her in that mood. I closed

the door and waited on the landing. My heart was racing. I heard her pacing the floor, cursing my name, along with the rest of the family's. 'Wankers. Evil wankers. I'll rip their heads off.' She growled again, and then it went quiet. I opened the door and looked in. Jodie was in bed looking calmly at a book. Apparently, the old Jodie had returned.

As a foster carer, I'd seen some pretty extreme behaviour in children and to a certain extent I was used to it – but not this extreme. This was new. Jodie's imaginary friends seemed to be taking her over.

'Who's Reg?' I asked later that morning, as we emptied the dishwasher together. Jodie looked up at me uncomprehendingly. 'Do you know someone called Reg? I thought you mentioned his name when I came into your room first thing this morning?'

She shook her head, and carried on sorting the cutlery. 'There's someone on Mum's telly called Reg, but he's horrible. I don't talk to him.'

'And there's no one else you know called Reg?'

'No.'

And I believed her. Reg, like Amy, seemed to have taken on a life of his own, without Jodie's knowledge or consent.

When I told Jill about this, she was very surprised. 'This is highly unusual. If I'm right, then it sounds like D.I.D. – Dissociative Identity Disorder.'

D.I.D. is a rare and complex response to stress,

she explained, where the personality splits into a number of different identities, in order to cope. Often, one identity has no idea what the others are doing.

'That sounds exactly what she's doing,' I said. 'It's very unnerving. Why is she doing it with us? It hasn't happened before. Why would it start happening now, when she's more secure than she's ever been?'

'Perhaps it's because it's only now that she feels safe enough to remember the abuse. I suspect that before, she wasn't even able to accept and process what was happening to her. She blotted it out in order to survive. You said that she was very calm and accepting at first – remember how she passively began to take her clothes off when you wanted to photograph her? There was no fight in her, because she needed to keep going. However, now that she's removed from the abuse, she can start recalling it and piecing together what happened.'

I told her about the remembered pain, and how real it seemed to Jodie.

'That makes sense as well,' said Jill. 'She couldn't afford to feel the pain at the time, so she's feeling it now. She's receiving an onslaught of information, physical and mental. Because she's remembering all these awful things, her brain's on overload, and can't cope. By splitting her awareness, at least part of the self can be kept safe. So far you've seen baby Amy and an angry adult male. Does she have an adult female side as well?'

'Now I come to think of it, yes. I thought she was just imitating her mother, but now I'm not so sure. She tries to chastise Lucy and Paula as an angry housewife.'

'Does she refer to her by name?'

'Not that I've heard, no.'

'It's the classic form. Baby, adult female, and adult male. We've all got these components in our personalities, but when we're mentally healthy they're all rolled into one.' Jill paused. 'To be honest, I'm really worried.' I was now feeling extremely concerned myself. Jodie, it seemed, was reacting to the terrible things that had happened to her. I had no idea what to expect or if I would be able to cope with the fall-out of her extraordinary emotional trauma.

Jill asked, 'Have you told Eileen?'

'No. She's been out of the office recently.'

'I'll try and get through to her. And make the psychologist aware of this. If I'm right, this is a severe personality disorder.'

'Jill?' I asked tentatively, as something occurred to me. 'When she's in one of these states, can she do things that she wouldn't normally do? I mean, this Reg seems like a very angry character, and she seems to be quite strong when she's being him.'

'If she was any bigger I'd be getting her out of there. Adults with D.I.D. can assume superhuman

227

strength and do things they wouldn't normally. But presumably you could restrain her if necessary, even when she's Reg?'

I paused. 'I think so.'

'And you want to continue?'

'Yes.' The further along this road I went, the more impossible it seemed to turn back. 'Now I know what it is, it doesn't seem quite so intimidating.'

'Good. It's really quite interesting, you know.'

Interesting for Jill, maybe, with her ability to assess the situation at one remove. For me . . . well, interesting wasn't quite the word.

That afternoon, I sat Adrian, Paula and Lucy down, and explained what Jill had said. They stared at me, open-mouthed.

'Jodie's got several personalities who possess her at different times?' said Adrian, trying to get it straight in his mind. 'And she has no idea that she's doing it?'

I nodded. It sounded crazy.

'Bonkers,' said Lucy. 'Stark raving bonkers. She's totally off her trolley.'

Paula laughed. 'I think I'll be the Queen of Sheba, and you can all wait on me and bring me gifts.'

I smiled. 'It's not an act, though, darling. She doesn't choose this. It just happens – it's her mind's way of dealing with what she's been through.'

'Will she be getting therapy?' Adrian asked, aware that she had seen a psychologist.

They all looked at me for an answer.

'Not until the assessments are complete, which won't be until nearer the final court hearing. Jill says this condition can pass of its own accord, and in the meantime the best advice is to ignore it. There's no point in challenging her because, as we've seen, she can't remember what the other characters have said or done.'

So we tried to ignore it and carry on, in the hope that it would pass, but now it escalated. Three or four times a day baby Amy, angry Reg or the nameless female matriarch suddenly took over and obliterated Jodie. It was often a very sudden change, usually lasting ten to fifteen minutes. Not only would Jodie's voice change, but each personality had its own type of body language. When she was in character as Reg, she would draw herself up to her full height, shoulders back, chest out, making herself big and masculine. As Amy, she cowered and her face was babyish and pouting. Her angry housewife stood aggressively, with short, angry movements and an unpleasant grimace. The change would occur in an instant, and revert just as suddenly when Jodie returned.

When baby Amy appeared at dinner, Paula couldn't resist cutting up her food and feeding her. 'I've never had a baby sister,' she grinned, as she wiped Jodie's chin. Conversely, when angry

Reg took over, we all ran for cover. And knowing what the problem was did help, even though anyone watching would probably have thought we were the ones who were stark raving bonkers.

I informed both Eileen and the psychologist of this new and disturbing facet of Jodie's mental health, but heard nothing from either of them. I could understand it in the psychologist's case – it wasn't her role to offer me advice or therapy tips – but I was disappointed that Eileen still wasn't able to offer any support or even show much interest, although by now I didn't expect anything different. It was just another small piece of Jodie's tragedy that she had been assigned a social worker who was, to say the least, ineffectual.

Jill remained highly supportive – and the best we could do was just to hope that things would somehow get better.

The spring term began, and to my utter relief the secretary at Abbey Green School finally phoned to confirm that funding had been approved, and Jodie could start the following Monday. She suggested we visit the school on the Friday afternoon, so that Jodie could spend some time with her class, and get to know her support teacher. I wondered whether to tell her about the D.I.D. Should I try to warn her about Jodie's erratic and bizarre behaviour? Would the school even have heard of D.I.D.? I decided not to mention it. They had Jodie's Statement of Educational Needs, and if anything untoward happened I was sure they'd call me. Besides, I wanted Jodie to start with a clean slate.

Now that Jodie had a school place, there was no further need for a home tutor. Nicola phoned to wish Jodie luck and say goodbye, and Jodie spoke sensibly to her for a good twenty minutes. After she hung up she came over to me solemnly.

'Nicola is a good adult, isn't she, Cathy?'

'Yes, sweet, she is. Most adults are, as you'll discover.'

Jodie nodded thoughtfully. I felt a spark of hope. Perhaps she was taking tiny, slow but definite steps towards being able to regain her trust in adults.

Later that day, Jodie's social worker Eileen paid us a visit, her second in almost ten months. Predictably enough, it went much like the first and was not a success. Jodie was hostile from the start, and Eileen had great difficulty relating to her. It is usual to leave the social worker and child together, so that they can talk privately, but each time I tried to busy myself away from the lounge, one of them would immediately call me back in. Jodie would want another drink, or a jigsaw, or the television turned on, or Eileen would want to ask something trivial. For some reason Eileen seemed to want me there; I suspected she was anxious, or possibly even afraid of Jodie. After going back and forth a number of times, I decided I might as well join them, so I sat down with Jodie, and tried to get her to calm down and speak more quietly. A quarter of an hour later Eileen picked up her briefcase and, with a tight-lipped smile, left. She had done her duty.

'Good riddance,' said Jodie, and slammed the door behind her.

I didn't disagree.

CHAPTER 22

THE FOX AND THE OWL

It was mid-January. After a brief lull, the weather had turned bitterly cold, and we had three full days of snow. Jodie relished the excitement, and on the few occasions when I couldn't immediately take her out into the snow, she would gaze out of the window, transfixed.

The children's moods had lifted too. Now that they were back at school they seemed to have found a new burst of empathy for Jodie. Paula, in particular, appeared to have benefited from venting her frustrations before Christmas. We hadn't actually arranged the sleepover yet, but she had had a number of friends round, and had made a point of encouraging Jodie to join in as part of the group, bless her.

One such afternoon Paula's friend Olivia came for lunch, and they decided to go for a walk in the snow. My street is on the rim of a large valley, and the views are quite spectacular. Jodie pouted when she realized they were leaving, so Paula asked if Jodie and I would like to join them. Jodie was thrilled, so the four of us wrapped ourselves in coats, scarves and boots, and headed out.

As we walked up towards the high street, Paula and I each took one of Jodie's hands, as the pavement was icy. However, despite our best efforts Jodie kept slipping over, each time falling on her bottom. The third time it happened, she remained sitting on the pavement. She crossed her arms, rolled her eyes, and sighed theatrically, 'Here we go again!'

Paula and I grinned at each other in delight. Jodie's usual response to this kind of adversity would have been a bitter tirade: 'Who put that bloody ice there? Why are they doing that to me? It's your fault! Hate you!' and so on. Instead, she'd seen the funny side, and actively made an effort to try to make us laugh. It might not sound like much, but for us it felt like progress, and we joined in gratefully.

Jodie's first day of school was approaching, so I took her shopping for her new school uniform. We bought two navy skirts, two jumpers with the school logo printed on them, and three white short-sleeved shirts. Jodie had behaved well in the shop, enjoying the attention, but she became angry when I opted for knee-length socks rather than tights. She wanted to have tights like Lucy and Paula wore, but I knew she'd have difficulty putting them on again after P.E. In the end, I came up with a sensible compromise, and bought Jodie a pair of white, lacy tights that she could wear at weekends.

As we arrived home, Jill phoned and told me

apologetically that the couple she had been considering for respite wouldn't be able to do it. Reason left unstated.

'Great,' I said tetchily. 'I'm promised regular breaks because of the high level of Jodie's needs, but because of that high level of needs it's impossible to find a carer.'

'I'm sorry, Cathy. I'll keep looking.'

'Yes, please do. Outside the agency if necessary.' What I meant by this was that Jill should approach a different fostering agency for a carer. This wasn't ideal, as standards varied, and the carers could be some distance away, but it was only one weekend and I needed a break.

On the Friday of that week we had arranged a visit to Jodie's new school. The visit wasn't till the afternoon, but Jodie was up early, as usual, and she immediately got dressed in her new uniform. I didn't think this was a good idea, but I was anxious to avoid any unnecessary confrontation, so I let her keep it on, and tucked an apron round her while she ate. Despite my efforts, by the time she'd had her breakfast and lunch her uniform contained a good helping of both. I sponged off the stains as best I could, and we arrived at the school gates looking reasonably smart for the afternoon session.

Abbey Green hadn't been my first choice, but as we arrived I was immediately impressed. The small, carpeted reception area was bright and welcoming, and the smiling receptionist greeted us warmly.

'Hello there, Jodie. It's very nice to meet you,' she said, and then phoned through to the Head, who appeared with courteous promptness.

'Adam West,' he said, shaking my hand. 'Hi, Jodie. Very pleased you can join us.'

He could only have been in his mid-thirties, but his friendly, informal manner quickly put me at ease. 'I thought we'd start with a tour of the school, then you can spend some time with Jodie's class, if that sounds all right?'

'Fine,' I said, then turned to Jodie. 'That sounds good, doesn't it?' She hid behind me, clinging to my skirt, all her bravado evaporated.

He led the way through the double doors and along a short corridor. 'There are six classrooms leading off the main hall,' he explained, 'which doubles as a canteen and gym.' As we went in, I could smell the residue of boiled greens and gravy, one constant factor shared by thousands of schools all over the country. The walls of the hall, like those of the corridors, were lined with examples of the children's work, and Mr West proudly described the various projects that had inspired this work. There were paintings, drawings, essays, poems and computer printouts, all based on a handful of themes, such as faraway lands, water, animals and designing a house. He was so enthusiastic and child-centred in his approach that I thought to myself: if this school can't cater for Jodie's needs, then no one can.

We arrived at Jodie's classroom, and the Head

knocked before we went in. A sea of faces looked up curiously, before returning to their work.

'Caroline Smith,' he said, leading us to the class teacher. 'This is Cathy Glass, and this is Jodie.' We shook hands. 'The lady over there is Mrs Rice, the classroom assistant. She'll be helping Jodie.'

I glanced over to the table and smiled. Mrs Rice was a homely woman in her early fifties, wearing a floral patterned dress. She gave us a little wave. Jodie's confidence had increased during the tour, and she started wandering between the tables, peering over the children's shoulders. One boy shifted uncomfortably.

'Jodie, come here,' I called. But she ignored me.

'Don't worry,' said Mrs Smith. 'They're just finishing a piece of creative writing from our literacy hour. She can look.'

Mr West took his leave. 'If you have any questions, I'll be in my office at the end of the day.'

I thanked him, then spent some minutes with Mrs Smith, as she explained how the tables were grouped. She suggested I have a look around, so I did, feeling intrusively conspicuous. I felt like a giant as I walked among the miniature tables and chairs. The blue group was obviously the brightest; their writing was neat and detailed, with few grammatical mistakes. Mrs Rice's table, the orange group, was a different matter. These children were struggling to produce a handful of legible lines, and their work was full of corrections. Nonetheless, even the weakest of these was well above Jodie's standard. Jodie could barely write her own name.

'Would you like to join your table now?' Mrs Smith called to Jodie, from across the room. 'The spare chair beside Mrs Rice is your place.' Her request was gentle but firm. Jodie, who apparently wasn't quite ready, sized her up. I could see Jodie had one of her take-me-on-if-you-dare expressions, and my heart was in my mouth. Not now, Jodie, I thought, please let's not have a refusal and a tantrum on your first visit.

Now the other children were looking too; presumably they were used to responding immediately to any request from their teacher. Jodie stared at Mrs Smith, but then, to my relief, she lowered her gaze and plodded heavily over, flopping in her chair with a dramatic sigh.

Mrs Rice gave Jodie a pencil and paper. I crept round the edge of the room and perched myself on a stool by the window. The classroom overlooked the playground, and an older class was in the middle of a P.E. lesson. The room was quiet save for the occasional scraping of a chair and the hushed voice of Mrs Rice giving assistance to her group. I noticed that there were more boys than girls, and wondered whether, with their friendships already established, the girls would allow Jodie in. The poor girl needed to make friends just as much as she needed the education, and children can be very forgiving if they feel it's justified.

The children finished their essays, and Mrs Smith asked who would like to read one out. Half a dozen hands shot up, including Jodie's. A boy called James was chosen first, and he'd written about the night-time adventures of a fox called Lance. The story had a clear structure, and used lots of adjectives, and when he was finished the other pupils gave him a big round of applause. Next came Susie, whose story cleverly centred around the observations of a wise owl, from his vantage point high up in the trees. I gathered, from the content of the essays, that they'd been told to write about nocturnal animals. Susie was given her round of applause, and the teacher said they had time for one more. Jodie's hand flew up again, waving for all she was worth.

Mrs Smith exchanged a glance with Mrs Rice. 'Come on then, Jodie. Let's hear yours.'

I cringed with embarrassment; I could see she'd only produced a handful of scribbles. 'Class, this is Jodie,' said the teacher. 'She'll be joining us from Monday.'

Jodie stood up, and proudly held the paper at eye level, as she'd seen the others do. She pretended to read loudly and confidently, but her story was simply a string of unrelated words, punctuated by the occasional 'owl' and 'fox', with nothing intelligible in between.

'I saw the fox, to see, and I say don't, and the fox was him, and he . . . No. And then the owl. Where he was . . . He got far, and Mr Owl. Watch it. I told

239

you, over there. So the fox went and in the night, you see, I said! Then they went. Then the fox was at night and the owl, but he was not, and I said. So I go to fox, and the owl . . .'

Fortunately Jodie was oblivious to the nonsense she was producing. I looked at the blank stares of the other children, and prayed they wouldn't laugh. After a couple of minutes, with no end in sight, the teacher thanked Jodie and told her to sit down. There was no applause, but neither was there any sniggering, and for that I was truly grateful. Jodie didn't appear to notice anything amiss at all – in fact, she was full of high spirits and rather triumphant.

The last hour was given over to self-chosen activities, during which the children worked on any aspect they liked of the topics covered during the week. I walked round the classroom once more. Some of the children were on the computers, adeptly cutting and pasting, while others were devising crosswords, stories, or producing pictures to complement their writing. Jodie was drawing a series of large boxes, and colouring them orange, blue, green, red and yellow. She explained to me that these were the class's different groups. I praised her, impressed that she'd picked up this much, then I wrote the names of the colours beneath them for her. Five minutes before the bell, the children packed away their things, and sat on the carpet in front of the teacher. They chanted, 'Good afternoon, Mrs Smith!' and the teacher wished them a happy weekend. As they collected their bags and coats and filed out, the teacher asked Jodie how she'd enjoyed her first afternoon.

'Brilliant,' she said. 'I want to come every day. For ever and ever!'

CHAPTER 23

GRANDDAD

One of the remarkable things about Jodie that I had noticed right from the start was that she had absolutely no conception of time. She would discuss events from years ago as if they were happening right now. Equally, if we had something planned for a few weeks' time, she would expect it to happen immediately. The day after the school visit she wanted to go again, and no matter how many times I explained to her that schools didn't open on Saturdays, she couldn't understand. Instead, she was convinced it was my fault.

'It's Saturday,' I explained, for the fifth time. 'No one goes to school on Saturdays. Be a good girl and take off your uniform, and we'll hang it up ready for Monday.'

'No! Don't want to! Shut up! It's mine and I'm going!' She sat cross-legged on the floor, with her arms folded, angry and defiant.

I crouched down. 'I know it's yours, sweet, and so are all these other lovely clothes. How about you wear your new lacy tights, as we're going to see Grandma and Granddad later.' I took the tights out of the drawer, and placed them with a skirt and jumper on the bed. 'It's up to you, but they'll look very smart with your denim skirt.'

I left the room, came downstairs and made breakfast. Half an hour later Jodie appeared in the clothes I'd laid out.

'Well done, Jodie. That's a wise choice.'

Every situation had to be handled with infinite care, if there was to be any chance of cooperation. I couldn't simply say, 'Put on your shoes, it's time to go.' Jodie would have to believe that it was her decision, and that she was in control. I knew where this had come from. When Jodie was being abused she had had no control over anything, so now she needed to be constantly in charge, just to feel safe. Unfortunately for me, the result of this was that even the simplest request would be met with a stubborn refusal, unless she could be persuaded that she herself had made the decision. I had to use diplomacy and coercion if I wanted anything done, and it could be very draining.

A visit to Grandma and Granddad's was just what we all needed, to smooth away some of the tensions within the family, and boost our morale. Jodie thought the world of my parents, as did Adrian, Lucy, Paula and all the other children we had looked after. Mum and Dad were in their early seventies, and they were the archetypal grandparents, with endless patience, and all the time in the world to indulge their grandchildren.

As we arrived, Jodie was on good form, and

greeted my parents warmly. We all went into the living room, when Jodie caught sight of my parents' dog, Cosmo, a rather sad, passive, old rescue greyhound. Jodie suddenly screamed, then rushed across the room and started whacking him with her fists. The poor dog yelped, but Jodie was on top of him and he couldn't move. Dad and I rushed over and pulled her off, and I asked her what on earth she was doing.

'It looked at me!' she shouted, still glaring at the frightened dog. She had never shown any fondness for animals but she had a particular aversion to dogs. Perhaps it was because of her father's dog, or that, in the pecking order she was used to, the dog was the one she could kick and hurt without any fear of reprisal. She certainly never had any empathy for anything more vulnerable than she was.

'But it didn't mean any harm,' I said firmly, as my dad stroked the poor animal, then let him out into the garden. 'Now behave yourself. We said we were going to have a good day, didn't we?'

Jodie nodded sullenly.

'I tell you what,' my father said. 'Why don't you help me feed the fish? They haven't been fed yet, because they were waiting for you to arrive. We can all do it together, if you like. How does that sound?'

Jodie liked that idea, so she took Paula's hand, and the two of them followed my father into the garden while Cosmo watched from a safe distance.

Adrian and Lucy, who considered themselves too mature for this kind of entertainment, sat in the living room, listening to their mp3 players, which had so far kept them mute since Christmas.

I joined Mum in the kitchen, and helped her prepare lunch, as we caught up on the latest news. As usual, I was soon doing most of the talking, and it was mainly about Jodie. I found it very cathartic to discuss abnormal behaviour in the context of my mother's very normal existence, and it helped that my mother was a good listener.

'Anyway,' I said at last, 'hopefully we'll turn a corner soon. So tell me, what have you two been up to?'

She recounted the various hobbies and interests which filled their very active retirement. Eventually the girls and my father streamed in through the kitchen door, while Jodie loudly enthused about the Golden Orbs which had come to the surface to feed. Mum and I served lunch, and I seated Jodie between the two of us. Her plate was piled high with chicken, roast potatoes, three vegetables and gravy.

'I wish I lived here,' she said, gazing adoringly at Grandma. Mum believes everyone needs 'feeding up', even when it's obvious they really ought to be on a diet.

As the meal progressed, I noticed Jodie taking more than a passing interest in my father, who was seated opposite her. She watched him intently, as he peered down through his spectacles at his plate, then over them to retrieve his drink or to talk to one of us. I assumed she was wondering about the way he used his spectacles, which were only for close focusing. Mum offered us second helpings, and I limited Jodie's. She sulked at this, resenting the fact that my father had filled his plate, but he needed it: age had thinned him down, rather than piling on the pounds.

'Granddad?' she asked suddenly, setting down her cutlery.

He looked up over his glasses. 'Yes, dear?'

'Are you Cathy's daddy?'

'That's right. She's my daughter.'

She thought for a moment, clearly trying to work something out. 'So, you're their granddaddy?' She pointed at Adrian and Paula. I smiled at Lucy, hoping she wouldn't be offended at Jodie's faux pas.

'Yes, that's right,' Dad replied. 'Well done.'

She glowed at the praise, and I was impressed that she'd finally made the connection, which she'd struggled with since she first met my parents. 'So if you're their granddad,' she said, still watching him, 'did you do naughty things with your willy to them when they was little, like my granddaddy did to me?'

Everyone fell silent. My father stopped eating and looked at me.

'Jodie! Of course not!' I said sharply. 'I've told you before, normal families don't do those things.

Granddad is a good man. Now finish your dinner, we'll talk about this later.'

Jodie, blissfully ignorant of the shocking impact of what she'd said, picked up her knife and fork, and carried on eating contentedly.

My parents were shocked; I could see it on their faces. Jodie had asked her question with such ease, as if it were a perfectly natural assumption. We quickly changed the subject, and talked loudly of other things, but meanwhile I was thinking about what she'd said. Her grandfather? I wasn't even aware she had grandparents; there was no reference to them in the records. I wondered if she was confusing Dad and Granddad, or if there really was a grandfather involved? Did this mean there was yet another abuser present in Jodie's life? Was there anyone who hadn't had a part in destroying her? I glanced at my father, who was still subdued after Jodie's bombshell, and wondered again at the great divide between healthy and abusive families. Could her perception ever be changed? Perhaps one day she'd be able to accept that what happened to her was abnormal and wrong, and that most families functioned very differently. But at times it seemed a forlorn hope.

I kept a close eye on Jodie for the rest of the afternoon, and Mum helped her with some colouring and cutting out. We were never able to leave my parents without a final cup of tea and slice of homemade cake, and we didn't say our

goodbyes until just after six. There was an accident on the motorway, so it was well past Jodie's
bedtime by the time we finally arrived home. I
decided to leave asking her about her granddad
until the following day, but as I tucked her into
bed and dimmed the lights she suddenly asked,
'Why didn't Granddaddy do naughty things to
Adrian and Paula? Doesn't he love them?'

I looked at her in the half-light. She was snuggled deep beneath her duvet, with only her blonde
hair visible, falling in strands across the pillow.
How could I begin to unravel the confusion
between normal affection and the warped gratification that she had known?

'It's a different kind of love, Jodie. Completely
different from the one between two grown-ups.
And what was done to you wasn't love of any
kind. It was cruel, and very, very wrong. You'll
understand more when you're older.'

I wanted to leave it at that, to go downstairs and
make a cup of coffee, then maybe sit in the lounge
and read the paper. But if I didn't follow this up
now, Jodie might have forgotten it in the morning,
sucking the awful memory back into the black
abyss of denial.

With a now familiar surge of anxiety at what I
was about to hear, I turned up the light a little,
and sat on the chair beside her bed. Her eyes
peered over the duvet, and I stroked her forehead.

'Jodie, pet, did your granddad hurt you in the
same way your daddy and uncle did?'

She shook her head. 'No, Cathy. They was nicer.'

'They? How many granddads did you have?'

'Granddad Wilson and Granddad Price.'

'So there were two then. And how were they nicer, Jodie?'

She thought for a moment, as the lines on her forehead creased, and I hoped she was about to tell me that they'd taken her to the zoo, or bought her an Easter egg, the kind of things normal grandparents do.

'They lay on top of me, but they didn't hurt. They just peed in the bed. It was because they loved me, Cathy.' She said it so matter-of-factly, she might as well have been recounting a trip to the zoo.

'No it wasn't. It was wrong, Jodie. Adults don't show love like that. What they did was cruel. It's got nothing to do with love.' But I could see how ejaculation without penetration might have seemed kinder to her, when compared with the other abuse.

'Were Mummy and Daddy in the room when this happened?' I asked.

'Sometimes.' She nodded. 'And Uncle Mike, and someone I didn't know.'

I held her hand and stroked her forehead. 'Is there anything else? Can you remember any more?'

She shook her head. 'Can I have a story now, Cathy? *Topsy and Tim's New Shoes?*'

She wasn't upset, and I found that I wasn't

either. I was becoming as desensitized as her. I read her the Topsy and Tim story, then said goodnight and went downstairs. I made a note of the conversation in my log, then stepped outside for a cigarette. As I stood there in the freezing night air, I wondered if there was a course I could take in basic psychotherapy. I decided not. If I made an amateur attempt to help Jodie, it would probably do more harm than good. All I could do was continue along the same lines as I had been, using a common-sense approach which restated normality, but did little or nothing for the profound psychological damage that had already been done. Not for the first time since Jodie's arrival, I felt completely inadequate.

On Sunday morning Jodie was buzzing with energy, and I had to deal with a barrage of questions about school. Would she have homework? Was there playtime? Did the teacher have a husband? A daddy? Would it rain? Adopting my usual policy of trying to burn off some of her nervous energy, I took her out on her bike.

'It's so cold,' I remarked, pulling up my collar. 'I think it could snow again.'

'What's snow?' she asked, as we climbed the hill. I tried to remind her as best I could, telling how much she had loved it earlier in the month when it had snowed over three days, but Jodie suddenly decided that she wanted snow immediately, and became angry when I couldn't or, according to her, wouldn't produce it. A fullscale tantrum ensued, and she lay prostrate on the pavement, banging her fists and demanding snow for a good fifteen minutes. It would have been comical if I hadn't been so cold. When we got back to the house, I sat her in front of a video until dinner was ready. She was just as hyperactive after dinner, and had another tantrum when I wouldn't go out to buy her some ice cream. I managed to persuade her to take a bath, and this calmed her down enough for bed at seven. Tomorrow would be her first day at school for more than a year, and I was praying that it would be a good one.

CHAPTER 24

FRIENDS

Jodie was up and down all night, but in the morning she was bright and excited, whereas I was just exhausted. She changed into her school uniform, and we only had one small hiccup when she demanded to wear her lacy tights, but I eventually managed to dissuade her.

We arrived at school early, so we sat in the car for a while, listening to the radio. Although Jodie was excited, I could tell she was also a little nervous, and I was nervous too, on her behalf.

I held Jodie's hand as we walked up to the school gates. I gave it a squeeze, and we entered the school building. Mrs Rice came and met us in reception. Because of Jodie's learning difficulties, it had been arranged that I would hand her over to Mrs Rice every morning, and she would hand her back at the end of the day. I gave Jodie a hug, and watched anxiously as Mrs Rice led her down the corridor.

As soon as I arrived home, the phone rang. It was Jill; she'd received the notes I'd emailed on Sunday about Jodie's granddads, and she'd already spoken to Eileen. They had checked the records,

and confirmed that there were definitely no grandparents on the scene; it was done with such speed
that I wondered if Eileen's manager had spoken
to her. Jodie's maternal grandmother was alive,
but had fallen out with her daughter years ago,
and there was no contact between them. Jodie had
never known her grandfathers on either side.
There was a pause, as Jill waited for me to come
to the obvious conclusion.

'They're in the same category as the so-called
uncles, paedophiles in the guise of family
members?' I said. Jodie had previously described
some of her other abusers as uncles and aunts,
but it appeared that these were not actual relatives; rather, they were friends of Jodie's parents,
who had been described as family members as an
easy way of introducing strangers into the home
environment.

'We think so. It looks as though Jodie's parents
must have been part of a network. The police are
running a check now for registered offenders,' Jill
replied. 'If the names Wilson or Price come up on
their list for the area they'll take them in for questioning. But I have to be honest, Cathy, I'm not
optimistic. If these people haven't been convicted
before, they won't be on the list. There's another
thing too. Eileen's had the results of the forensic
medical back.'

'Yes?'

Jill lowered her voice. 'It confirms that Jodie's
been penetrated, but without DNA, or third-party

evidence, there's not enough for a criminal prosecution. She has been abused, but to get a conviction you need to prove who was responsible.'

'Who on earth do you think must have been responsible? Isn't it clear that Jodie's telling the truth? The forensic result just confirms everything she's been saying.' I sighed. 'So what now?'

'We keep going, and hope something comes up. Eileen's realized that Jodie's due for an LAC review – it's actually overdue. Is it all right if we have it at your house? She's suggested Thursday afternoon at two o'clock.'

'Yes, that's fine.'

'Eileen wants Jodie to be there. I know . . . an afternoon off school when she's just started, and I know she won't be able to contribute anything. But Eileen's suddenly one for the rule book, and she is within her rights to insist.'

I felt the mixture of anger and frustration that so often seemed to dog me when dealing with Eileen. 'OK, I'll pick her up from school at lunchtime,' I said, and, after a quick goodbye, hung up.

LAC stands for Looked After Children, which is the official term for children in care. A LAC review is a regular meeting, required under the Children's Act, and attended by all those involved in the child's case. The purpose of the meeting is to report on the child's progress and decide on any actions which need to be taken. Jodie's parents wouldn't be present, of course, because contact had been suspended, but the guardian ad litum, the child's social worker, her team leader, the headmaster, Jill, Jodie and myself would all be there. However, since Jodie was still functioning at the level of a four-year-old, her presence was likely to offer little more than disruption.

With Jodie at school, I vowed to make the most of my first free day in months. I sat on the sofa and started to plan my day. Three hours later I woke up, and as I came to I chided myself for the time I'd wasted. It was now 12.45, and I had less than two hours before I'd have to make the return journey to school. I rushed to the supermarket, but by the time I got home I realized I'd have to give up my fantasy of reading in peace for an hour. Still, I comforted myself, I must have needed the sleep. I was getting so little at night, and that was broken every few hours by Jodie's night-time torments. No wonder I couldn't keep my eyes open the minute I had the opportunity to relax.

I arrived back at the school and waited by the gates, exchanging smiles with a few of the other mothers. Had they heard about Jodie already, I wondered? How would the other children have described her? Mrs Rice appeared, with Jodie jumping up and down beside her, and told me Jodie had had a good day. This was confirmed in the car, as Jodie wouldn't stop talking all the way home. She told me over and over again about all the children in her class, most of whom were now her new best friends – and she wanted all of them to come round for tea, just like Paula's friends did.

Adrian, Lucy and Paula were already in when we got home, so Jodie had a new audience for her excitable monologue, and they listened with patience. It continued throughout dinner to the extent that I had to remind her to eat, which was definitely a first. She settled easily that night, as she was physically and emotionally exhausted, and I did much the same.

Just after midnight I was woken by the sound of Jodie sobbing on the landing. I pulled on my dressing gown, hurried out of my room and found her lying on the carpet outside Paula's bedroom. Her face was crimson, and she could hardly breathe for crying. I put my arm around her, and led her back to her room. I sat beside her on the bed and cuddled her until she was able to speak.

'Cathy,' she said, through sobs, 'when I was at my school I had a friend, but then she wouldn't be my friend any more.' I passed her a tissue, and waited while she blew her nose.

'Don't upset yourself, pet. You'll make lots of new friends now.'

'But she was my best, best friend. And she came to my house. But then she wasn't allowed, because of what I said.'

My sleep-fuddled brain started to focus. 'What did you say? I'm sure it wasn't that bad. Friends fall out all the time, Jodie, even best ones.'

She shook her head. 'I told her. About Mummy and Daddy and Uncle Mike. And she told her mummy and daddy, and they said she couldn't come and play. Her mummy said it was a bad house. But I'm not bad, am I, Cathy?'

I held her closer to me. 'No, sweet, of course you're not bad. She meant what was happening to you was bad. It was never your fault. You mustn't think that.' As I comforted her, my mind was whirring. She had told someone. Other adults had been made aware of the abuse. Could this be the third-party evidence that was needed to secure a prosecution? I was fully awake now.

'You did right to tell, Jodie. Her mummy and daddy should have told the police instead of stopping her from playing. What was her name? Can you remember? It's important.'

She sniffed. 'Louise Smith. She lived next door. I won't tell my new friends, will I, Cathy?'

'No, there's no need. You can tell me anything you want, and you know that I'll do something about it.'

She sniffed and managed a smile.

'Good girl. You did the right thing. Now I want you to try and get some sleep. We don't want you tired for tomorrow.'

I tucked her in, and stroked her forehead until her eyes closed. I was tense and focused. Jodie had had the courage to tell someone, but that courage had not only gone unrewarded but, in her eyes, it had led to further punishment, as she had been prevented from seeing her friend. I could imagine why Louise's parents had kept quiet: they hadn't wanted to get involved, and they'd wanted to protect their own child. However, by keeping quiet they'd left an innocent victim open to further abuse. All they needed to have done was to make an anonymous phone call to the NSPCC, the Social Services or the police, and that would have been enough to start an enquiry. Whenever this kind of allegation is made, the police or Social Services have to look into it.

I went back to bed, but I couldn't settle. In the end I gave up, and went downstairs and made myself some hot chocolate. I stood in the kitchen, warming my hands on the hot mug. There were wider implications to what Jodie had said. Living next door, the Smiths must have seen the comings and goings. They probably knew who these so-called aunts, uncles and granddads were, by face, if not by name. If the police interviewed the Smiths now, with the allegations out in the open, surely they'd have to tell the truth? I knew the council estate where Jodie had grown up well; I'd looked after kids from there before. It was a tight-knit, closely bound community, where everyone seemed to be in and out of each other's houses. How many other residents had known what was going on, but remained silent, fearful of the potential consequences? How did they sleep at night?

CHAPTER 25

DENIAL

'But they must know something!' I insisted to Jill, when she phoned a few days later. 'They were in and out of each other's houses all the time. The girls were best friends.'

'Yes, but the Smiths claim they still are friends. They say they're astonished by the allegations, and have even offered to give a character reference for Jodie's parents. I'm sorry, Cathy, but I don't think we're going to get anything useful out of them.'

I went quiet. I could feel the walls of conspiratorial silence that had imprisoned Jodie closing in again, and it was frightening. 'So why did they stop their daughter from going to play, if her parents were so bloody respectable?'

'Well, they say they never did. Look, Cathy, I don't doubt what you're saying, or what Jodie's said. But Eileen's actually spoken to them, and it seems there's no chance of them talking, and the police are of the same mind. If these so-called granddads were registered offenders it would be different, but they're not. The fact is, all we've got is the word of a confused eight-year-old with learning difficulties, who won't even speak to the police. It's not enough to bring a case.'

'She's not that confused,' I snapped. 'Not when it comes to this; she's clear and focused.' I took a breath; there was no point shouting at Jill. 'I'm sorry, I'm just frustrated. It looks like they're going to go scot-free, while Jodie has to bear all the consequences of being brave enough to tell the truth.'

'I know it's frustrating, but Jodie doesn't need to know there won't be a prosecution. At least it's good for her that she's been able to disclose, but we'll have to accept that's as far as it's likely to go at present. The police have said they'll keep the file open, in case anything new comes up.'

'I'm going to have to distance myself,' I said wearily. 'I'm becoming too involved.'

'You wouldn't be such a good carer if you weren't, Cathy. And I'm still working on that respite. I haven't forgotten.'

I felt like going round to the Smiths' myself, and begging them if necessary to come forward. I stood on the patio smoking, working out what I would say. If I looked into their eyes, could I shame them into admitting what they knew? If I told them about Jodie's nightmares, about how her life had been destroyed, could I change their minds? I inhaled deeply, but as I stubbed out the cigarette I realized I couldn't do it. It would have been a completely inappropriate, unprofessional thing for a foster carer to do, and I would probably have lost my job, and therefore lost Jodie. Besides which, I doubted it could have done any good. If they'd resisted the best efforts of the police and Social Services, they weren't likely to be swayed by me. I went inside and closed the kitchen door. Yet again I felt Jodie's frustration.

I took some comfort from the fact that Jodie was finally in school, and hoped that the routine of it would give her something else to occupy her mind. But this routine was doomed to be interrupted by constant reminders of her past. Thursday arrived, and I had to pick her up from school at lunchtime, so that she could attend the LAC review.

By three o'clock there were six of us in my lounge, sitting with coffee and digestives. Astonishingly, Eileen had turned up a whole hour late, with no explanation beyond a half-hearted, 'Sorry, I was held up.' She proceeded to distribute copies of her agenda, and the meeting finally began.

Jodie was suddenly the centre of attention for reasons she didn't understand, so naturally enough she played to the audience. With hands on hips, she strutted up and down, shouting instructions, and telling everyone off for talking every time they spoke. She said she was 'playing at schools'. Jill and I exchanged knowing glances; we'd had a feeling this might happen.

Despite Jodie's disruptions, Eileen persisted in working through her agenda, and raised her voice above Jodie's when necessary. It quickly turned into a circus. Adam West gave his report, which was minimal, since Jodie had only been in school for three and a half days. Then, as he had another meeting to go to, he made his apologies and left. Jodie wasn't happy at this. Why should he get to go back to school and have fun, if she couldn't? She was on the point of a full-scale tantrum, which I averted by replenishing the biscuits, and reassuring her she could go tomorrow.

Because of Jodie's behaviour I was constantly in and out of my chair, and as a result I could barely contribute to the discussion. I was also uncomfortable, as I felt that talking about Jodie while she was there was demeaning for her, and likely to reinforce the very issues and behaviour that we were trying to move on from.

'Would you like to contribute anything, Jodie?' Eileen eventually asked. 'This meeting is after all about you.'

'Contribute means to say something,' I explained, as Jodie gawped blankly.

'No!' she shouted. 'And I've told you before to stop talking, or you'll miss your playtime.' I was pleased the headmaster had left, and was no longer here to see this Dickensian portrayal of his award-winning school.

An hour and a half later we were finally finished, having fulfilled the statutory obligation, but accomplished next to nothing. I would have liked us to address Jodie's desperate need for therapy, but this didn't seem to be an option until the childcare proceedings had been resolved. The team leader and the guardian left first, then Eileen made a move to follow.

'It was nice meeting you again, Jodie,' she said, tucking her notes into her briefcase.

'Was it?' she said. 'Why?'

Eileen forced a smile. 'Because you're a lovely little girl.'

The condescension and insincerity was evident even to Jodie. There was a moment's pause as her features changed into a set that I knew well, while Eileen remained blissfully ignorant of what was coming.

'No, I'm not!' Jodie boomed, in her deep masculine voice. 'I'm Reg, and I'm angry. Have you locked up that fucking father yet?' And before I could stop her, she kicked Eileen on the shin.

I quickly enfolded and restrained her, as Eileen rubbed her leg.

'I'll see you out,' said Jill, leading her down the hall.

'That was very naughty,' I said to Jodie. 'You don't kick, whoever you are.'

But as quickly as Reg had appeared, he vanished, and by the time Jill returned Jodie was sitting happily on the floor, engrossed in her Lego.

'So that's Reg,' said Jill grimly. 'I know you told me about this, but nothing prepares you for seeing it in action. It's so chilling. I've seen it before years ago, but my goodness – only the severest kind of trauma could provoke this in such a young child.'

'This is the first time she's turned into Reg in front of strangers,' I said.

'Well, I'm pleased I've had the opportunity to witness this first hand.'

'Yes, I expect Eileen was as well,' I replied dryly. We both smiled.

Now that Reg had been released in front of others, he had no hesitation in making another appearance, this time with a different audience. I had just returned from taking Jodie to school when the secretary phoned. 'Hello, Cathy, we have a problem. Jodie's not hurt, but the Head has asked if you could come straight away.'

My coat was still on, so I retrieved my keys from the hall table and headed back, my mind racing. What could she have done now? When I arrived, the secretary showed me straight through to the Head's office. He was seated sombrely behind his desk, and I sensed that the distance between us was deliberate, to emphasize the seriousness of the conversation we were about to have.

'Thank you for coming so promptly,' he said, briefly standing and waving to the seat opposite. 'I'll come straight to the point. We've had rather an unfortunate incident this morning, which resulted in Jodie slapping another child's face.' One incident of slapping wouldn't necessitate my being summoned before the Head; we both knew that. 'I'll be perfectly frank, Mrs Glass. It wasn't so much the slapping that upset the child, and the rest of the class, but the behaviour that accompanied it.'

I raised my eyebrows questioningly.

'Jodie was completely out of control over something really quite minor. She was kicking and shouting vile abuse, then blamed it on someone called Reg. We don't have anyone with that name in the class, but she was adamant. It took two members of staff to calm her down. Now, obviously I haven't known Jodie for very long, but her reaction was very disturbing, and seemed quite out of character.'

Out of character indeed. I decided I had no alternative but to come clean. I told him about Jodie's D.I.D., and what we'd witnessed at home, then reassured him that there was a psychologist involved. I omitted to mention that the psychologist was only conducting assessment, rather than therapy. I also touched on her two other characters, and he nodded in recognition.

'Mrs Rice mentioned that Jodie sometimes talks in a babyish voice. We had put it down to nerves – you know how children can regress if they're anxious – but you're saying it's part of the same problem?'

'It could be, yes.'

'And presumably her social worker's aware?'

'She is.' Even more so after yesterday, I thought.

'And you say it could disappear of its own accord?'

'That's what I've been told, yes.'

'Normally we'd exclude a child for the rest of the day after an incident of this nature, but there seems little point if she doesn't even know what she's done. I'll keep her here and monitor it.'

I thanked him, and asked him to pass on my apologies to the other child, and the staff. 'I'll speak to Jodie later,' I said, feeling duty bound to offer something. 'I'm sorry you've had to deal with this in school.'

I came out of the office, aware that I'd had a narrow escape. It was clear that Mr West wouldn't tolerate Reg's behaviour indefinitely. I spoke to Jodie about it that evening, but it was a waste of time. Sometimes she appeared to remember nothing at all, and sometimes she appeared to know what I was talking about when she blamed it on Reg or Amy. We could both begin to lose our sanity if we went on too long trying to work out what was happening. As far as she was concerned, I was accusing her of something which she herself hadn't done, and I didn't pursue it for fear of undermining the trust that she'd placed in me. Yet again, this was another incident which demonstrated that Jodie desperately needed therapy to start as soon as possible. It simply wasn't good enough to wait until the end of the court proceedings. I decided to pressure as much as I could for treatment to begin.

'She does need to be in therapy,' the psychologist agreed, when I took Jodie for her next appointment

266

at the clinic the following week. 'How long is it until the final court hearing?'

'It's set for May.'

That was almost four months away. She sighed and rolled her eyes. 'And have you noticed any improvement, generally?'

I looked at Jodie, walking in circles in the middle of the room, muttering to herself. 'She hasn't defecated for some time. And on a good day I have some level of cooperation, although she's plagued by flashbacks even then. Yesterday she was convinced she could see her dad's face on the curtains in the lounge.'

'She was hallucinating?'

'Yes, but it was completely real to her. She said I must have let him in without telling her, and she was hysterical. At night she wakes up screaming, and when I go in she's convinced there are people in the room who want to hurt her. I can see her eyes focusing on them, even though she's staring at blank space. It can take hours to reassure her. She seems to be actually reliving the pain she felt at the time.' I shuddered. 'My family find it very upsetting.'

'They would. With post-traumatic shock the abuse is constantly being revisited. Are you having regular breaks?'

I smiled stoically. 'I'm still waiting. There's a problem in identifying suitable carers, because of the level of Jodie's needs.'

She made a note in her pad, then looked at her watch.

'Cathy, there's one more test I'd like to do with Jodie. Would it be all right if you waited outside? It's just a game,' she reassured Jodie, who clung to my arm, wanting to come with me.

I sat on one of the chairs in the corridor, and Dr Burrows closed the door. It may have only been a game, but Jodie was in no mood to play; I could hear her shouting at the doctor to shut up and go away. Dr Burrows' even tone persisted for ten minutes, then the door opened and Jodie rushed out.

'Blimmin' doctors,' she cursed. 'Why don't they mind their own fucking business?' She had reached the exit by the time I caught up with her.

Over the following weeks Jodie continued to enjoy school, although there was no noticeable improvement in her behaviour or condition. In fact, rather than the school having an effect on Jodie, it seemed instead that Jodie was affecting the school. One afternoon when I arrived to collect Jodie I noticed that Mrs Rice's eyes were red and puffy. 'Are you OK?' I asked, hoping this wasn't too intrusive.

'Yes, I'm fine,' she laughed, still sniffling. 'I just got a bit emotional.'

'Oh, I hope it's not anything that Jodie's . . .'

'No no no. Well, not exactly,' she interrupted. 'Actually, could I have a quick word?'

Mrs Rice obviously didn't want to talk in front of Jodie, so I sent her off to run around the playground for a few minutes, while Mrs Rice and I walked over to a quiet spot.

'Some of the children had their hearing tests today, and Jodie started talking in class about some kind of medical she'd had. We were pleased that she had something to contribute, obviously, but then suddenly she started saying these awful things about . . . She said she preferred it when a man did it, and it became clear she was talking about . . . well . . . you know.'

'Oh, I am sorry. She doesn't know the difference between what's appropriate and what's not.'

'No, it was fine. I interrupted her before the other kids twigged, but she seemed to want to talk about it, so I spoke to her at playtime, just the two of us. Anyway, I just wanted to make sure you were aware of the details. The only new aspect seemed to be that she mentioned an aunt being involved, as well as her mother, but she didn't give a name for the aunt. That was all.'

'OK, thank you for letting me know. She has told me about the aunt before. I'm really sorry you've had to deal with all this.'

'Oh, don't worry, I'm sure it won't be the last time!' She smiled. I patted her on the arm, and Jodie and I headed home.

On the Friday the school held a fête for Comic Relief. The sun was out, so the stalls were set up in the playground, rather than in the hall as had been expected. The children wore red, the teachers wore wigs and silly costumes, and even some of the parents were wearing red plastic noses. There were stalls with sweets and cakes, games and tombolas, and a set of stocks where the braver teachers allowed themselves to be pelted with wet sponges. It was great fun, and Jodie revelled in it. I stood watching her, as she hared around the playground, being chased by three of her classmates. They were all soaking wet, and their faces were flushed with the excitement. Jodie's pigtails swung in the air as she dodged and ran from her new friends, laughing wildly. It was probably one of the happiest moments of her life.

CHAPTER 26

LINKS IN THE CHAIN

The school handovers were not just designed to ensure Jodie's safety; they also allowed the teaching assistant and me to keep each other fully updated with Jodie's progress. Each morning I gave Mrs Rice a brief summary of how Jodie had been the night before: how she'd slept, what her mood was like, any problems to look out for and so on. In the afternoon Mrs Rice would do the same for me, which was useful, especially when Jodie was upset or angry at school.

As Jodie settled into her class she seemed to get on reasonably well with the other children, largely because most of them were bright enough to stay on polite terms with her while keeping their distance. However, there was one other pupil in the orange group who had behavioural problems, a boy called Robert, and he was Mrs Rice's other main charge. She sat between Jodie and Robert in class, and spent most of her day working with the pair of them on a one-to-two basis, keeping their work loosely related to what was going on in the broader lesson. This kind of teaching is known as 'differentiating work'.

One afternoon, as Jodie trudged unhappily down the steps, Mrs Rice explained to me what had happened. The class had been drawing with pastels, and Robert and Jodie had both reached for the red pastel at the same time. Robert got there first, so Jodie sat back in a huff. She glared at her picture, glared at Robert, then got up out of her chair, walked behind Mrs Rice and grabbed the pastel out of Robert's hand. Robert started crying, and Mrs Rice naturally told Jodie off and made her hand it back. Jodie was furious, and shouted that it was Robert's fault, and called him 'four eyes'. This upset Robert even more, as he'd only recently started wearing glasses, and Jodie was eventually persuaded to apologize. When the lesson finished, the children went out for play-time. In the playground Jodie spent some minutes standing in silence, while staring at Robert. Then she walked over and punched him, and the pair of them had to be separated.

On the way home she was still furious, thumping and kicking the back of the passenger seat. 'He's bullying me, Cathy! I hate him, I hate him!' Jodie often had tantrums in the car, as she knew there was little I could do to stop her.

'Jodie, calm down and sit still. I won't tell you again.'

'No! Shut up!'

'Jodie, there'll be no television tonight, I'm warning you. You haven't had the best of days. Enough!'

She pouted in silence and I tried to explain the rationale behind her being told off. 'You grabbed the red pastel from Robert, then called him a very hurtful name. That's why Mrs Rice was annoyed.'

'Yes, but I needed it. Why won't anyone believe me?'

Over the following weeks, Jodie's complaints about Robert became a regular feature of our drives home, and often our evenings too. Jodie was adamant that Robert was bullying her, no matter how many times it was explained to her that she in fact was bullying him. I did feel sorry for Robert. He was a quiet, anxious boy, with more than enough problems of his own, and Jodie brought out the absolute worst in him.

Jodie's relationship with Robert was just one of numerous problems at the school, and I quickly came to dread the sound of the secretary's voice, as it usually meant we were in trouble. However, the next worry I was faced with regarding school was unrelated to Jodie's behaviour. One evening at dinner she was telling me about her classmate Freya, and my attention had wandered. Jodie's stories tended to ramble, and rarely had a point or resolution. However, when Jodie mentioned Freya had visited her at her old house I quickly paid attention.

'Did you say Freya came to your house when you lived at home?'

'Yeah.'

'The house you grew up in, with your mummy and daddy?'

'Yes,' she sighed.

'And she's in your class now?'

'Yeah.'

'So were you and Freya friends from your last school?'

'No, she didn't go to my school.'

'So how did you know her?'

'Because she came round, and we played Barbie.'

'So did your mummy and daddy know hers?'

'Yeah, from the pub.'

'I see. And do they still see each other, do you know?'

'S'ppose so.'

Oh shit, I thought.

The next day at school I went in to see the Head. If Freya's parents were still friendly with Jodie's parents. it was almost certain the news of which school Jodie now attended would filter back. This raised the possibility that her parents might come to the school and confront us, or even try to snatch her. Jodie would be terrified at the sight of her father in what she thought was a safe place, let alone if he approached her. The school run is fraught with anxiety when you're fostering, as you're an exposed target. Parents do occasionally try to grab their children at the school gates, and the advice we're given is that we have to let the child go, and call the police.

The Head suggested that Jodie and I should use

the staff entrance from now on, and he gave me the security code. Although this was a sensible precaution, it meant that in yet another small way Jodie had been made different from her classmates, and her past was once again hampering her future.

The following Sunday, Jodie, Paula and I went for a walk in the park. We were walking up the hill through the centre of the park, when an elderly lady coming towards us slipped and fell. It was dreadful to witness; her wrists failed to break her fall, and she cracked her nose on the tarmac. Paula and I ran up to her, and I gave her first aid, while Paula phoned for an ambulance on her mobile. I used a wad of clean tissues from my bag to stem the bleeding, all the while talking to her, making sure she didn't go into shock. Her name was Maureen and she was clearly badly shaken; her frail body was trembling. Her face was grazed, her nose appeared to be broken and one of her wrists had swollen up. We waited until the paramedics arrived, and explained to them what had happened. The ambulance took her off to hospital, and we returned home. Throughout all of this, Jodie had stood by quietly watching.

'That evening at dinner it was still on our minds.

'I hope that poor woman's all right,' Paula said. 'I could have cried.'

'What do you want to cry for?' Jodie asked.

'That poor lady, who fell over in the park.'

'Why? She didn't hurt you.'

'No, I know that,' Paula said patiently. 'But she was badly hurt and she was old. When you see something like that it makes you sad, doesn't it?'

Jodie stared back at her, clearly not understanding the emotion she was trying to describe.

I decided to try and help. 'We don't like to see other people get hurt, Jodie, because we know how bad it feels ourselves. If you'd fallen over, you'd be hurt, wouldn't you?'

Jodie thought for a second. 'Yes. That poor lady.' She then repeated the phrase throughout the rest of the evening. I was glad to hear her making the right noises, but it sounded hollow and I wasn't actually convinced she felt it. It wasn't that Jodie was being wilfully callous, she just didn't seem to have any sense of empathy. I wondered if this was why she could be so cruel to animals, and so rude and violent to other people. In all the time she'd been with us, I'd never once seen her cry out of sadness; her tears had only ever come from rage and frustration. However, although she hadn't yet learned to empathize, she had learned that people expected her to sound sympathetic, so she would mimic the reactions of others, to appear normal and fit in. Looking back, she'd done the same thing at Christmas, when she'd copied the others' reactions when opening her presents. Likewise, when I pointed out a beautiful sunset, she might repeat the phrase, 'What a beautiful sunset!', but again it sounded hollow, as though she couldn't actually see or appreciate its beauty.

Some weeks later I arrived at the school to collect Jodie at the end of the day. As she came down the corridor, I saw she was being escorted by the Head, rather than Mrs Rice. I took a deep breath and braced myself. What had she done now? We exchanged hellos, then he took me to one side, out of Jodie's earshot.

'Don't worry,' he said, 'she hasn't done anything. I just wanted a quick word. Mrs Rice has decided to take some time off, so we have a new teaching assistant starting tomorrow.'

'Oh, I see,' I said, taken aback. 'It's rather sudden. She didn't mention it. I hope she's OK.'

He nodded. 'I think she just needs to take some time out. You know what it's like working with children, and TAs tend to be on the front line. Like you foster carers.'

I nodded in agreement.

'Sometimes you just need a break, don't you?'

'Yes, I know the feeling.' I smiled weakly, wondering if I would ever get the break I'd been promised at the beginning of the year.

As I left, I felt sad for Mrs Rice. I'd seen her upset often enough to realize that Jodie was partly responsible for wearing her out. She wasn't used to hearing about the awful things that Jodie had been through, and she'd never dealt with a child this difficult and disturbed before. Jodie was constantly on edge, and alert for danger: fight or flight. If she heard the slightest noise, she'd spin round, ready for action. When you spend long enough in the company of a child like Jodie, you can soon find yourself on a heightened state of alert, and it becomes very difficult to switch off and relax.

I certainly felt myself becoming increasingly overwhelmed by Jodie's life, and all the pain, fear and distress she had suffered.

CHAPTER 27

SILENCE

The poet T.S. Eliot wrote that April is the cruellest month, and it seemed that this year he was exactly right. As April approached, the gloomy days and permanently grey skies gave no hint of anything different, in the past or the future. The winter seemed endless, as the temperature plummeted. It was hard to believe that Jodie had been with us for almost a whole year, but the anniversary of her arrival was near.

I drew up my collar, and loitered outside the travel agent's window. I fantasized about the cut-price offers to the Caribbean. How I'd have loved to put us all on a plane and head for an island in the sun. But it was impossible. Although my purse might just have coped with it, I knew Jodie wouldn't. On top of all her other problems, she had become so fearful of adults that even a visit to our local newsagent, with whom she previously used to chat, would now produce a panic attack. A packed flight would have been intolerable for her, and I doubted the airline would charter a plane just for us.

I moved away from the tempting window display, and turned towards the supermarket. My mobile phone rang; it was the school secretary.

'I'm sorry, Cathy,' she said. 'Jodie's inconsolable. She's convinced her father has come to take her. Can you come straight away?'

I turned and headed back to the car.

Fortunately the roads were quiet, so twenty minutes later I was walking down the path towards reception. A high-pitched scream erupted from inside, and I knew it was Jodie. I pressed the security buzzer, and the secretary showed me through to the medical room. Jodie was clinging to the radiator, her eyes wide and staring, her body rigid with fear.

'Don't make me go with him! Please, Cathy, please,' she begged.

The new assistant, Miss Walker, who got on well enough with Jodie, knelt beside her, talking softly, trying to reassure her, but I could see Jodie was way past that.

I moved towards her, but she backed away. 'No one's taking you away, Jodie,' I said firmly. 'He's not here, I promise, and you know I don't lie.'

She opened her mouth, about to scream, but I didn't give her a chance.

'No, Jodie. I mean it. Stop it. There's no one here. Now calm down, let go of the radiator, then we can have a cuddle.'

The young assistant eyed me suspiciously. Jodie looked from one to the other, then at the door.

She started to relax her grip. 'Good girl. That's better.' She finally let go.

I went over and took her in my arms, as Miss Walker quietly slipped out.

'He was here,' she sobbed. 'At my old school. He came to collect me, then we went in his car.'

The rest was muffled by her sobs, but I knew how it would go. The past had once again transposed itself on to the present, with flashbacks that felt as real now as when the abuse had happened.

'It's all right, pet, I promise you. It won't happen again. There, there. It's OK.'

Once she was calm I led her to the car, and we drove home. It was eleven in the morning, but she wanted to go straight to bed. She said she was tired, and her bed was nice and safe. I took her upstairs and helped her out of her uniform. I tucked her in, and she fell asleep straight away. I came back every half hour to check on her, but she didn't stir. At two o'clock in the afternoon I decided to go in and wake her, as I knew if she slept too long she'd be up all night.

She had changed position, and was now lying flat on her back. Her eyes were open and she was staring at the ceiling.

'Feeling better?' I asked, but she gave no acknowledgement. I opened the curtains, took her jeans and jumper from the wardrobe, and laid them on the bed. 'Put these on, pet, and I'll make you a snack, then we could take your bike to the park for a bit. You'd like that.'

Usually she was adept at telling me exactly what she did or didn't like, but this time she made no sound or movement. I looked closely at her, then I perched on the bed and eased the duvet from under her chin. 'Jodie, are you all right, sweet?'

Her eyes were focused on some distant point above her head. I tried chivvying her along. 'Come on. Get dressed while I make you a sandwich, then we'll go out.' She remained staring, giving no clue that she'd even heard me.

I decided it was probably best to leave her, in the hope that she'd think about the park, and rally round. A quarter of an hour later, when she still hadn't appeared, I went up to check on her again. She was exactly as I'd left her: flat on her back and staring into space. I sat on the bed and started talking, reassuring her that I understood how difficult it was, but that eventually everything would be sorted out; she had her whole life ahead of her. Still she said nothing, and remained immobile. I tried firmness, then coercion, then bribery, then finally I tried to physically lift her from the pillow, but none of it worked. She flopped back like a rag doll, and I was really starting to worry. I hovered in the doorway, then, leaving the door wide open, went to the phone in my bedroom. I called Jill and told her about the day's events.

'It could be part of the post-traumatic shock,' she said. 'The flashback she had at school could have caused her brain to shut down for protection.'

'So she'll come out of it?'

'She should be recovered by the morning. I suggest you let her sleep it off. If you need help during the night call the emergency social worker, but I doubt it'll be necessary.'

I returned to Jodie's room and tried once more to rouse her. When this failed, I reluctantly closed the curtains and came out, leaving the door ajar. A little later the children arrived home, and I explained what had happened. They came with me as I checked on her every half hour, but there was no change, and an eerie hush descended on the house, as music and televisions were kept low. By the time I went to bed her eyes were closed and she seemed to be sleeping. I left her light dimmed and her door open, and went to my room.

At four in the morning I was woken by a small voice outside my bedroom door. 'Cathy, Amy's wet the bed.'

I leapt up and hugged her. 'No problem.' At least some part of Jodie was back. I changed her sheets and pyjamas, as she continued chattering in her baby voice. 'Amy's good girl. She tells Cathy. Amy wants potty.' I didn't mind; anything was better than that dreadful comatose silence. I tucked her in, then left her snuggled up with a teddy, contentedly sucking her thumb.

In the morning I was surprised to find Amy was still in occupation, and she remained so throughout breakfast.

'Stop babbling in that silly voice,' Lucy eventually snapped; she was never at her best first thing in the morning.

I shot her a warning glance. 'I'm sure she'll be gone by the time we get to school,' I said. But an hour later, as I kissed Jodie goodbye and passed her over to Miss Walker, she toddled off still in character as Amy, with the tottering gait of an infant just learning to walk.

As I drove home I got stuck in traffic, so I phoned Jill from the car and updated her. She asked me to email my log notes over as soon as possible, so she could forward them to Eileen, the guardian ad litum and Dr Burrows. It was after midday by the time I'd finished typing, and I was about to make some lunch when the phone rang. Please let it not be the school again, I thought. I hadn't even started the housework yet, and I still had to do the supermarket run.

It was the school. 'Hi, Cathy,' the secretary said, and I braced myself for the bad news. 'Mr West asked me to call to let you know Jodie's been fine today.'

'Thank you,' I sighed with relief. 'Thank you very much.'

Jodie's good behaviour continued through the evening, but it turned out to be a false dawn. The next morning she was sobbing uncontrollably and despite my best efforts I couldn't get her to tell me why. As I sat on her bed, watching her weep,

I again felt completely ineffectual as a carer, and tried to remind myself that this was no ordinary childhood trauma.

By 9.00 a.m. she was no better, so I phoned the school and told them she wouldn't be coming in for the morning, but that if there was an improvement I'd bring her for the afternoon. There wasn't. Nor the following day. By the end of the week Jodie had been in school for a total of one and a half days, and she was deteriorating before my eyes. When she wasn't crying she was staring into space, removed and distant from anything I could say or do. She was hardly eating, and my previous policy of restricting sweet and fatty foods went out of the window.

'What about a chocolate biscuit?' I asked, trying to get a spark of interest out of her. 'Or there's ice-cream in the freezer?'

But nothing could tempt her, and she was surviving on the odd mouthful of sandwich and occasional handful of crisps.

It was extremely distressing. I'd never seen any child like this before and I was at a complete loss to know how to deal with it, or how to help Jodie. I phoned the only person I could think of who could give me support and advice at a time like this. Jill agreed to come round at once.

'This can't go on,' she said when she saw Jodie's state, which alternated between the heart-rending crying and total blankness. 'She needs help. Now.'

She phoned Eileen, but was told she was on

annual leave once again, and the new team manager, Gail, was in a meeting. Jill left a stern message, requiring a call back as soon as she was free.

'Jill?' I asked. 'Is it possible for a child this young to have a nervous breakdown?'

'There are cases, yes, but it's very rare.'

We looked at each other, both thinking the same thing. The extent of Jodie's abuse was rare – so why shouldn't she be suffering a nervous breakdown? If there was any child who was a prime candidate for a complete mental collapse, it was her.

Jill tried talking to Jodie, who'd spent all morning propped on the sofa staring silently into space. It was a slightly different approach to mine. Jill didn't ask her any questions. Instead, she just recounted stories of various children she knew, hoping these would prompt a reaction. However, the end result was the same: a blank stare, which eventually gave way to silent tears. I did the only thing I could: I held her tightly, and reassured her it was going to be OK. Jill had nothing else to offer, so she left, saying she'd phone regularly, and promised to alert Dr Burrows.

The doctor phoned within the hour and asked to see Jodie first thing Monday morning. She said she'd cancelled an appointment to fit her in, and although I was grateful I wasn't even sure I'd be able to get Jodie out of the house. I asked if she could make it a home visit.

'I'm afraid not,' she replied apologetically. 'I'm only allowed to see children at the centre, because of the insurance.'

I said I'd make sure Jodie was there.

The weekend passed, and Jodie showed no improvement. The whole family spoke in whispers, in recognition of her suffering. We took turns sitting with her on the sofa, reading her favourite stories or trying to involve her in games, but not even the *Mary Poppins* video could produce a reaction. All she wanted was to go to bed, where she now spent an increasingly large part of the day, and from which it was a struggle to coerce her in the morning.

I prayed that Dr Burrows would have some answers for us.

CHAPTER 28

ASSESSMENT

On Monday morning I washed and dressed Jodie, then watched as she sat at the kitchen table, staring into space. Eventually I threw away the porridge she hadn't touched, tucked a packet of crisps into my bag and helped her on with her coat and shoes. I had told her we were going to see Dr Burrows, but she was as lifeless as ever. I helped her out of the house, strapped her into her seatbelt and turned up the volume on her favourite singalong cassette. As we drove to the clinic she stared straight ahead at the seat in front of her, and said nothing. She was completely unreachable, and I wondered if she even knew where she was.

We arrived at the clinic and I gave our names to the receptionist, who told us to go straight through to the consulting room. I knocked and entered; Dr Burrows was arranging crayons on the child-size table. As soon as Jodie saw the doctor, her previous lethargy vanished and she erupted into a violent tantrum.

'Don't want to! Go away!' She kicked the small plastic chairs across the room.

'All right, Jodie,' Dr Burrows soothed. 'There's nothing to be worried about. I'm here to help you.'

'Don't want your help! Piss off!' Jodie covered her ears, screwed up her eyes and screamed for all she was worth.

The doctor motioned for me to do nothing, so I stayed where I was, as the cry reverberated around the walls in an agonizing crescendo. Eventually she ran out of breath, and the scream ended as abruptly as it had begun. She lowered her hands and darted to the table, throwing it against the wall. She overturned the toy boxes, kicked the contents across the floor, then turned to the filing cabinet, which had one drawer half open. Dr Burrows intercepted her.

'No. You can't go in there,' she said calmly, placing herself between the filing cabinet and Jodie. 'That's mine and contains important papers. Not in there.'

To my surprise, Jodie accepted this, but her unspent anger turned inwards, upon herself. She grabbed a clump of her hair and tore it out. At this, I got up and restrained her. It might not have been the correct approach in the doctor's eyes, but I wasn't prepared to stand by and watch her harm herself. I held her wrists, then crossed her arms, enfolding her as I did at home. She struggled, spat and then finally went limp. I led her over to the sofa and put my arms around her. Whether Dr Burrows approved or not, I couldn't tell. She sat opposite, and the room was quiet. I looked at the mess; the floor between us was covered in debris, a sea of destruction.

We sat in silence, then Dr Burrows leaned towards Jodie. Her voice was soft and low, and she was searching for eye contact. 'I know you're hurting, Jodie, and I want to try and stop that hurt. You let Cathy help you. Will you let me help you too? It would be really good if you did.'

It was a relaxed, non-threatening approach, which I was sure had worked with countless children before, but although Jodie was quiet, it was a silence I recognized as being withdrawn.

Dr Burrows gave me a reassuring smile, then repeated her request. Jodie didn't move, and gave no indication that she'd even heard. The psychologist tried again, this time rephrasing it. 'Jodie, Cathy has told me about how brave you've been; you've had an awful lot to deal with. But I think you're finding this problem is too big to fix on your own. That's why Cathy's here, and that's why I'm here too. Will you let me help you?'

Jodie continued staring at some indistinct point a yard or so ahead, remaining as closed off and removed as ever.

Dr Burrows sat back, and opened the notepad on her lap. 'Cathy, perhaps you could tell me how Jodie's been since we last met. I know you've been worried about her.'

I assumed this was a strategy to encourage Jodie to share her feelings, so I explained that she'd been doing extremely well, but that horrible memories from her past had been making her unhappy. I gave a couple of examples, to make it clear to Jodie that Dr Burrows knew her history and that she could be trusted. I said that the whole family was very worried; Adrian, Lucy and Paula cared a great deal for Jodie, and didn't like to see her upset. Dr Burrows leaned forward again.

'I see lots of children who are upset and angry because of things that have happened. It's not their fault. I know ways to help. I help them get rid of some of the hurt, so they can be happy again. I'd like to help you, Jodie.'

The nature of our visit appeared to have changed from assessment to therapy, but unless Jodie engaged, and the pathway of communication opened, it would all be in vain.

'I'd like you to help us,' I said, hoping the 'us' might spark Jodie's confidence, but she remained inert, staring straight ahead. Dr Burrows made another note in her pad.

'Would you like to play a game, Jodie?' she asked. 'I could bring in the doll's house.'

I looked at Jodie hopefully, but she made no move.

'How about a drawing? You drew a lovely picture on your first visit. I've still got it.'

Jodie didn't even look up.

'I tell you what.' The doctor rose from her chair. 'Before we do anything, Cathy and I are going to put these toys back in the boxes. We'd like you to help us, please.'

I took my cue, slipped my arm from Jodie and joined the doctor on the floor. Presumably the aim was to engage Jodie in physical collaboration, in the hope that it would ease her into saying something. But as we repacked the toy boxes and picked up the crayons I could see out of the corner of my eye that Jodie wasn't even looking at us, perhaps wasn't even aware of us. A few minutes later we finished, and returned to our seats. Dr Burrows made some more notes in her pad, while I sat with my arm around Jodie. I couldn't begin to guess what she was writing, but I supposed to her professional eye there were indicators, and possibly even a diagnosis, despite Jodie's non-cooperation.

She closed her pad and smiled kindly. 'That's enough for today. Thank you both for coming. I'll be in touch.'

I was taken aback, and wondered if this was another ploy to spark Jodie into communication. The psychologist stood up. 'I'll see you again soon, Jodie.' The session was definitely finished.

I looked at Jodie, who was still motionless, wearing the same impenetrable stare.

'OK, sweet, we can go home now.' I took her hand and lifted her from the chair, as the doctor opened the door. As we walked out into the daylight I had an awful sense of foreboding.

CHAPTER 29

THERAPY

My sense of foreboding persisted through the following day. Jodie and I sat on the sofa as I read her one of her favourite rhymes by Shirley Hughes. 'Bathwater's hot, seawater's cold. Ginger's kittens are very young, but Buster's getting old.' In the past she had turned the pages eagerly, repeating the words, enjoying the pleasant sound of the rhyme. Now she seemed impervious; deaf and mute.

Jodie's disturbance had reached a new level and I knew that what I could offer was grossly inadequate. There was something frightening as well as deeply saddening about watching her distress. How far could a personality fracture before it was impossible to put it back together? Where would all her misery and hurt take her in the end? It seemed as though it was leading her to a place of darkness and silence where, finally, no one would be able to reach her. I knew she needed help urgently. But what kind of help? And how could I comfort her?

I put the book down and held her close, as I re-played the previous day's session with Dr Burrows in my head. I hadn't expected a miracle cure, but I had hoped for at least a hint of progress. Instead the session had only served to demonstrate how disturbed Jodie was, and how powerless even the psychologist was to reach or help her. I stroked a few strands of hair from her forehead, and looked at her pale, unresponsive face. Was it possible that she would be trapped like this forever?

'I feel so helpless, Jodie,' I whispered. 'I wish I could do something. I wish I was a fairy godmother and I could wave a magic wand so all your troubles would go away.'

I looped my arms under her shoulders, eased her on to my lap and rocked her gently. She remained impassive. My gaze drifted to the window as a rogue snowflake floated past. It was followed by another, and then another. They drifted down as if from heaven, and then melted as they touched the patio.

'Look, Jodie!' I raised her head towards the window. 'It's trying to snow and it's April!'

She looked up, and her eyes seemed to focus for a second.

'Shall we go outside and have a look? You like snow, don't you? Please look.'

But the moment passed, and she turned her head back to the floor, showing no emotion or recognition.

I put her to bed at seven and, with the girls at their piano lessons and Adrian coming home much later, I had the house to myself. I tried to read, but I couldn't concentrate. I put on a CD of classical music, but it only made me sad. In the end I sat watching TV, keeping the volume low so I could hear if Jodie stirred. I went to bed early and, as I lay awake, I prayed for the first time in thirty years.

In the morning I fancied there was some small improvement. Jodie came downstairs on her own, and managed a few spoonfuls of Weetabix. Sadly, though, it didn't last. Half an hour later she was curled foetally on the sofa again, silent and withdrawn.

Jill phoned at 9.30. The new team leader had called an emergency planning meeting for 11.00, and my presence was required. She didn't know exactly why the meeting had been called, but said it suggested things might be starting to move. Dr Burrows may have recommended that therapy start immediately. Alternatively, if we dared hope, new evidence might have emerged that would finally put Jodie's abusers behind bars. Jill's colleague, Lisa, had offered to babysit, and would arrive in about an hour. Finally, some action, I thought. I looked down at Jodie, and felt my hopes begin to rise.

Lisa arrived in good time, and I introduced her to Jodie, who did at least manage to look in her direction. I showed her where the coffee and biscuits were, then left, as she began reading a Barbie magazine to Jodie. I'd changed into my smart 'meetings' suit, and my spirits continued to lift as I drove to the Social Services. Perhaps something good was going to come out of this; finally other people had begun to understand what I had known for some time – that the extent of Jodie's troubles was extraordinary and that she needed specialist help and immediate therapy. Someone had to know how to unlock her and restore her to life.

I parked in the multi-storey car park nearby, and took the lift down to the street with ten minutes to spare.

The ornate stone building, which had once been the old town hall, was now surrounded by high-rise flats, and retained only the façade of its previous gentility. I heaved open the double doors and walked in. As usual, it was full. People of all ages and nationalities were sitting, standing or pacing as they waited anxiously for their numbers to appear on the electronic display suspended from the ceiling. As I walked through the mêlée a toddler grabbed the hem of my skirt, before his mother whisked him back on to her lap, smiling an apology.

I approached the reception desk. 'Cathy Glass,' I said, as the receptionist slid the glass partition just far enough to hear. 'I'm here for the eleven o'clock meeting in respect of Jodie Brown. I'm her carer.'

With stoic resignation she ticked my name off a printed list, then handed me a stick-on security pass, with 'Visitor' printed in large black letters. I pressed it on to my coat.

'Room seven,' she said. 'Through the double doors, up the stairs, and it's on your left.' The partition slid shut before I or anyone else could poke a head in.

I knew the layout of the building, having attended many meetings here in the past. Room seven was one of the largest, and as I climbed the stairs I realized that it was also where Jodie's pre-placement meeting had taken place almost a year earlier. It was hard to believe that it had been so long. I thought back to that day and cringed at my cavalier assumptions at the time. Back then I had been in no doubt that all any child needed was care, firm guidelines, encouragement and attention, and I had had no doubt that this Jodie would end up as another success. I had been so confident that I would reach Jodie just as I had reached so many troubled children and helped to put them back on the road to recovery and as normal a life as possible. But for once my tried and tested methods had failed me. At least I wasn't alone in not being able to reach the source of Jodie's torment. Nevertheless, I wondered if anyone in room seven would show their disappointment.

Jill, Sally and Gail, the new team manager, were already seated along two sides of the polished mahogany table. They smiled as I walked in, and Gail introduced herself. I exchanged a 'Good morning' with Sally, and sat next to Jill.

297

'We're just waiting for Dr Burrows and Mary from finance,' Gail said. 'Eileen's on leave, I'm afraid. And Jodie's headmaster won't be coming, but he has submitted a report.'

I slipped off my coat, draped it over the back of my chair, and took heart from the fact that finance had been invited. Usually, finance people were only present when funding needed to be found. And funding would be required in order to embark on therapy.

'How is she?' Jill asked quietly.

'Pretty much the same. But once she's in therapy I'm sure things will start to improve.'

'Let's hope so,' she smiled.

The door opened and Mary rushed in, clutching a thick wad of papers; she apologized for being late. She sat opposite me, and I was dying to ask how much therapy their budget would stretch to, but I knew it would be poor protocol to do so before the meeting had even started. Gail and Mary spoke quietly between themselves, discussing a different case. Then the door opened again, and Dr Burrows appeared carrying a briefcase, looking more like a city worker than a psychologist in her smart grey suit. 'Sorry to keep you waiting, but the cab was late.'

Gail waited for her to sit down, and then opened the meeting. She thanked us all for coming, minuted the date, the time, and the names of those present, and then asked us to each introduce ourselves.

After the introductions she looked down the length of the table. 'We're here to assess the present situation with regard to Jodie, and to decide how best to proceed. I think it would be helpful to start with you, Cathy, then, Sally, if you could go next. I'll read out the school's report, and perhaps if you would conclude, Dr Burrows.'

We murmured our agreement.

I'd rehearsed what I was going to say during the drive over. I was going to be positive about Jodie's initial progress, without minimizing her need for help. I took a deep breath, and began.

'As you know, Jodie showed very challenging behaviour when she came to me, to such a degree that she had been through five carers in four months. She was extremely aggressive and confrontational, and suffered from delayed development. She had poor bowel control and very low self-esteem. She exhibited sexualized behaviour towards men and women.

'Over time, she settled into our household routine and began to respond to the clear boundaries I set, and the positive encouragement. As her anxiety decreased she became less violent and was learning to manage her anger. However, as she began to feel safe she started to disclose. The extent of the sexual abuse she has suffered at the hands of her family is horrendous.

'As the disclosures continued, her progress halted, and she became increasingly disturbed. Since that time she has suffered from night terrors,

299

vivid hallucinations, and her personality seems to be fragmenting.

'Over the last two weeks, as you know, Jodie's condition has deteriorated further, and faster. Despite all my encouragement and reassurance, she now spends large parts of the day in bed, and takes virtually no interest in what is going on around her. She rarely speaks or eats, and I often find her crying silently to herself. In January she joined the Abbey Green Primary School, where she was supported by a full-time assistant. Initially she made some progress, but since her deterioration she's been unable to attend. She's missed more than three weeks in total.'

I looked them in the eye as I spoke, and saw concern and disquiet reflected back. 'I admit I am at a loss to know how to reach Jodie, and help her come to terms with her experiences. In my view she needs the help of a professional psychotherapist. Given our earlier success, I'm optimistic that once therapy has begun we can resume making progress.'

Gail thanked me, and handed over to Sally, the guardian ad litum. Sally listed the dates when she'd visited, and praised my success in gaining Jodie's trust, which had allowed her to disclose. She said that while she hadn't had the chance to observe Jodie recently, she had been in close contact with Dr Burrows and Eileen, and was thus fully abreast of the current situation. She'd seen Jodie's parents, and made them aware of how badly Jodie had been affected by the disclosures. Jodie's father had been unmoved and was still adamant that Jodie was making it up, but Mrs Brown had broken down in tears. She said nothing more about Jodie's parents – and with her professionalism, there was no question that she would – but there was an inference that there was not much doubt of their joint culpability in what had happened to Jodie.

I felt no sympathy on hearing that Jodie's mother had broken down; my immediate reaction was that it was a sham, to cover up her own guilt. I had no doubt that what Jodie had told me was the truth. There was no other way a child of her age could know the things she knew and describe the things she had described; and I only had to look at her disintegration to know that what she had said had happened.

I could hardly bear to think about her parents. I hated the thought that they were free to continue their daily lives and whatever degradations they got up to, while their daughter was imprisoned inside the pain and suffering they had caused. What they had inflicted on Jodie had condemned her to a life sentence.

'Jodie is a very badly damaged child,' Sally concluded, 'and my recommendations will be wholly in line with Dr Burrows' findings.'

There was silence, as Gail made a note, then she took a sheet from her file and read out the headmaster's report. At the time of writing, Jodie had attended a total of seventy-two days, and Mr West had based his observations on both her academic ability and how she interacted with her peers. At present she was learning to sequence the alphabet and the numbers up to twenty. She had no sight vocabulary but had been working on a target of learning five new words a week. Her concentration was very limited, and she was being encouraged to spend longer on tasks, and to work independently. She had found difficulty in making friends, largely due to her erratic and strange behaviour. The test results showed she was at about the average level of a four-year-old in terms of reading and writing. His concluding sentence summed it up perfectly:

'Jodie's education and social development are being severely restricted by her experiences, and until these have been addressed I feel her achievements will be negligible.'

Gail filed away the report, and I felt my pulse quicken as Dr Burrows opened her file. She would be the final speaker, and after she had given her recommendations Mary would do her sums and then funding would be confirmed, so that we could start Jodie on the path to recovery. I only hoped it would be adequate. My feeling was that she needed at least two one-hour sessions a week.

'As you know,' Dr Burrows began, 'I have been appointed by the court to assess Jodie in respect of the full care proceedings. While this was originally intended to determine the feasibility of her returning to live at home, what has come out since confirms that returning home is impossible, so I am now addressing the issue of her present mental health.' She proceeded to give a clinical appraisal of Jodie's condition, making reference to our last two appointments. I appreciated that Dr Burrows' presence and her report indicated just how seriously everyone was now taking this matter. The psychologist was only supposed to submit her comments at the final proceedings later in the year, but she had stepped outside her remit from the court to give her analysis earlier. What she had observed about Jodie had caused her such concern that she knew immediate action had to be taken – hence her presence at this meeting, despite her extremely busy schedule.

I looked along the table at the others, as they took detailed notes. The doctor drew to a close.

'It is therefore my recommendation that Jodie requires nothing less than intensive, long-term therapy with a paediatric psychotherapist experienced in child sexual abuse.'

Thank God, I thought. All we need now is the funding.

'What level of therapy do you have in mind?' Gail asked. Mary slid her calculator in front of her.

'Jodie has learning difficulties,' said Dr Burrows, 'and functions at the level of a much younger child. As a result she has difficulty in engaging with concepts and retaining them. In view of this, and the severe nature of her condition, I do not think even a high level of sessional therapy would be of any help. It is therefore my professional opinion that for therapy to have any effect in Jodie's case it must be constant and immediate. I therefore recommend the best chance of recovery would be in a therapeutic residential unit.'

I heard the last two words, but it took a moment to sink in. The room fell silent, as the others finished writing. I could feel my pulse pounding in my neck, and my stomach churning. Jill touched my arm.

'Thank you, Dr Burrows,' Gail said. 'That was very helpful.'

I could feel their eyes on me, as I stared down at my notepad.

'Cathy,' said Sally, 'how do you feel about this? I know you've become very close to Jodie.'

I lifted my head and swallowed. My voice was uneven, and I was struggling to hold back the welling tears. 'It's difficult. I wasn't expecting this. I was hoping that once Jodie started regular therapy we'd be able to see her through.' I paused for a second. 'To be honest, I feel it's all been for nothing.'

Sally looked at Dr Burrows, who gently shook her head.

'Even before this present crisis,' said the doctor, 'I doubt Jodie could have functioned successfully in a normal family. She's deeply traumatized, and it's affecting all aspects of her life. Very few carers would have invested as much as you have, and it's to your credit that she's come this far.'

Gail, Sally and Jill all muttered their agreement.

I shrugged despondently. 'Would it not be worth trying sessional therapy for, say, six months?'

They looked again at Dr Burrows.

She looked over at me sympathetically. 'In my opinion, no. Not only would it not be effective, but it could exacerbate her condition. Jodie's personality is disintegrating, and the longer it's left, the more profound the long-term damage may be.'

I said nothing.

'What time scale are you looking at?' Gail asked.

'If I make a recommendation immediately, she could be in within a month.'

I flinched.

'Do you have somewhere in mind?' Gail continued.

The doctor delved into her briefcase, and brought out some coloured pamphlets which she distributed along the table.

'It's called High Oaks, and it's run by Dr Ron Graham and his wife Betty. They're practising child psychologists. You may have heard of them. They're well respected in their field.'

Jill opened the pamphlet between us, and I stared at the first page. All I could see were blocks of fuzzy print, juxtaposed with pictures of smiling children. I blinked and tried to focus.

The doctor continued her explanation. 'They've

been established for twelve years and have built up an excellent reputation. It's a lovely old manor house set in an acre of wooded parkland on the outskirts of Cambridgeshire. The Grahams live on site, together with a support staff of highly trained therapists. The children are taught by qualified teachers who come into the schoolroom in the morning. They cover all the curriculum subjects up to GCSE. The afternoons are given over to recreational activities and one-to-one therapy. At weekends they do what other families do, outings to the cinema, swimming and so on, and of course they take them on holiday. I've had close links with the Grahams since they first opened, and they have a very high success rate. Ninety per cent of the children eventually move on to live in a family. But of course it doesn't come cheap.'

'How much?' Gail asked.

'It depends on the package, but for someone with Jodie's needs it will be approximately four thousand pounds a week. I would make an initial recommendation for three years, but of course that would be under regular review.'

I glanced up, Mary tapped some figures into her calculator and showed the result to Gail, who made a note.

'Would she be able to receive visitors?' Jill asked, knowing that's what I would have asked if I had been thinking straight.

'Absolutely,' replied Dr Burrows. 'In fact, it's essential. If a child has no family then High Oaks

306

arranges for a befriender. It's very important that the children maintain ties with the outside world.'

'And Cathy, you'd want to continue contact?' asked Sally.

'Yes, of course,' I responded automatically.

Gail looked along the table. 'We'll have to take it to panel, but as it's your recommendation it's likely to be approved. Is there anything else?'

Dr Burrows leaned forward. 'Only to thank Cathy for all she's done, and the offer of contact in the future.'

The others concurred, and immediately began gathering together their papers. They dispersed quickly, leaving Jill and me alone. I placed my hands palm down on the table, and took a deep breath.

'How am I going to explain this to Jodie? She trusted me, and now I've got to tell her she's going. She'll think I've rejected her like the others. What's that going to do for her mental health?'

Jill touched my arm. 'I know, I'm so sorry, Cathy. Listen, I wouldn't say anything to her just yet. In my experience, these organizations tend to have a set procedure for introductions. I'll contact High Oaks and see how they want to handle it. We'll take it from there.'

I sighed and stood up. 'OK. I'd better be getting back, she'll wonder where I am.'

Jill joined me in the corridor. 'It may not seem like it now, but it is for the best. You couldn't have done any more. You'll be keeping in touch, so she'll know you haven't rejected her. And who knows: three years down the line . . . ?'

'Yes, I know what you're saying. I understand that it's for the best. The question is, will she?'

I walked out of the building fighting my feelings of failure. Jodie was going to leave me in a worse condition than she'd arrived in – that was a first for any child who'd been placed with me. I could tell myself all I liked that it wasn't my fault, but it was hard not to feel that it had all been a waste of time – all those sleepless nights, the endless draining days of tantrums and violence, the scenes in public, the awful mealtimes, the disruption to my children's lives. Now, after everything we'd suffered, Jodie was going to be moved on again.

I knew intellectually that Jodie needed proper help and intensive therapy of the kind I simply couldn't offer, not with all the love, kindness and common sense in the world. But still, I felt like I'd let myself down. And, most importantly of all, I'd let Jodie down.

How could I tell her that she had to leave?

CHAPTER 30

GREEN GRASS AND BROWN COWS

That night, while the rest of the house slept, I took out the photo album containing pictures of all the children I've fostered; I call it my Rogues' Gallery. I flicked through the photographs. Some of them were posed, others captured unaware, on an outing to the coast or running round the garden. There were children of all ages and races, from little Jason who was only two days old when he arrived, to Martha, an angry and defiant seventeen-year-old, who went on to become a doctor.

I'd lost contact with some of them, but many still wrote to me and phoned. Four of them had stayed with me for a year or more, and all four now visited regularly, and had become part of our extended family. As I turned the pages, remembering the children's various personalities and problems, there wasn't one that I felt I'd failed. At least, not until now. There were no pictures of Jodie yet, but when I did come to add them I knew they would be the last. Whatever aptitude or ability I'd had seemed to have been lost. My confidence was shattered and I decided I wouldn't foster again.

Three days passed before I heard anything further, and all the while Jodie remained shuttered and distant. I didn't even raise the possibility of school any more; there was no point, she was in a world of her own. Somehow, we got through the days. I read to her, cuddled her and tried to tempt her to eat, while Adrian, Lucy and Paula made their own efforts to try and cheer her up.

I had sat the children down not long after I'd returned from the emergency meeting and told them that Jodie would be leaving us. They didn't say much but their solemn expressions and quiet acceptance told me that they already knew how serious Jodie's condition had become. It was always a sad moment when a child left us, but usually it was in the knowledge that they were going forward in a positive way – back to their families, or on to an adoptive family – and they left us better than they had arrived. With Jodie there was no such comfort; despite our best efforts, we had not managed to help her, and no one was unaffected.

'Don't blame yourselves,' I said, echoing Jill's words to me. 'We've done our best. That's all we can do.'

But it sounded as hollow to them as it had done to me, and I knew that they shared my sense of failure.

Four days after the meeting a letter arrived from Ron Graham. Inside the envelope there was a letter for me, and a second envelope, addressed to Jodie. In my letter, Ron introduced himself and wrote that he would phone soon to arrange a visit. In the meantime, would I give Jodie the enclosed? I handed her the envelope as she picked at her lunch. She took it from me suspiciously, then peered at her name on the front. Suddenly her eyes brightened. 'For me? Who's it from?'

'You'd better open it and find out. It looks very important.'

I moved her plate away as she carefully picked open the flap and unfolded the pale yellow sheet. It was typed in bold red print, with a little smiley face in one corner; it was immediately appealing.

'For me?' she said again.

'Yes. Shall I read it?'

She held it between us protectively, and I pointed to the words as I read.

Dear Jodie
My name is Ron and my wife is called Betty.
We have lots of children living with us, in a big house in the country.
We sort out their problems and have lots of fun too. We are good at sorting out problems and we'd like to come and tell you about us.
We look forward to meeting you.
Bye for now,
Ron and Betty

It was a simple but cleverly crafted introduction, and she was thrilled at having a letter of her own.

She asked me to read it to her again, and then a third time.

'When are they coming?' she asked, showing more enthusiasm than she had done in weeks.

'I don't know yet. They're going to phone.'

'I hope it's soon. They sound nice, don't they, Cathy?'

'Yes, they do, sweet.'

She tucked the letter back into the envelope, and carried it around with her for the rest of the day. When Adrian, Lucy and Paula arrived home, she got them to read it to her, and they were as surprised by her enthusiasm as I had been. None of us actually said so, but we were all feeling a little bit slighted. How had one letter from strangers succeeded, where months of care from us had failed?

That night when Jodie was in bed, Ron phoned. I told him about her positive reaction.

'Children like Jodie very rarely form attachments,' he said, instinctively registering my unspoken feelings. 'It's no indictment of you, Cathy.' He asked about the make-up of my family, and how Jodie had interacted with everyone. He explained the introductory procedure: it started with the letter, and would continue with a visit from him and his wife the following week.

'We never rush the introductions,' he said. 'Jodie has put her trust in you, and now we have to transfer some of that trust to us.'

As he spoke, I was impressed by how much of

Jodie's background he had at his fingertips; he must have read the file from cover to cover, and we were on the phone for over an hour. It was a relief to talk to someone who seemed to know what they were doing and to be fully conversant with the case. It made such a difference. Although Jill had done all she could, she was just a small cog in an enormous wheel, with very little power to change anything. She could only make suggestions and ask questions. Eileen, Jodie's supposedly dedicated social worker, had proved uncommitted, inefficient and, if I was honest, negligent in the handling of the case. After a year she still didn't seem to know the details of Jodie's file, neither had she taken the trouble to get to know Jodie, or fulfilled her statutory duties. It was only when I talked to Ron that I felt some of the burden I had carried for so long beginning to lift from my shoulders. I hadn't realized how lonely I had felt. For so long, it had been Jodie and me struggling along together as best we could while the system ground slowly on, hampered by its vastness and bureaucracy. Now, at last, I felt as though someone was truly interested in her.

When I asked what I should tell Jodie about their visit, he said to tell her as little as possible, but to write down any questions she had, and to reassure her that they would be answered when Ron and Betty arrived.

I went to bed feeling happier than I had done in a long while; Jodie had responded positively,

313

and Ron seemed to be sensitive and direct. Perhaps everyone was right, and this was for the best.

The following morning, when the others had left for school, I told Jodie about Ron's phone call the night before.

'What's he want?' she snarled, pushing away the porridge she'd just asked for.

I wondered if she understood that Ron was the one who had sent the letter. 'To find out how you are. He wrote you that lovely letter, remember? They're going to come and see you next week.'

'Don't want to. Shut up. Go away.'

'Jodie . . . ?' I started, but I decided not to pursue it. I'd do as Ron had asked, and take my cue from her.

She didn't mention Ron, Betty or the visit for the rest of the day, and remained silent and withdrawn. At bedtime I found the letter torn into pieces, scattered across the floor. It would have been ridiculous to ignore this, as I knew Jodie well enough to realize that this was her way of communicating anger. I gathered together the scraps of paper and sat on the edge of the bed.

'I know it's difficult, sweet. It's difficult for all of us. Can you tell me how you're feeling? What your thoughts are? Maybe I can help.'

Her face crumpled and she threw herself into my arms. I held her close, her head pressed against my chest, as she cried pitifully.

'What is it, Jodie? Try and tell me, please. I do really want to help.'

She thought for a few seconds, then blurted out, 'They'll do what the others did. I don't want to. It hurt. You said it wouldn't happen again.'

'Oh, sweetheart, no. They're good, kind people. They'd never hurt you, honestly.'

But Jodie's perception was very different to mine. In her world, a new adult usually meant someone new who would abuse and hurt you, with only a handful of exceptions. The idea of any new adult must have been terrifying for Jodie. Ignoring Ron's advice to say as little as possible, I tried to explain.

'Ron and Betty are like me. They help children who have been hurt, only they can do it better than me. They know the right things to say. They've helped hundreds of children, and they want to help you. I'll be with you the whole time they're here. All they want to do is to talk. They're going to tell us about the house where they live, and the other children who stay there.'

She sniffed. 'They won't go in my bedroom, will they? And I don't want to go in their car.'

'No, of course not.' I turned her to face me. 'Look, Jodie, you've met lots of new people since you've been with me, and none of them has hurt you. I wouldn't let them come here if I didn't think it was for the best. You do trust me, don't you?'

She nodded. 'Then please trust me on this,

315

sweet.' She let me dry her tears with a tissue, but I wasn't sure that she'd accepted my assurances. After all, her time with me had been relatively short, compared with the eight years beforehand. In Jodie's experience, my world was still the exception, not the norm.

I read her a story, and settled her for the night. As I came out of her room I heard Amy telling Jodie, 'You can trust Cathy. Really, you can.'

As the day of the visit drew nearer, Jodie became increasingly unstable. She lapsed in and out of the Reg and Amy characters, and in between she offered little else. Occasionally I saw the real Jodie, and I tried to make the most of it, but she quickly retreated back into her shell, and I was again met with that blank, unrelenting stare. School remained out of the question and, apart from essential shopping expeditions, we hardly left the house.

On the morning of Ron and Betty's visit she was no different, and I was anxious that she'd deteriorate further with strangers coming into the house. Betty phoned from the car to say they'd be with us in fifteen minutes, and I warned her of my concerns.

'You've done well to see it through,' she said, as positive and perceptive as her husband. 'Once we're in the house, and she's met us, it will become easier.'

I wasn't convinced.

I returned to the lounge, where I'd started a

jigsaw in the hope of trying to entice Jodie into doing something. 'That was Ron and Betty,' I said brightly. 'They'll be with us shortly. Shall we start this puzzle?'

To my amazement she slid off the sofa, picked a piece and passed it to me. I put it into position, and the face of a cat took shape.

'Where's our cat?' she asked suddenly.

'Toscha's asleep in her basket by the radiator.'

'Have they got a cat?'

'I don't know. That's something we could ask.'

She passed me another piece, and I snapped it into place. When the doorbell rang, Jodie was still on the floor, to all appearances playing contentedly like any other child.

I took Ron and Betty's coats, and showed them into the lounge. They were a well-built couple in their late forties, smartly dressed in country casuals, with warm, likeable faces.

'Hi, Jodie,' Betty said brightly. 'It's very nice to meet you.' She bent down to examine the jigsaw. 'That's good. Do you like puzzles?'

Jodie nodded.

'This is my husband Ron.'

Jodie looked up and smiled, as Ron sat unobtrusively in the armchair a short way from her.

'Jodie was wondering if you had a cat,' I said.

'Not a cat,' replied Betty, 'but behind the house is a field with lots of cows.'

'Cows?' said Jodie, suddenly interested.

'Yes. In the morning you can hear them mooing,

317

and then the farmer comes and takes them for milking. The children love to watch that. Sometimes the cows come right up to the fence, and you can stroke them.'

'Really?' She was beaming now. I slipped into the kitchen and made some coffee.

Toscha, hearing new voices, rose languidly from her basket and went in to take a look. I heard Jodie introduce her.

'This is Toscha, but she's smaller than a cow.'

'That's right,' said Betty. 'A lot smaller.'

Jodie must have seen something in Ron and Betty, because she was so unlike the child I'd described, I felt my account could have been called into question, if there hadn't been all the other reports.

I carried the tray through, as Betty helped put the finishing touches to the jigsaw. I sat and admired the result. Jodie passed around the plate of biscuits, then sat beside Betty on the sofa.

'Tell me what other games you like, Jodie,' said Ron, gently introducing himself into the conversation. He was softly spoken, and could never have been described as intimidating.

'Painting, I like,' she said, 'and going to the park.'

'That sounds good.' He smiled at her, and Jodie smiled back.

We spent some minutes talking about the park, then Ron subtly drew the conversation to High Oaks, and the activities and outings they did there. He took a leaflet from his pocket: it was a children's

318

version of the one I'd seen at the meeting, and we gathered around Jodie as we read through it. As Jodie turned the pages, Ron described their daily routine, and mentioned some of the other children. Jodie asked if they had a television, and what time they went to bed.

Ron and Betty stayed for nearly two hours, talking and playing, and showed us a short video of High Oaks, which included the rooms and the grounds. Once they were satisfied that Jodie was ready, they suggested we make a date to visit High Oaks the following week.

'I want to go now,' laughed Jodie, jumping up.

'Oh no,' Betty smiled. 'We want to have your room ready, so you can see it when you come.'

This was the first time any of us had mentioned 'her' room, or the possibility of her living there, and I watched Jodie to see her response.

'Can Cathy come?'

'For the visit? Of course,' replied Ron. 'She'll bring you in the car, and you'll both see your room and meet everyone. Then the next time you come, you can stay the night, and Cathy will come home and pick you up the following day.'

'Will I stroke a cow?' she asked.

'You'll certainly see one,' said Betty. 'Whether you stroke it or not depends on how close it comes to the fence.'

I smiled to myself. Cows had clearly replaced cats in Jodie's affections, as surely as Ron and Betty were replacing me. We saw them out and waved goodbye, and Jodie remained lively and excited for the rest of the afternoon. She spent some time painting in the conservatory, and when I came in to check on her she grinned proudly as she showed me her latest work. It was a bright, colourful picture of a big red house, set in a green field, with three brown cows.

CHAPTER 31

HIGH OAKS

A week later there was an air of hushed expectation as we pulled into the drive at High Oaks, and the imposing manor house came in view. Jodie had spent much of the long drive dozing, or talking to Julie, her life-size doll. As we approached High Oaks she fell silent and pulled herself forward for a better view. We recognized the house from the video, but I was surprised at its size close up. It was enormous, with fourteen bedrooms stretching out over two wings, and an annex to the right, which had once been the servants' quarters and was now the therapy and 'quiet' room. The roof was gabled, dipping over an arched brick porch, which was draped with ivy. I guessed the buildings had been built in the mid-nineteenth century.

'This is very grand,' I said. 'We'll have to make an appointment to speak to you.'

Jodie grinned, not quite understanding what I'd said, but appreciating that it was special, and that it applied to her.

I parked behind a line of three cars on the carriage drive and opened Jodie's door to let her out. She slipped her hand in mine, and we crunched across the gravel towards the oak door. I pulled the brass bell cord, and we heard the bell echo inside.

'Me do it,' she said, and gave it another three sharp tugs.

The door opened and Betty appeared, smiling. 'Do you like our bell, Jodie? We thought about having a modern one fitted, but everyone voted to keep it.'

Jodie immediately swapped my hand for Betty's, and I was surprised, as that morning she'd claimed she didn't even know who Betty was. We walked into the hall, which was decorated by white-painted panels with stencilled rosettes in the centre of each square, giving the space a light, cheery feel. Ron appeared from within the house. 'Hi Jodie, hi Cathy. Did you have a good journey?'

'Yes, thank you,' I answered for us both. Jodie took refuge behind Betty.

Ron had phoned the previous evening, and I'd updated him on Jodie's state of mind. There had been no change, and Jodie hadn't raised the subject of the visit. We'd only discussed it once, the day before, when I'd reminded Jodie that we were going, and Reg had replied that he 'fucking wasn't'.

'This way to the lounge,' said Betty, leading Jodie down the hall. 'The children are out for a walk, which is why it's so quiet. They'll be back later.'

The lounge was at the back of the house, and

it must have been three times the size of ours at home. Through the French windows was a concrete patio area, and beyond that there were swings, a climbing frame, a seesaw and a magnificent tree house. Beyond the fence at the back I could see the field, which was at present empty of cows. The lounge was furnished practically, with four sofas around the walls, as well as two armchairs and half a dozen beanbags, arranged at angles facing the widescreen television.

'We use this room in the evenings and weekends,' Ron said, 'when we're all together. We'll show you the rest of the house later.'

Jodie sat next to Betty on one of the sofas and propped her doll between them. I sat on the adjacent sofa, and Ron took the large armchair. We were like Goldilocks and the Three Bears, with the father bear having the largest. Betty offered us a drink, but we declined, having stopped on the motorway for breakfast.

'We have ten children with us at present,' said Ron, looking at Jodie, 'and nine carers to help. Clare and Val will be your special adults. You'll meet them next visit. Betty and I are always here, so is the housekeeper, Shirley. She makes our meals, then we all help clear away. I know you like helping, don't you, Jodie?'

She didn't answer but smiled sheepishly, and inched into Betty.

Ron continued to explain how the children had turns in choosing what they wanted for the evening meal; meanwhile I glanced around the room. I wondered how they kept it so clean and tidy with so many children, and supposed it must be down to the housekeeper.

'Now, have you thought of any questions?' asked Ron.

'Where's the cows?' she said, becoming more confident, and wriggling to the edge of the sofa.

'At this time of day they're usually in the upper fields. You'll be able to see them from your bedroom. Would you like to look round now?'

She nodded vigorously, and slid off the sofa. With the doll clutched under her arm, she followed Betty into the dining room, which also overlooked the garden and had a long refectory table and fourteen chairs. Next to this was the office, which the children were not allowed to go into without knocking first. Next door was the playroom, which was as big as the lounge and brimming with toys, beanbags and equipment. There were three computers, various small plastic tables, and cupboards stacked with games, soft toys and books. There was also a 'home corner', which was equipped with a toy cooker, a sink, a microwave, a settee and a cot. Around one little table sat half a dozen teddy bears, with plastic cups and plates neatly laid out in front of them. Jodie pointed at it excitedly.   −

'We had a teddy bears' picnic last night,' said Betty. 'I bet your dolly would like to join in next time.' Jodie shook Julie, so that the doll appeared to be nodding. 'Good, then we'll lay an extra place.'

We moved on to the kitchen, where a woman was busy at the sink.

'Shirley, this is Jodie,' Ron said, 'and her carer Cathy.'

Shirley was a rotund woman in her late fifties with a kind, open face. She wiped her hands on her apron and came over. 'Hello, Jodie, nice to meet you. And who's this?' She was referring to the doll, but Jodie had hidden her behind Betty's back.

'I'm sorry,' I said, shaking her hand.

'No problem. I expect she'll show me next time.'

'Now your bedroom,' Betty said, sensing Jodie's eagerness to move on. Jodie released her hand and took mine, and we followed Ron up the winding staircase with an impressive balustrade, along the landing to the door second from last.

'You go in first, Jodie,' Betty encouraged. 'This is your room, and we're your guests.'

Jodie proudly turned the handle and went in, and we heard her gasp with delight. The room had been freshly decorated in two-tone peach, with complementary flowered curtains and a matching duvet. A new pine bed was against one wall, with a matching wardrobe, chest of drawers and bookcase against the other.

Jodie was at the window. 'Over there! I can see cows!'

I stood behind her, as we looked out on half a

325

dozen Friesians gathered around a massive oak tree to the right of the property. 'Cows at last,' I said, as much to Betty and Ron as to Jodie. But it was a beautiful view, with the grounds stretching to the field on one side and rolling hills on the other. I couldn't have imagined a better start to Jodie's recovery than opening the curtains every morning and gazing on such tranquillity.

She stood staring for a while, then turned to explore her room. She opened and closed all the drawers, investigated the wardrobe and then sat heavily on the bed.

'Next time you come,' Betty said, 'you could bring one of your toys and leave it in your room if you like.'

'I can leave the doll now,' she exclaimed, holding her up by the arm.

'Are you sure? If she's your favourite, you won't see her again until next week.'

'I want her to stay,' she said determinedly.

Betty and I exchanged approving glances, as Jodie pulled back the duvet and tucked Julie in. Clearly, this was a positive sign.

We moved on to the bathrooms, which were each shared by three children. We then walked past the other bedrooms, but we didn't go in; Betty explained to Jodie that these were private. As we headed downstairs, the front door opened, and the children returned from their walk. The quiet house suddenly erupted into excited chattering, and Jodie grabbed my hand and froze.

'It's OK,' I said. 'There's nothing to worry about.'

'We'll say a quick hello,' said Betty encouragingly, 'then I think that's enough for today. You've done very well, Jodie.'

I coaxed her down the rest of the stairs but, confronted with so many new faces, she stayed hidden behind me. The children began taking off their muddy boots and hanging up their coats. They all had their own pegs and shoeboxes.

'This is Jodie and Cathy,' Ron said.

There was a chorus of 'hi's and 'hello's, but Jodie said nothing and stayed where she was.

'Is the hot chocolate ready?' one boy asked.

'Shirley's doing it now,' replied Ron. It seemed that a long walk followed by hot chocolate was a regular routine, and the children streamed off in the direction of the dining room like one big family returning from an outing. With the hall now clear, Jodie came out from her hiding place.

'Have you thought of any more questions?' Betty smiled.

Jodie shook her head and moved towards the front door.

'OK, well if you do think of anything, you can tell Cathy. We'll give you a ring tomorrow, and then see you next week.'

I thanked them as we left, and they waved until we were out of sight.

Jodie, having risen to the occasion, was now physically and emotionally exhausted. She lay on the back seat moaning, then stuck her thumb in her mouth, curled into a ball, and was asleep within five minutes. I phoned home to say we were on our way, and told the children the visit had gone well.

'So she's definitely going then?' Paula asked. I could hear the sadness in her voice.

'Yes. You know, it really is the best place for her, and I think she knows that. I'll tell you all about it later.'

I settled in the traffic on the southbound carriage, at a steady 65–70 miles per hour. Every now and then I glanced in the mirror, as Jodie slept on the back seat. She'd been so calm and normal today, I was tempted to overlook the months of disturbed behaviour, and believe once again that she could possibly have stayed with us. Maybe with regular therapy, love and patience she could recover and learn to function within a family. In my mind I replayed Dr Burrows' diagnosis, and wondered if she was ever wrong. Did she make mistakes? Was her conclusion 100 per cent certain, or just the best guess she could make at the time? We were the only family Jodie had, and however good High Oaks might have been, it was still a children's home. I turned Radio Four on quietly, and focused on the car in front.

Twenty minutes from home, Jodie woke with a cry. She was desperate for the toilet. 'I can't wait, Cathy. I'll wet meself!' This was at least one area where she clearly had improved; a year ago she would have simply done it on the back seat.

I pulled off the motorway and found a quiet lane, then I spotted an entrance to a field. I pulled in and led Jodie behind a clump of trees. 'You can squat here. No one can see.'

She lifted her skirt and grinned. 'Do you want to watch?'

'No. Of course not.' I turned my back.

I heard the stream of water, then her voice. 'My daddy did. I had to pee on his face. He said it was the drink of the gods, warm and sweet.'

I said nothing. Hiding my revulsion had become as much a part of caring for Jodie as showing love and affection.

CHAPTER 32

OVERNIGHT STAY

Jodie's normality was short-lived, and it took all my energy to see her through the following days. The morning after the visit, she woke up expecting to see cows out of her bedroom window, and became angry when I told her that they were at High Oaks, and that she'd see them again the following week.

'You've taken them,' she sneered. 'It's your fault. You hate me.'

'I don't hate you, Jodie. I like you very much.'

'Give me the cows, then,' she persisted. 'I want them now.'

'I can't, sweet. They're not here. It's impossible.'

I wondered if her confusion was due to the impending move. Bringing her to a realization that she would be going was a subtle and gradual process. I had obviously never said, 'You are going to leave us, Jodie,' which would have made her feel rejected and negated the positive feelings about High Oaks that we had carefully been nurturing. Instead, we worked on bringing her to an understanding that she would be going to High Oaks in the near future, first for a visit where she would have her own room and stay the night and have lots of fun. It all had to be very positive, which it was. It was moving on, not leaving behind. She appeared to listen as I emphasized all the progress she had made during her stay with us, how much she would enjoy herself at High Oaks with Ron and Betty, how we would all miss her, and that we would still visit.

'Will my mummy and daddy visit?' she asked.

'No. Definitely not.' But whereas in the past this would have given her some comfort, she now seemed to see it as another rejection.

'You lot! You're all the same. I hate you. Get out!' Reg suddenly appeared and lunged at me, spitting abuse. I hurried out and shut the door, then hovered on the landing. Ten minutes later the door swung open. Amy appeared, with her thumb in her mouth and a wet stain down the front of her pyjamas.

And it was a measure of how strange and distorted our lives had become that I was pleased to see Reg and Amy back. It meant that some level of 'normality' had been regained.

As the days brought us closer to Jodie's next visit to High Oaks, she flipped between acute lethargy and violent anger, so I was administering sympathy and discipline in equal amounts, sometimes within the same minute. I was also struggling to come to terms with my own feelings about her leaving, as well as having to try to keep the rest of the family's spirits up. I felt I was being stretched in all directions.

Wednesday morning finally arrived, and we found ourselves at High Oaks again, this time with Jodie's overnight bag. Jodie rang the bell enthusiastically, and Ron and Betty answered. They'd advised me to keep my goodbye as short as possible, but in practice I was given no choice in the matter. Jodie wanted nothing to do with me, instantly transferring her affections and attention to Betty.

'Bye, then, Jodie,' I said cheerfully. 'Have a lovely time and I'll see you tomorrow.'

She said nothing, and met my offer of a kiss and a hug with sullen refusal. Betty gave me a sympathetic smile, as if to say 'don't take it personally', but that didn't stop the pang of rejection I felt. Jodie and I had been together almost constantly for a year and I felt that everything we'd been through had bonded us and brought us close. It was hard seeing her turn her back on me and walk away without a second thought.

It was not her fault, I reminded myself. Her ability to form attachments was yet another piece of her personality numbed and stunted by the abuse. I was the normal one, not her, and I ought to be grateful to have the capacity to love and miss other people. On the way home, though, I had to stop for a strong black coffee and some quiet time to help me recover.

By the time I arrived back, there wasn't much

of the day left. I made dinner for the children, cleared up the plates, and then collapsed in front of the television.

After a fitful night's sleep, I returned to collect her at 1.00 p.m. However, as much as our first visit had been a success, this one had not. Ron took me aside on the gravel drive and updated me.

'She had a couple of tantrums, which weren't entirely unexpected. Betty had to restrain her once after she attacked one of the boys. But please don't worry, Cathy. This move is obviously going to cause a reaction. We're well prepared for it.'

Jodie was due to move there permanently in only five days' time, and I now had misgivings about the timetable. 'Do you think we ought to consider pushing the move back, to give her more time to adjust?' I asked.

'No,' he replied firmly. 'In my experience, delaying it now would only confuse her and make it worse.'

We stepped into the hall, and Betty and Jodie appeared from the playroom. Jodie wasn't happy. 'What you doing here?' she scowled. 'Why do you always stop me having fun?'

'It's time to go home, Jodie,' I replied patiently.

'But I want to stay here. Why won't you let me stay?'

The same old Jodie, with her unfathomable switch-arounds and contrary behaviour.

'You can stay very soon, Jodie, but just not today, OK? Now come on, we have to get going.'

Ron and Betty saw her into the car with her bag.

We were up most of the night. Jodie was scared and disoriented, and adamant that there were people in her room. The next morning I was exhausted, but I was kept busy by a battery of phone calls from the various professionals involved with Jodie's case, all wanting updates, and arranging their final visits. Sally the guardian came round to say goodbye. Her report was now complete, so her practical involvement with Jodie was over. As she explained this to Jodie, I could see that Sally had developed a genuine affection for her. I realized how difficult her job must be, always having to say goodbye. Jodie, however, couldn't remember who Sally was, and told her to fuck off.

Jill arrived the next morning and gave Jodie a present for her new bedroom. It was a pretty china ornament of a cat, and Jodie seemed pleased, and even thanked her.

Now that Jodie was leaving me, Jill would end her connection with the case, so she had wanted to come round and say a proper goodbye to Jodie. It was not only that she was a nice person – it's good social work practice to say goodbye to children when you are no longer going to see them. For a child who is constantly moving and meeting lots of new adults, it can be disorienting if people simply vanish from their lives with no explanation, and it can make them feel even more abandoned and out of control. So when children leave me, there are always visits and goodbyes and a little farewell party.

'Goodbye then, Jodie,' Jill said, as she left. 'Lots of luck.'

'Say goodbye to Jill,' I said, and Jodie obediently waved her off. However, as soon as Jill had gone, Jodie threw the china cat on the floor, smashing it into pieces.

Dr Burrows phoned that afternoon, and said she would need to see Jodie one last time before filing her assessment in court. To my relief, she added that she would prefer to leave it until Jodie had relocated to High Oaks, so she could include this in her report.

The final visitor, two days before the move, was Eileen, who breezed in more than an hour late, again offering no apology. In her case it was not goodbye, as Eileen would continue being Jodie's social worker and should visit Jodie and monitor her progress. I felt a little sad that the only person who was going to stay in official contact with Jodie was the one who seemed to care least about her – but there was not much I could do about that.

'Are you looking forward to going?' she asked insensitively. 'You'll be living with other boys and girls just like you.'

'I'm going to kill them all!' Jodie thundered, rising to the occasion. 'I'm going to rip their heads off. And yours. You bleeding cow.'

Eileen declined my offer of coffee, and was with us for just fifteen minutes, as usual. It was probably the last time I was going to see Eileen – another social worker might have continued the connection and kept me informed out of courtesy, but I had a feeling that wouldn't happen in this case. And I couldn't stifle a sense of relief that I wouldn't have to deal with her any more myself.

I showed her to the door, and she turned round with a cheery and unconcerned, 'Bye then!' There were no words of thanks or gratitude for the hard work I had put into Jodie over the past year, or any sense that we had been bonded by this tragic little girl.

'Goodbye, Eileen,' I said. If anyone had needed a damn good social worker it was Jodie, but maybe, between the rest of us – Dr Burrows, Sally, Jill and myself – we had done our best to make up for it.

After Eileen left it took me an hour to calm Jodie down again, and I promised her she wouldn't be seeing much more of Eileen. Given Eileen's performance to date, this was probably true.

Despite Jodie's negative outbursts about High Oaks, she also said on more than one occasion that she wanted to 'go and live with the cows'. The following afternoon I found her in the kitchen, trying to open the cupboard doors.

'What are you looking for, Jodie?'

'Carrier bags,' she muttered, as if it was none of my business.

'Can you tell me why? I might be able to help.'

'I need to pack,' she answered wearily.

I took her upstairs, fetched the suitcases from the top of my wardrobe, and carried them through to her room. We worked slowly, side by side. 'It's like going on holiday,' she said, stuffing handfuls of toys into the holdalls.

'Yes, a little. Have you ever been on holiday, Jodie?'

She looked at me blankly, and I realized that, like many deprived children, she'd probably never had a proper holiday, but was simply repeating what she'd heard at school or on TV.

'This is more like moving home,' I added, which was something she could relate to. I felt a pang of regret, for, if things had been different, I could have taken her on her first holiday.

During these last few days, Adrian, Paula and Lucy were unusually quiet, and showed enduring patience in the face of Jodie's tantrums and insults. I knew that they, like me, were finding Jodie's departure more difficult than that of any other child we'd fostered. To say goodbye when a child is returning to parents who have overcome their problems has an optimistic feeling of success. Even those children who can't return home, and are found adoptive families or long-term foster placements, leave with a fresh start and the knowledge that they will be welcomed and loved by a new set of parents. The only consolation in Jodie's case was that she'd be in safe hands, and would finally receive the therapy that I hoped would set her on the path to recovery.

CHAPTER 33

GOODBYE

On the morning of the move Jodie refused breakfast and sat at the kitchen table, waiting impatiently. I finished my coffee, then began stacking her cases in the hall. She stood at the bottom of the stairs watching me, but turned her back when I asked her if she wanted to help. Eventually all the bags were piled up in the hallway, just as they had been a year before.

'Where are we going?' asked Jodie, trying to reach her coat.

I lifted it down. 'To High Oaks. Remember? You're going to your new home.'

'Oh goody. Is it today? I thought it was next year.' Next year, next week, it was all the same to Jodie.

Adrian, Lucy and Paula got up early so they could see us off before going to school. They gathered in the hallway, uncertain what to say. Paula took the lead and tried to give Jodie a hug, but she stuck out her tongue and turned sideways.

'We'll miss you, Jodie,' Lucy said, 'and we'll speak to you soon.' Jodie just shrugged. She seemed to be quite indifferent to the parting, even though it was obvious Paula and Lucy were quite upset. The three of them helped me load the car, then stood on the doorstep waving.

'You going home?' asked Jodie, as we pulled out of sight.

'I will be once I've settled you, yes.'

'Good. Don't want you. I've got Betty. You can go home, Cathy.'

I knew this was her way of dealing with the separation. She was feeling an emotion, but couldn't acknowledge what it was, or even that she was feeling it.

'I'll phone you on Saturday,' I said. 'And when Betty and Ron tell me it's OK, we'll all come and visit.'

'Don't want to,' she said again. 'Hate you all.'

She'd only been awake for an hour, but she was soon asleep again. She had been reasonably quiet in the night but, as I glanced back at her, lying on the back seat, I wondered how well she could have slept. I turned the radio on low, then switched it off again; the busy string quartet only added to my gloom. I concentrated on driving, and reminded myself of all the positive aspects of where Jodie was going. Nonetheless I kept returning to the guilty question that made me feel hollow inside: had I really done all I could to help her?

When we arrived at High Oaks, Jodie still had her eyes closed, but I sensed that she wasn't asleep.

'Jodie, pet.' I gently rocked her shoulder. 'We're here. Shall we go and find Ron and Betty?'

340

Her eyelids flickered, then opened, and she smiled directly at me. She gave me her hand, and I helped her scramble out. Ron and Betty appeared on the doorstep, but Jodie dashed straight past them and up to her room. The three of us went inside, and had coffee in the lounge. As it was a weekday, the children were having lessons in the playroom and I could hear the steady hum of their voices as we talked. We completed the paperwork and I handed over Jodie's bank book, where I'd been depositing five pounds a week. The allowance from the Social Services that is supposed to cover pocket money and treats is minuscule, so I made it up with my own money to a half decent sum to provide a little fund for the future. It was the only money of her own Jodie would have.

I also handed over the book in which I had kept a record of the things we had done, and which I knew would be part of her life story work.

'This looks good,' said Ron, flicking through the pages and seeing photographs of us all and the places we had been, pasted-in drawings, bus tickets, train tickets, pamphlets and other memorabilia from days out. I had written a few lines under each entry, with an explanation and the date.

'Great,' he said. 'This will really help with the life story work, and of course we'll be continuing it here as well. It's one of the best I've seen. So many foster parents don't seem to have the time to do it, and it's so important for these children to have evidence of their past, particularly when they start therapy. Hopefully Jodie's social worker will be able to give us some things as well, from the time before she came to you.'

Don't count on it, I thought, but said nothing.

Ron smiled. 'You've done magnificently for Jodie, you really have. Thanks, Cathy. She couldn't have asked for better.'

I welcomed Ron's praise. I already greatly admired the work he and Betty did at High Oaks, and a compliment from him was valued and much appreciated.

Before I knew it, it was time to leave, and Ron advised me to make my departure as brief and low key as possible. While Jodie played in her room we unloaded the car and stacked the cases in the hall. When we were finished I stood there uncertainly, wondering if I should just slip out.

'I'll fetch her,' Betty said, sensing my indecision. 'It's important to say goodbye.'

I waited with Ron while Betty disappeared upstairs. A child's voice erupted in the playroom, followed by the soothing tone of the teacher.

'Try not to worry,' Ron said. 'Really, she'll be fine.'

Betty appeared on the landing, holding Jodie's hand, and as they descended they counted down the steps together, just as we had at home. 'Eleven, twelve, thirteen . . .' Jodie hesitated.

'Fourteen?' I offered.

'That's right, Cathy, but let Betty do it. It's her job now.'

I couldn't help but smile. 'I'm going now, Jodie. Will you give me a hug goodbye?'

She rolled her eyes, then held out her arms sullenly, waiting for me to come to her. I walked over, bent down and put my arms around her. She was stiff and unwilling, but then as I moved to pull away I suddenly felt her arms tighten round my waist. Her head pressed against my stomach. I stroked her hair and blinked back my tears. This would be the last time I hugged her like this, I knew that. I tried to put everything I could into that last embrace: how much I cared for her, how I hoped that she would get better – and how sorry I was that I hadn't been able to help her in the way she needed. She had been the most testing of all the children I'd fostered, and yet that had brought a bond of such closeness that it was difficult to let go, even though I knew it was for the best.

After a few moments I eased her away and drew back. 'OK, sweet, I'll be off now and leave you to unpack. I'll phone in a couple of days.'

'Where you going?' she asked, frowning.

'Home, pet. I have to do the housework, then make Adrian, Lucy and Paula their dinner. You'll be busy too.'

She moved towards Betty, looping her arm around her waist, and snuggled into her side. 'OK, Cathy, I understand. This is my home now, and Amy's. You go. Bye.'

I glanced at Betty, then turned towards the door. Jodie was behind me, repeating her explanation to Amy. 'Betty looks after us now.'

Ron opened the front door, and I crossed the gravel towards the car. I didn't look back until I was in my seat. The three of them gave a little wave, then disappeared inside.

CHAPTER 34

PROGRESS

The house was quiet save for the intermittent ringing of the phone. I listened as the answer phone clicked in, then turned over and closed my eyes. Was it the same person, or a number of different callers? It didn't matter. I'd deal with it in my own time.

It was the day after Jodie had left. I'd gone back to bed after seeing the children off to school, and although I didn't sleep, the enveloping warmth of the duvet safely embraced and cocooned me. Had she slept, I wondered, or had she been plagued by nocturnal demons? What was she doing now? It was mid-morning. Was she in the playroom, out for a walk, or finishing her unpacking? Was she happy? Or had she been taken over by one of her characters? How was she engaging with the other children? That was my biggest concern. Would they be more tolerant, having had similar experiences to hers? Or would their anger and bitterness turn on the stranger in their midst? I feared for her, but I knew I had to let go.

The phone rang again and I snatched it up.

'Cathy?' It was Jill. 'Sorry to disturb you, but

I thought you'd want to know. The police have picked up Jodie's parents, and three of the grand-dads and uncles, and they're going to charge them. The Smiths have accused them of abusing their daughter, and the police have got evidence this time.'

My mind snapped into focus as I pulled myself up the bed. 'The Smiths.'

'You remember. Jodie's neighbours? They stopped their daughter, Louise, going round to play.'

'Yes, yes, I know, but I thought they wanted to give the parents a character reference?'

'They did, until all this came out. DNA has identified Jodie's father and others. The police raided the house, and found thousands of photographs. It is a paedophile ring, and it looks pretty widespread.'

I stared at the curtains, with the floral pattern illuminated by the morning sun. The enormity of what was happening suddenly hit me. The burden of proof had at last swung in Jodie's favour. There was a chance that she would get justice and that the vile people who had abused her would be punished.

'Eileen wants to know if you'll give evidence. I said I was sure you would. And they'll need your log. I'll arrange to have it collected.'

I was still staring straight ahead, as the peonies on the curtains glowed fiery red. 'Yes, of course, anything. Oh, thank goodness. Do they know when it started? Have they got any idea?'

'They're still investigating, but apparently some of the photos show Jodie very young.'

I paused. 'Eighteen months. That's when her development stopped.'

'Yes. And there's some before that. I'll keep you posted.'

I replaced the receiver and remained sitting up in bed. I thought of poor Louise Smith, who had suffered despite her parents having been warned, because they'd failed to take action. How many others had had their lives ruined because Jodie had been ignored? All those years she had been on the at-risk register, supposedly receiving regular visits from social workers, yet no one had noticed anything untoward.

I thought of Jodie's parents, and remembered something I'd been told during training on sexual abuse, some years before. The speaker had said that paedophiles were harder to catch than other criminals, because they didn't believe they were doing anything wrong, so they didn't act guilty.

Heaving myself out of bed, I walked along the landing and into Jodie's room. The emptiness was stark, compared with the cluttered chaos of before. The room still smelled of Jodie, that personal scent which individualizes us all, the most evocative reminder of an absent friend or relative. I stared at the bed, which hadn't been touched since she'd left. Dust motes hung in the shaft of sunlight. I stood silently, taking in the lingering presence of Jodie, still palpable, as though at any moment she could have reached out and touched me. As I turned to leave, I caught sight of an envelope propped on the chest of drawers behind the door. 'Cathy' was printed on the front, in what appeared to be Paula's handwriting. I picked it up and opened it. Inside was a sheet of lined paper, torn from an exercise book.

Dear Cathy,
Paula is writing this as I don't know my words. It was kind of you to look after me and I wish I could have stayed. I'm sorry for all the bad things I did. I can't help it. Something makes me. You are the only person who has looked after me and not got angry. I think you understand. I hope you forgive me. Adrian, Lucy and Paula are very lucky. When they have made me better can I come and live with you? Will you be my new mummy? I don't want my old one.
Love,
Jodie

She'd signed her name herself, and the rest of the page was filled with kisses in red crayon. I looked up, and my eyes brimmed. Somehow I had reached her. It made everything worthwhile. It helped to assuage some of my sense of failure.

Yes, Jodie, of course I will. Whenever you're ready, pet.

EPILOGUE

Initially Jodie found the move very difficult. She had two full-time carers, Clare and Val, who were allocated solely to her, working in shifts. I wasn't told very much about her progress, as I no longer had an official role; I wasn't a relative, or her carer, I was just a visitor. Nonetheless I gathered that she had often been violent and disruptive, and had continued with roughly the same patterns of behaviour as during her last months with me.

In those first few months she would phone regularly. Clare or Val would make the call, we'd have a brief chat, and then they'd hand the phone over to Jodie. Usually she was calling to complain about Clare or Val, because they weren't letting her do exactly as she wanted. I would listen patiently as that familiar voice shouted, 'I'm bleedin' going to kick 'em!', and then I'd try to reason with her, to get her to understand that her carers' requests were for her own good, just as mine had been.

Although we were frequently in touch, Jodie rarely gave us any sign of affection. I could tell she felt rejected and upset about the move, and she made this clear every time we visited. As we prepared to leave I would try to hug her, but instead of returning the affection she would wallop me on the arm or, worse, stand sullen and silent.

What we did during our visits varied, depending on Jodie's mood. If she was reasonably stable we might go bowling, or to the park, or some local site of interest, usually followed by lunch at Pizza Hut, which had become her favourite. If she was having a bad day we'd stay in the house, playing in the home corner, with Jodie making dinner on the toy oven or remonstrating with her baby doll.

But however hostile she'd been she would always ask when our next visit was going to be, and phone within the week. After about six months she managed to say goodbye properly at the end of a visit, without thumping me, and it felt like a breakthrough. We praised her immensely. Jodie never spoke of her feelings, except of the hatred she still felt for her father, so all we could do was to try and interpret the few clues she gave. She never told me she resented me or felt rejected. Equally, she never said she missed us or looked forward to seeing us. I felt that her finally being able to say goodbye was a good sign, as it suggested she was reconciled to being at High Oaks, if nothing else.

During this time there was some discussion about whether to start contact between Jodie and her brother and sister, who had been found an adoptive family. In the end the decision was made to leave things as they were. Jodie hardly ever mentioned her siblings, except during therapy, and the general feeling was that they weren't close, so it would be best to allow Ben and Chelsea to have a fresh start. In many respects Jodie had lost her childhood, but they still had theirs, having been taken into care that much younger and, it was thought, having escaped the kind of abuse Jodie had suffered.

Jodie did make progress at High Oaks, but her therapy and recovery were hampered by her learning difficulties. A CAT scan revealed brain damage, which had probably been caused by repeated blows to the head when she was an infant. Perhaps as a result of this, there was little progress in Jodie's education, speech or motor skills, even though her behaviour did show some improvement.

Jodie put on a lot of weight at High Oaks, and quickly. She had been overweight when she had come to me, but I had managed to stabilize it. At High Oaks, however, some of the children were anorexic, so the house policy was to allow the children to eat pretty much what they liked. Jodie, given a free rein, had two helpings of everything, and within months the rolls of fat had reappeared round her middle and thighs.

In the months after Jodie left, the two court cases took place: the final care hearing, and the criminal prosecution of the abusers. The care hearing came first, and resulted in Full Care Orders for

Jodie, Ben and Chelsea, which in practice meant that they all remained where they were.

During the care hearing my logs were requested by the judge to be used as evidence, but I didn't have to attend in person.

A few months later the criminal case was heard. The crimes against Jodie weren't actually included in the charges, as there was felt to be insufficient evidence. Instead, Jodie's father and the other men were charged in respect of another child, and the possession and making of indecent photographs. Again, I had no involvement in the court case, and I only found out the outcome from Jill. Jodie's father and two other men were found guilty on all charges. Jodie's mother, and two other defendants, were acquitted. The three convicted men were all given custodial sentences.

Jodie had been on the at-risk register since birth, and by the time she was taken into care she'd had more than fifty visits to casualty, with injuries including broken bones, burns, scalds and cuts. Jodie's Social Services file was apparently so large that it filled two suitcases.

Jodie's case history was a catalogue of errors, and a shameful indictment of the failings of the Social Services. For Jodie to have been on the at-risk register for eight years was bad practice in itself. Children are placed on the register to allow Social Services to monitor and investigate; either an investigation should take place, or Social Services should satisfy themselves that everything is in order, with the child then being removed from the register. In Jodie's case, neither course was followed.

One reason for this appears to have been the high turnover of social workers: there had been over twenty involved in Jodie's case. It appears that Jodie's social workers had avoided making visits to the house, or had allowed themselves to be intimidated into not asking the proper questions. As a result of this intimidation, the family were frequently passed on to new social workers.

As bad as this sounds, I did have some sympathy. The majority of social workers are women, and they are expected to visit violent households on their own. They are frequently attacked, but they hardly ever press charges, because their job requires them to try to build a relationship with these parents. As a result, parents who know the system know that they can treat social workers with impunity. In this context it's no wonder that some social workers avoid visiting aggressive families, or accept unconvincing excuses.

As the Brown family were passed from one weary social worker to the next, their file at Social Services quickly expanded – social workers are plagued by paperwork. The file soon became prohibitively large, in that its sheer size meant that no one involved in the case seemed to have time to read the whole thing. If anyone had seen the overall picture, including all of Jodie's hospital visits, they would surely have acted sooner.

However, Jodie's case isn't the first to be over-looked in this way, and, sadly, I doubt it will be the last.

Today, three years on, Jodie continues to make slow, limited progress. Much of her anxiety has gone, and she's probably as happy as she's ever going to be. The intensive therapy has helped her to bring the various parts of her personality together, and Amy and Reg now make only rare appearances. She feels safe at High Oaks, and knows that the protection of those identities is no longer needed.

Jodie is now in a special school. As she has grown older her learning difficulties have become increasingly apparent. When I take her out, people now treat her like a disabled child, going out of their way to speak to her, behaving with exaggerated kindness. She's very overweight, and this makes her even more cumbersome and accident-prone. Her delayed development and poor speech are also obvious, and every year she falls further behind her peers. At some point, perhaps quite soon, she will reach her ceiling in terms of what she can learn, and her disability will become even more pronounced in contrast to her peers.

She rarely mentions her parents now, other than in the context of her ongoing therapy. She does exchange birthday and Christmas cards with Ben and Chelsea, and she has spoken to them on the phone once. This phone call, however, was not a success, and is unlikely to be repeated, as she became very confused and hostile. Much of what happened to Jodie remains deeply buried, and will probably stay buried indefinitely. Only time will tell.

The children and I still visit Jodie, making the return trip of two hundred miles every four to six weeks. We also speak to her on the phone most weeks. On our most recent visit, Paula and I took her to a steak house (as a change from pizza) and while we waited for our order to arrive Jodie suddenly looked directly at Paula and said, 'I like your top. It's very pretty.' We were delighted. It was the first compliment we'd ever heard Jodie offer, and it suggested real progress, as it showed the beginnings of empathy: Jodie had complimented Paula because she wanted to make her feel good, and because she wanted us to like her.

I still find it hard to understand what happened to Jodie. I can somehow accept that there are parents who neglect their children, through drink or drugs or mental illness, and whose cruelty is a side-effect of other problems. But the dreadful abyss that Jodie lived in is a mystery of such darkness and evil that it beggars belief. When I look at my own children and, thank goodness, the majority of children, who are loved and cared for and nurtured, it is hard to comprehend the mindset of parents who seem to care nothing for their child, and do not simply neglect her but actively set about destroying her for their own perverted gratification.

Jodie is a damaged child. She has been vandalized. Her mental processes and her emotions have been destroyed. I doubt she will ever recover sufficiently to lead a normal life, and she will never get the pleasure from life that should have been hers. She has been condemned to an endless punishment by the very people who should have cared for her the most. To me, that is the worst crime imaginable.

I still visit Jodie at High Oaks. Many of the children who were there when Jodie arrived have now left, having recovered enough to move on to long-term foster families. Whether Jodie will ever be able to do the same remains to be seen, but if ever she can, and I'm not too old, my offer stands. And I am still fostering. There's always another child out there who needs help.